DONG XOAI, VIETNAM 1965

DC COMICS
THE JOE KUBERT LIBRARY

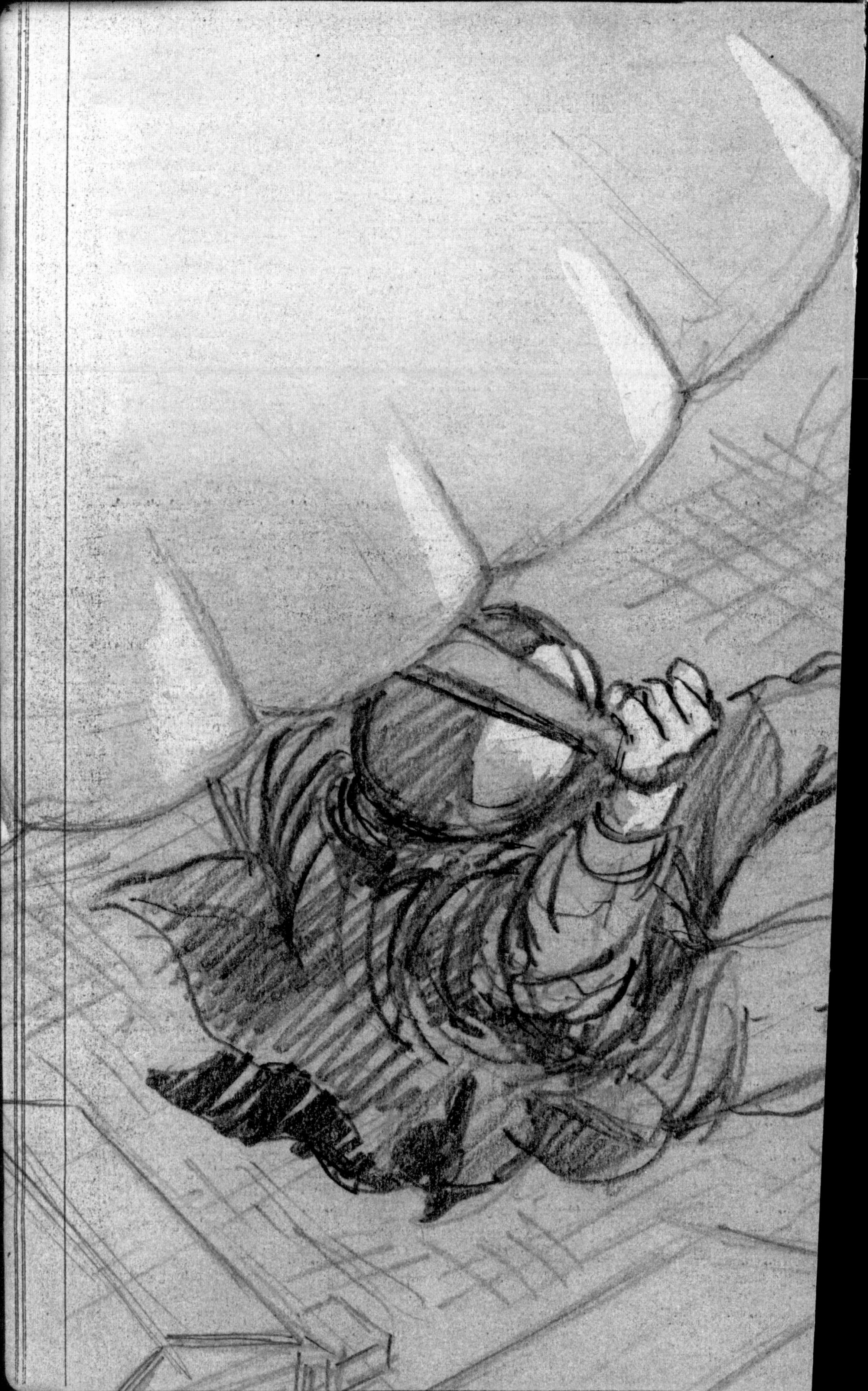

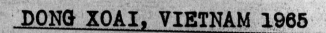

DONG XOAI, VIETNAM 1965

Written and Illustrated by **JOE KUBERT**

Lettering and Production by **Pete Carlsson**

INSPIRED BY ACTUAL EVENTS

Karen Berger SVP - Executive Editor
Will Dennis Editor
Mark Doyle Associate Editor
Robbin Brosterman Design Director - Books
Louis Prandi Art Director

DC COMICS
Paul Levitz President & Publisher
Richard Bruning SVP - Creative Director
Patrick Caldon EVP - Finance & Operations
Amy Genkins SVP - Business & Legal Affairs
Jim Lee Editorial Director - WildStorm
Gregory Noveck SVP - Creative Affairs
Steve Rotterdam SVP - Sales & Marketing
Cheryl Rubin SVP - Brand Management

THE OLD C-118 SHUDDERS ON THE LAST LEG OF A FOUR-DAY TRIP TO SOUTHEAST ASIA. THE MEN ABOARD SHIFT INTO A VARIETY OF POSITIONS. IT'S BEEN A LONG RIDE.

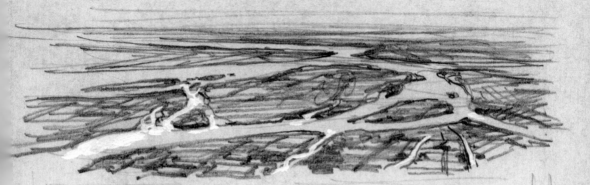

SOME CHEW ON CANDY BARS. SOME SMOKE. SOME TALK INCESSANTLY. SOME SIT SILENTLY, LOOKING OUT OF THE SMALL PORTHOLE WINDOWS, THINKING OF THEIR FAMILIES. SOME SLEEP.

THESE ARE THE TWELVE MEN WHO COMPRISE A SPECIAL FORCES A-TEAM, DESTINED AS ADVISORS IN THE SMALL WAR-TORN COUNTRY OF VIET NAM.

THEY HAD LEFT POPE AIR FORCE BASE IN NORTH CAROLINA FOUR DAYS AGO. THE SCHEDULED BOEING 707 TURNED OUT TO BE AN OLD C-118.

"HELLUVA RIDE."

"YEAH. WHAT HAPPENED TO THAT 707 WE WERE SUPPOSED TO RIDE, CAP'N KEANE?"

"DON'T KNOW, MARTINEZ. HEARD THEY WERE GONNA USE IT TO EVACUATE DEPENDENTS."

THE TWELVE MEN ABOARD ARE FROM THE **5TH SPECIAL FORCES GROUP, AIRBORNE**. ORIGINALLY *DETACHMENT A-414*, LATER DESIGNATED *A-313* AND *A-342*.

ALL OF THEM HAD FORMED FRIEND- SHIPS, HAVING TRAINED TOGETHER FOR THIS MISSION AT FT. BRAGG IN NORTH CAROLINA. FIVE OF THEM SERVED PREVIOUS TOURS IN VIET NAM.

THE C-118 CUTS A WIDE ARC OVER THE JUNGLE BELOW...

BUSBY:
"HOW DOES IT LOOK, ALLISON? LIKE YOU LEFT IT?"

ALLISON:
"YEAH. STILL **GREEN AND HOT**. LIKE A MEXICAN TAMALE."

MARTINEZ:
"COMIN' INTO SAIGON SOON."

SHEER:
"AND MY REAR IS STILL **SORE** FROM THAT GAMMA GLOBULIN SHOT YOU GAVE US, BUSBY."

BUSBY:
"YOU'RE **WELCOME**, I'M SURE."

25 FEBRUARY, 1965 - LANDING IN SAIGON, VIET NAM

CARTER:
"WE COULD'VE USED MORE THAN JUST THE FIVE MONTHS' TRAINING AT BRAGG, LIEUTENANT."

KELLY:
"WE HAD MORE'N MOST, CARTER."

ALLISON:
"HEY, WHEN WE GET BACK STATESIDE, WHAT SAY WE LET MARTINEZ MAKE US ANOTHER TACADO AT HIS HOUSE? WHAT SAY, MARTY? *LOVE* THEM TACOS."

MARTINEZ:
"OKAY BY *ME*, ALLISON. ALL WE GOTTA DO IS CONVINCE MY *WIFE*. YOU GUYS PACKED AWAY A *LOT* OF TACOS BEFORE YOU LEFT MY HOUSE."

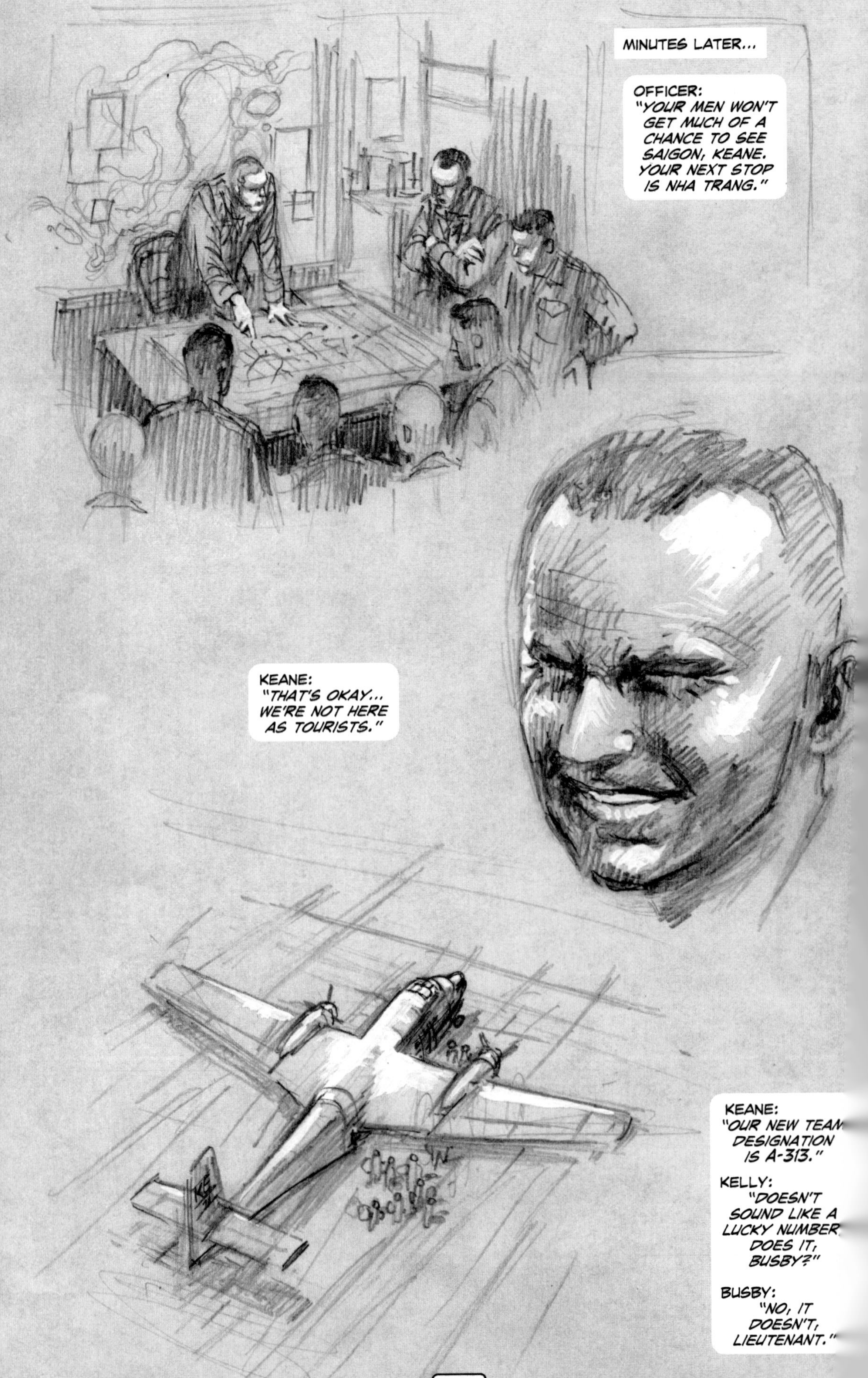

MINUTES LATER...
OFFICER: "YOUR MEN WON'T GET MUCH OF A CHANCE TO SEE SAIGON, KEANE. YOUR NEXT STOP IS NHA TRANG."
KEANE: "THAT'S OKAY... WE'RE NOT HERE AS TOURISTS."
KEANE: "OUR NEW TEAM DESIGNATION IS A-313."
KELLY: "DOESN'T SOUND LIKE A LUCKY NUMBER, DOES IT, BUSBY?"
BUSBY: "NO, IT DOESN'T, LIEUTENANT."

IT WAS A SHORT HOP TO NHA TRANG.
AFTER ONE DAY OF ORIENTATION
TRAINING IN NHA TRANG, A-313 WAS
ITCHING TO GET STARTED ON THEIR
MISSION...

STARK:
"ENOUGH
PRELIMINARIES
ALREADY.
WHEN DO WE GET
TO **WORK**, SIR?"

ALLISON:
"YEAH, CAP'N
KEANE. I'M
READY TO BLOW
THIS JOINT."

BUSBY:
"HEY—WHAT D'YA
SAY WE GO FOR
A CHANGE OF
PACE? DO SOME
JUMPING?"

"CHANGE OF PACE"
IS A JUMP OVER CAM
RANH BAY. THE THICK
GREEN CARPET OF
JUNGLE FLOWS INTO
THE SPARKLING BLUE-
GREEN WATER OF THE
BAY. BEAUTIFUL...
BREATHTAKING... AND
EXHILARATING.

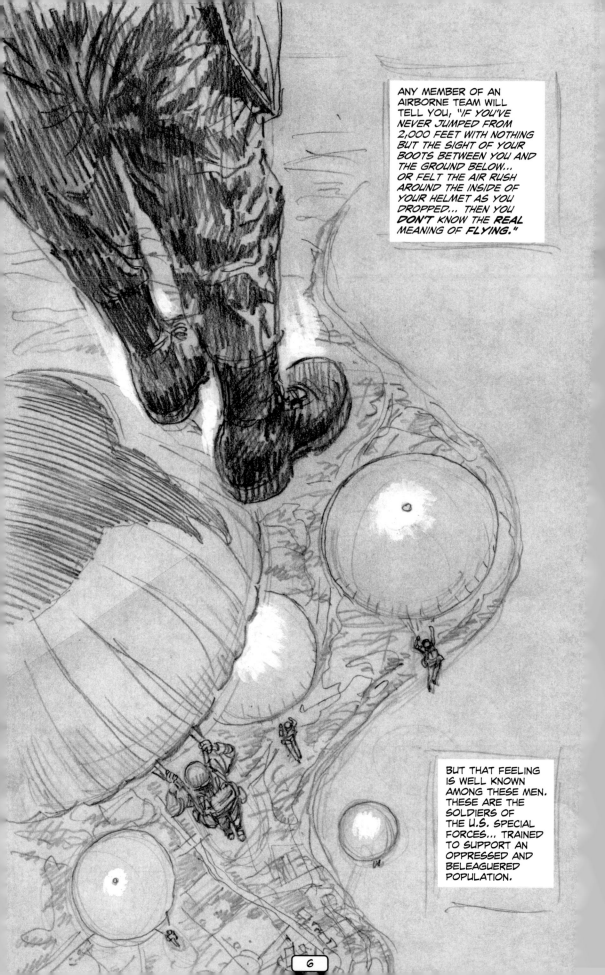

ANY MEMBER OF AN AIRBORNE TEAM WILL TELL YOU, "IF YOU'VE NEVER JUMPED FROM 2,000 FEET WITH NOTHING BUT THE SIGHT OF YOUR BOOTS BETWEEN YOU AND THE GROUND BELOW... OR FELT THE AIR RUSH AROUND THE INSIDE OF YOUR HELMET AS YOU DROPPED... THEN YOU *DON'T* KNOW THE *REAL* MEANING OF *FLYING.*"

BUT THAT FEELING IS WELL KNOWN AMONG THESE MEN. THESE ARE THE SOLDIERS OF THE U.S. SPECIAL FORCES... TRAINED TO SUPPORT AN OPPRESSED AND BELEAGUERED POPULATION.

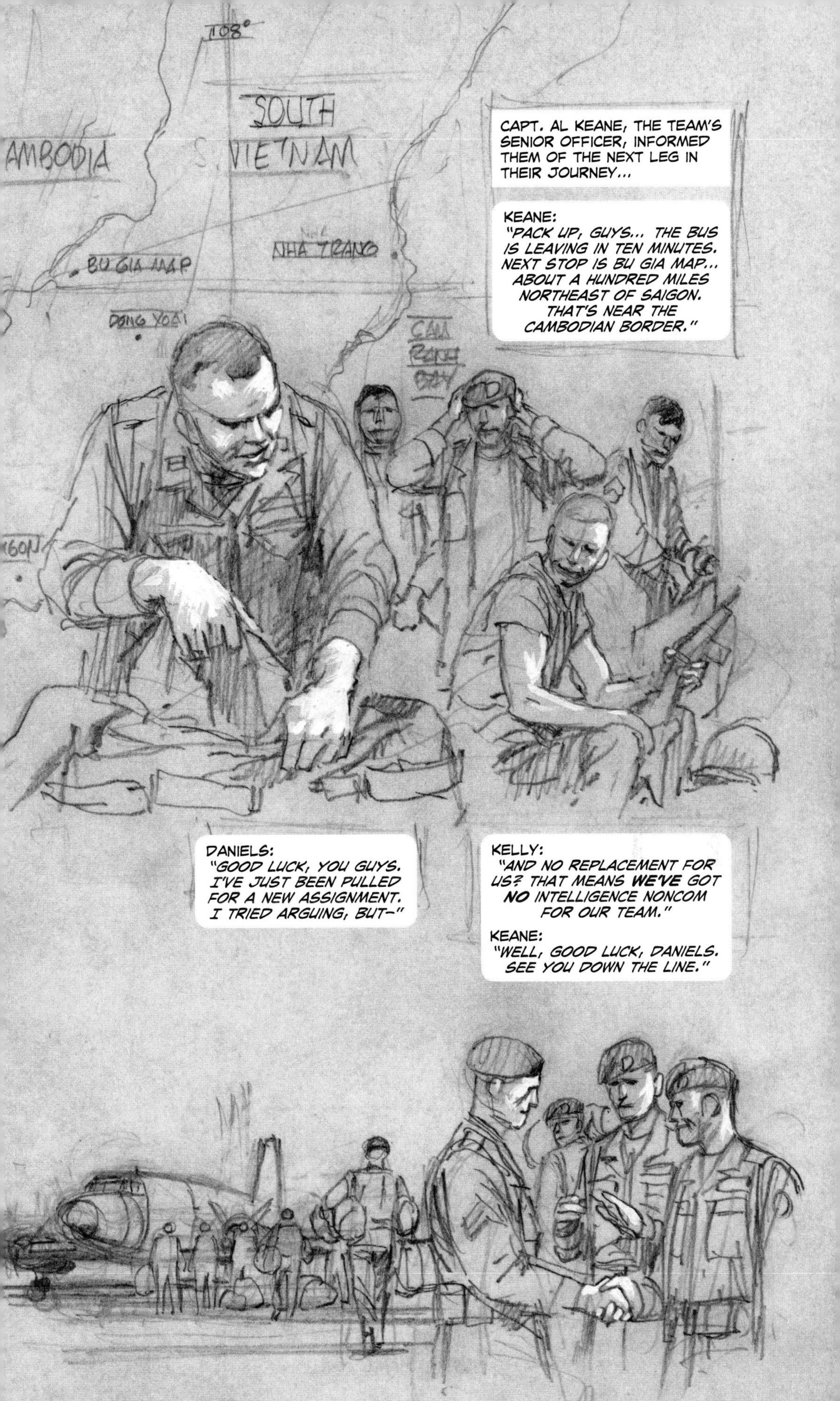
108°
SOUTH VIETNAM
NHA TRANG
CAPT. AL KEANE, THE TEAM'S SENIOR OFFICER, INFORMED THEM OF THE NEXT LEG IN THEIR JOURNEY...
KEANE: "PACK UP, GUYS... THE BUS IS LEAVING IN TEN MINUTES. NEXT STOP IS BU GIA MAP... ABOUT A HUNDRED MILES NORTHEAST OF SAIGON. THAT'S NEAR THE CAMBODIAN BORDER."
DANIELS: "GOOD LUCK, YOU GUYS. I'VE JUST BEEN PULLED FOR A NEW ASSIGNMENT. I TRIED ARGUING, BUT-"
KELLY: "AND NO REPLACEMENT FOR US? THAT MEANS **WE'VE** GOT **NO** INTELLIGENCE NONCOM FOR OUR TEAM."
KEANE: "WELL, GOOD LUCK, DANIELS. SEE YOU DOWN THE LINE."

MARTINEZ:
"WHAT'S WAITIN' FOR US IN BU GIA MAP, SIR? HOPE THEY GOT A SPA THERE."

KELLY:
"SURE... WITH HOT'N' COLD RUNNING BEER, MARTINEZ."

KEANE:
"OUR JOB IS TO TRAIN THE CIVILIAN IRREGULAR DEFENSE FORCES AND ACT AS ADVISORS TO THE VIETNAMESE SPECIAL FORCES."

KEANE:
"WE ALSO CHECK ON INFILTRATION ROUTES OF THE VIET CONG AND TRAIN THEM FOR ACTIVE DEFENSE AND AGGRESSIVE PATROLLING."

KELLY:
"OH, IS THAT ALL, CAP'N?"

KEANE:
"LOOKS LIKE WE'RE ALMOST THERE, GENTLEMEN. WHAT SAY WE MAKE A JUMP... BEFORE WE LAND? WE MAY NOT GET ANOTHER CHANCE FOR AWHILE."

KEANE:
"THERE IT IS...
BEAUTIFUL DOWN-
TOWN BU GIA MAP.
WATCH OUT FOR THE
THORN BUSHES."

BU GIA MAP IS LOCATED ON
A CLEARING SURROUNDED
BY DENSE JUNGLE.
MONTAGNARDS, THE
MOUNTAIN PEOPLE NATIVE
TO VIET NAM, OCCUPY A
SMALL VILLAGE NEARBY.

SEVERAL CIDG* COMPANIES
AND VIETNAMESE SPECIAL
FORCES OCCUPY THE CAMP.

BARTON:
"LOOKS LIKE A WELCOMING
COMMITTEE'S OUT TO GREET
US. CAREFUL YOU DON'T
LAND ON ANY OF 'EM."

*CIVILIAN IRREGULAR DEFENSE GROUP

THE TEAM MEETS WITH THE U.S. OFFICER IN CHARGE. DETACHMENT A-313 ASSUMES RESPONSIBILITY FOR BU GIA MAP FROM DETACHMENT A-223. TACTICALLY, THIS CAMP IS LOCATED IN THE MOST REMOTE AREA ON THE CHART... CLOSE TO THE BORDER OF CAMBODIA.

ROSEN:
"CAP'N KEANE? I'M ROSEN, C.O. OF A-223. WELCOME TO THE HINTERLANDS. WE'RE SURE HAPPY T'SEE Y'ALL."

KEANE:
"SAME HERE. WHAT CAN YOU TELL US ABOUT BU GIA MAP?"

ROSEN:
"THEY'RE GOOD PEOPLE HERE, BUT YOU'VE GOT A LOT OF WORK AHEAD OF YOU. THEY DON'T LIKE THE V.C.... BUT FOLKS NEED TRAINING. I'LL SHOW YOU AND YOUR MEN THE LAYOUT HERE... THEN I'LL BE TAKIN' OFF. GOOD LUCK... 'N' STAY HEALTHY."

THE NEW A-TEAM IS GREETED WARMLY BY THE MONTAGNARDS... ESPECIALLY BY THE CHILDREN... WHO SCRAMBLE FOR CANDY AND CHEWING GUM.

THE COMPOUND'S GENERAL CONDITIONS ARE GOOD. QUARTERS CONTAINED FOLDING COTS AND ELECTRICITY SUPPLIED BY GENERATORS. SHOWERS AND FLUSH TOILETS, TOO. COOKING STOVES ARE BUTANE-FED, AND WATER IS CLEAN.

THEY HAVE REFRIGERATORS THAT ARE KEROSENE-OPERATED.
LAUNDRY AND GENERAL CLEAN-UP IS DONE ON A REGULAR BASIS BY THE VILLAGERS.
NOT THE HILTON, IT'S TRUE. BUT A FEW LEVELS BETTER THAN EXPECTED.

KELLY:
"OKAY, MEN... LET'S CHECK THE BUILDINGS AND DEFENSES. LET'S GET TO WORK."

KELLY:
"ALL BUILDINGS AND FORTIFICATIONS LOOK TO BE IN GOOD SHAPE, CAP'N KEANE. WALLS'RE PROTECTED BY SANDBAGS, AND A PERIMETER OF BARBED WIRE SURROUNDS THE CAMP."

KEANE:
"SOUNDS GOOD, KELLY. HOW'S IT LOOK TO YOU, CANTRO?"

CANTRO:
"MINES AND BOOBY TRAPS ARE PRETTY PRIMITIVE – SOME OF 'EM NEED TO BE REPLACED."

CANTRO:
"THEY DUG A TRENCH AROUND THE ENCAMPMENT, BUT IT LACKS A CONNECTION WITH COMMUNICATION. THAT'S **NOT** GOOD."

THE TEAM GETS TO MEET THE STRIKE FORCE CONTINGENTS. THEY COME FROM DIFFERENT AREAS. ONE GROUP IS FROM CAMBODIA WHICH IS ON THE WESTERN BORDER OF VIET NAM. THE MEN ARE SHORT IN STATURE... BUT TOUGH.

THE MONTAGNARDS ARE INDIGENOUS PEOPLE WHO INHABIT THE MOUNTAIN AREAS. THEY'VE BEEN HERE FOREVER.

ANOTHER GROUP A-TEAM TAGS AS "SAIGON COWBOYS" ARE YOUNG AND FULL OF THEMSELVES. A GOOD NUMBER OF THEM ENLISTED IN ORDER TO AVOID A LONGER STRETCH IN THE REGULAR VIETNAMESE ARMY.

THESE ARE THE MEN THE ADVISORS MUST TRAIN AND DEVELOP INTO SOLDIERS.

MARTINEZ:
"WE GOT A **LOT** OF WORK TO DO, GENTLEMEN. THESE MONTAGNARDS ARE SERIOUS WORKERS AND NEED OUR HELP."

KELLY:
"YEAH. THEY'RE MOSTLY FARMERS. SO, LET'S GET ON IT."

BARTON:
"RIGHT, MARTINEZ. THEY WORK ALL DAY IN THE FIELDS AN' SING CHANTS ALL NIGHT... TO WARD OFF EVIL SPIRITS."

CARTER:
"IT'S GONNA TAKE MORE'N **CHANTS** OR **GRAND OL' OPRY** TO WARD OFF THE V.C.... THERE'S LOTS A' WORK T'DO."

FALLON:
"MOST OF 'EM LIVE IN THESE LONGHOUSES... SEVERAL FAMILIES TOGETHER, ALLISON."

ALLISON:
"YEAH, FALLON... BUT THAT WON'T HELP THEM MUCH... AGAINST A V.C. ATTACK. THEIR SELF-DEFENSE NEEDS **WORK.**"

ESTABLISHING A RELATIONSHIP WITH THEIR VIETNAMESE COUNTERPARTS IS NOT AN EASY TASK. BUT IT IS ESSENTIAL TO DO SO. TRUST IS A VITAL BUILDING BLOCK IF A-TEAM'S PURPOSE IS TO BE ACCOMPLISHED.

THE WORK INVOLVES THE IMPROVEMENT OF BUNKERS AND TRENCH WALLS..

...CHECKING DEFENSIVE BARBED WIRE...

...OBSERVING AND RECOGNIZING POTENTIAL FIELDS OF FIRE...

...AND HOLDING CONTINUAL PRACTICE ALERTS.

THOSE ARE THE ORDERS OF THE DAY... AND NIGHT.

BUT PUSH COME TO SHOVE, THE A-TEAM DEPENDS ON *EACH OTHER*. AT LEAST ONE USSF MAN WAS ON DUTY EVERY NIGHT. HE WAS ALSO RESPONSIBLE FOR MAKING SURE THERE WAS WARM WATER FOR SHAVING AND BATHING NEXT DAY.

FALLON:
"I PULLED GUARD DUTY LAST NIGHT, LOOTENANT. WATER HOT ENOUGH FOR YA?"

KELLY:
"NO, FALLON... BUT, IT'LL DO."

THE IMPORTANCE OF PATROLS CAN'T BE OVERESTIMATED. AS EMPHASIS, TWO USSF ADVISORS ALWAYS ACCOMPANY TWENTY TO FORTY CIDG SOLDIERS IN A PATROL GROUP.

THE PATROLS' MISSIONS ARE TO LOCATE THE V.C. AND DISRUPT INFILTRATION ROUTES. SOME OF THE PATROLS WERE REWARDING... OTHERS WERE... LESS INTERESTING.

THE A-TEAM TAKES IT AS IT COMES.

CARTER:
"Y'KNOW, ALLISON...
IT WOULD'A BEEN A LOT EASIER
– AND FASTER – IF THEY'D INSERTED
US BY 'COPTER."

ALLISON:
"YEAH... AN' IF MY MOM HAD BEEN
BORN WITH **PANTS**, SHE'D–"

CARTER:
"HOLD IT, ALLISON. LOOKS
LIKE V.C.'S BEEN USING THIS
AREA LIKE A MAIN BOULEVARD
THIS SIDE OF THE RIVER."

ALLISON:
"RIGHT! EYES OPEN FOR
BOOBY TRAPS."

ALLISON:
"WAIT A MINUTE.
DO YOU HEAR --?"

CARTER:
"**WOODCHOPPING.**
SOMEBODY'S CUTTIN'
TREES ON THE OTHER
SIDE OF THE RIVER."

ALLISON:
"THE WATER'S NOT DEEP HERE. WE CAN—"

A HIGH-PITCHED VOICE FROM THE PATROL:
"NO, WE CANNOT."

THE VIETNAMESE NONCOM SPOKE RAPIDLY
IN CLIPPED SENTENCES:
"ORDERS ARE TO STAY WITHIN COMMITTED
BOUNDARIES. NO EXTENSIONS. NOT TO
INSTIGATE COMBAT."

ALLISON:
"OKAY. NOTHIN' T'DO,
THEN... BUT HEAD BACK
TO BU GIA MAP."

CARTER:
"RIGHT."

THAT NIGHT BACK AT
THE ENCAMPMENT...

FALLON:
"JUST GOT A RADIO
MESSAGE, CAPT. KEANE.
VILLAGE OF DAK O...
'BOUT FOUR MILES FROM
US... HAS BEEN RAIDED.
BURNED..."

KEANE:
"BARTON, CANTRO...
GET A PLATOON OF
CIDG TOGETHER. CHECK
IT OUT. NOW."

18

HOURS LATER, AS DAWN SPREADS ITS LIGHT OVER A SMOKE-FILLED SKY COVERING DAK O...

BARTON:
"NO PEOPLE AROUND ANYWHERE, CANTRO. NO BODIES. NOTHIN'."

CANTRO:
"ALL THE FOODSTUFF'S BEEN TAKEN."

BARTON:
"YEAH. THE V.C. ARE GOOD AT THAT."

CANTRO:
"FROM THE TRACKS, LOOKS LIKE THERE MUST'VE BEEN LESS THAN A DOZEN V.C.... AND THE VILLAGERS JUST TOOK OFF."

BARTON:
"MAYBE WE CAN STILL CATCH THE BOYS THAT DID THIS. LET'S SEE IF WE CAN SNIFF 'EM OUT, OK?"

AS BARTON AND CANTRO MOVE THEIR GROUP
FROM DAK O, ANOTHER PATROL, LED BY CARTER
AND KELLY, SURVEY THE NEARBY AREA...

CARTER:
"GOOD THING BARTON ALERTED US
TO HIS FINDINGS AT DAK O."

KELLY:
"YEAH. KEEP A WATCH OUT FOR THOSE
PUNJI STAKES. V.C. DIPS 'EM IN EXCREMENT
AN' PLANT 'EM EVERYWHERE—"

A RUSTLE OF DRY LEAVES...
A SNAP OF A TWIG GIVE
EVIDENCE TO ELEMENTS OF A
V.C. COMPANY IN THE SHADOWS
OF THE JUNGLE UNDERGROWTH.

A WHISPERED COMMAND IS GIVEN TO TAKE COVER... FOLLOWED BY AN ORDER TO OPEN FIRE AT THE VIETCONG.

RETURN FIRE IS IMMEDIATE AS THE SOUNDS REVERBERATE SHARPLY THROUGH THE JUNGLE.

BUT THE HEAVY FOLIAGE MAKES IT DIFFICULT TO FOCUS ON A TARGET. THE SHOTS ARE RANDOM AND INEFFECTIVE.

KELLY:
 "WE GOTTA GET **CLOSER** TO 'EM, CARTER... MAYBE SHAKE 'EM OUTTA THE GRASS."

CARTER:
 "CHECK. I'LL MAINTAIN A BASE OF FIRE WITH OUR GUYS...WE'LL COVER YOU."

SEIZING AN OPPORTUNITY IN A MOMENT OF SILENCE, 2ND LT. KELLY MOTIONS SEVERAL OF HIS PATROL GROUP TO ACCOMPANY HIS ADVANCE ON THE CONCEALED VIET CONG...

...WHO IMMEDIATELY RESUME A LETHAL BARRAGE AT THE CHARGING FIGURES.

THE V.C. DID WHAT ANY NORMAL PERSON WOULD DO IN THE FACE OF THE SCREAMING CHARGE LED BY 2ND LT. KELLY. THEY RAN!

CARTER:
"THEY'RE GONE, SIR. TOOK TO THE HILLS."

KELLY:
"LOOKS LIKE, CARTER. OKAY... LET'S TAKE CARE OF OUR WOUNDED, FIRST. THEN, PICK UP ANY LOOSE GEAR... REPORT THE ACTION... AN' HEAD BACK TO CAMP."

KELLY:
"EVERYTHING SET? OKAY...LET'S GO HOME."

ON A TRAIL BACK TO BU GIA MAP, THE PLATOON LED BY SSGT. JIMMY CANTRO AND SSGT SAM BARTON CAME UPON AN ARVN* GROUP IN A SMALL CLEARING. IT WAS A FRIENDLY GREETING.

"AH... YOU ARE AMERICANS... WELCOME."

THE ARVN OFFICER SPOKE IN A CULTURED TONE:
"WE WERE SENT FROM DON BINH... RECONNAISSANCE. WE DISCOVERED THIS MISSIONARY SETTLEMENT. BURNED... DESTROYED. ALL THE INHABITANTS WERE GONE... NONE REMAINED. BUT, COME, SERGEANT... WON'T YOU AND YOUR COMRADE JOIN ME FOR LUNCH? WE HAVE DUCK... CHICKEN..."

BARTON:
"THANKS, CAPTAIN. HEY... WE'RE STILL IN THE JUNGLE, AREN'T WE? AND THE V.C. ARE CLOSE BY... WHITE DINNER CLOTH? NAPKINS? DINNERWARE?"

THE COOL ANSWER WAS:
"OF COURSE, SERGEANT. BUT THE SITUATION SHOULD NOT CEASE CONTINUATION OF NORMAL AMENITIES..."

*ARMY OF THE REPUBLIC OF VIET NAM

TOWARDS LATE AFTERNOON, THE USSF ADVISORS AND THEIR GROUPS MAKE THEIR WAY BACK TO BU GIA MAP. BARTON GIVES HIS REPORT TO CAPT. KEANE...

BARTON:
"THIS IS ONE CRAZY WAR, SIR. HE HAD A CHECKERED TABLECLOTH. SILVERWARE. THE WORKS. ONLY THING MISSIN' WAS THE CHINESE WAITER."

KEANE:
"DON'T BE FOOLED BY WHAT YOU JUST SAW, BARTON. THIS WAR'S HEATING UP. THAT'S WHY WE'VE GOT ORDERS TO GET ANY AND ALL ADDITIONAL INFO ON V.C. MOVEMENTS.
I GOT A FEELING THINGS'RE GOING TO GET REAL SERIOUS... SOONER THAN LATER."

CAPT. KEANE CONTACTS THE
ARVN OFFICERS IN CAMP. ANY
SUBSEQUENT ACTIONS CANNOT
BE ENACTED WITHOUT THE
AGREEMENT AND PERMISSION
OF THE VIETNAMESE. THE
USSF ARE ADVISORS...
NOT INITIATORS.

KEANE:
"I NEED MORE MEN FOR A
SPECIAL RECON MISSION. A
LARGER PATROL FORCE WILL–"

ASPIRANT*:
"SORRY... BUT, IN THE ABSENCE
OF MY COMMANDER, LT. LUC,
I CANNOT AUTHORIZE OUR
PERSONNEL TO DUTY PATROL."

KEANE:
"BUT THESE ORDERS
ARE FROM YOUR OWN
HEADQUARTERS–"

ASPIRANT:
"I AM SORRY, BUT UNTIL
MY SUPERIOR – LT. LUC
– RETURNS AND GIVES
SPECIFIC PERMISSION...
I CANNOT–"

KEANE:
"THIS CAN'T WAIT!
WHERE IS LT. LUC?"

ASPIRANT:
"LT. LUC IS ON
A VISIT TO HIS
HOME AND GAVE
ORDERS NOT TO BE
CONTACTED... OR
DISTURBED."

KEANE:
"I'M SORRY,
BUT THAT'S NOT
ACCEPTABLE."

ASPIRANT:
"I, TOO,
AM SORRY."

*ASPIRANT IS A GRADE CLOSER
TO WARRANT OFFICER. THEY ARE
"ASPIRING" TO BECOME LIEUTENANT.

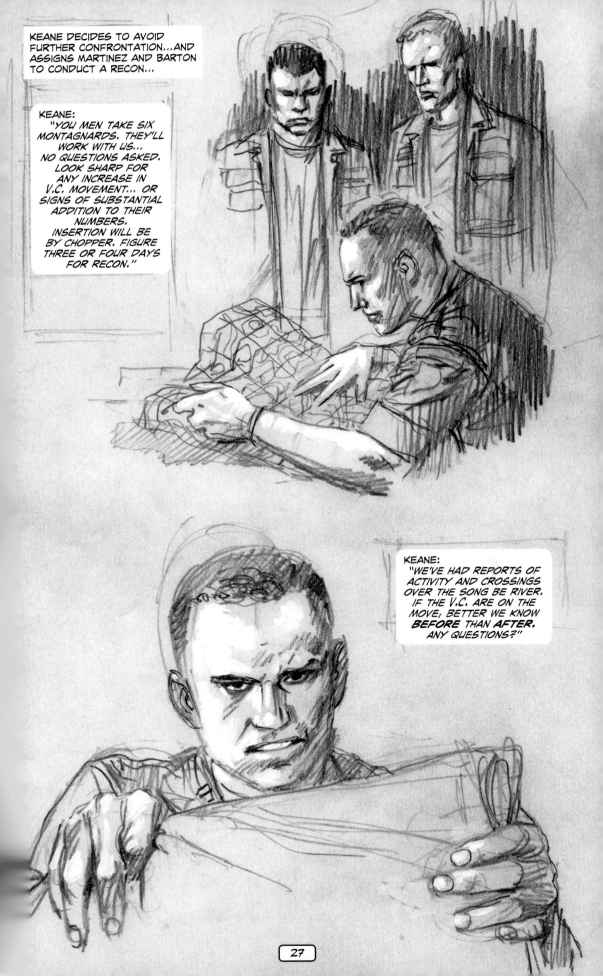

KEANE DECIDES TO AVOID FURTHER CONFRONTATION...AND ASSIGNS MARTINEZ AND BARTON TO CONDUCT A RECON...

KEANE:
"YOU MEN TAKE SIX MONTAGNARDS. THEY'LL WORK WITH US... NO QUESTIONS ASKED. LOOK SHARP FOR ANY INCREASE IN V.C. MOVEMENT... OR SIGNS OF SUBSTANTIAL ADDITION TO THEIR NUMBERS. INSERTION WILL BE BY CHOPPER. FIGURE THREE OR FOUR DAYS FOR RECON."

KEANE:
"WE'VE HAD REPORTS OF ACTIVITY AND CROSSINGS OVER THE SONG BE RIVER. IF THE V.C. ARE ON THE MOVE, BETTER WE KNOW **BEFORE** THAN **AFTER**. ANY QUESTIONS?"

AS THE HELICOPTER CARRYING THE RECON TEAM LIFTS OFF TOWARDS THE JUNGLE, KEANE'S MIND IS ALREADY OCCUPIED WITH OTHER THINGS...

KEANE THINKS:
"GOTTA MAKE SURE STARK AND BARTON KEEP THESE VILLAGE PEOPLE AND THEIR FAMILIES HEALTHY. THAT MEANS OVERSEEING SANITATION AND MAINTAINING A CLEAN WATER SUPPLY. THE VILLAGERS ARE GOOD PEOPLE... BUT THEY'VE GOT A LOT TO LEARN ABOUT BASIC HYGIENE AND HEALTH CARE.

THESE PEOPLE HAVE BEEN CONSTANTLY BESET WITH WORMS... MALARIA... TYPHOID... AND DYSENTERY. AND THEY'LL APPRECIATE THE HELP WE CAN GIVE THEM."

KEANE:
"THESE PEOPLE ARE
CLOSE-KNIT WITH THEIR
FAMILIES. THE MEN TAKE
THEIR WIVES AND CHILDREN
WHEREVER THEY GO.
THAT COULD PRESENT
PROBLEMS. IN CASE OF
A V.C. ATTACK — WHAT'S
THEIR PRIORITY?"

KELLY:
"MAYBE THE MEN'LL
FIGHT *HARDER* IF
THEIR FAMILIES—"

MARTINEZ:
"YEAH... AN'
MAYBE SOME OF
THE *FAMILY* ARE
GATHERING INFO
FOR THE V.C."

KEANE:
"POINT IS, THERE'S
NOTHING WE CAN DO
BUT WORK WITH THE
SITUATION WE *GOT.*"

KEANE:
"WE'VE GOT TO LEARN MORE ABOUT THEM... TRY TO UNDERSTAND *THEIR* WAYS. THAT'S OUR JOB."

KELLY:
"RIGHT. THEY'RE BASICALLY GOOD PEOPLE. THEY JUST WANT TO BE LEFT ALONE... IN PEACE."

McCAINE:
"YEAH...AND *WE'RE* HERE TO HELP THEM DO JUST *THAT*."

MARTINEZ:
"THE ORIENTATION WE GOT STATESIDE HELPED A LITTLE TO UNDERSTAND THEM...BUT..."

KEANE:
"...IT WAS ONLY AN INTRODUCTION TO A COMPLEX SITUATION. THERE'S A *LOT* MORE WE HAVE TO LEARN... ABOUT THEM AND THEIR WAYS."

KELLY:
"LET 'EM KNOW WE'RE *NOT* HERE TO *CHANGE* THEM. ONLY... TO *HELP* THEM."

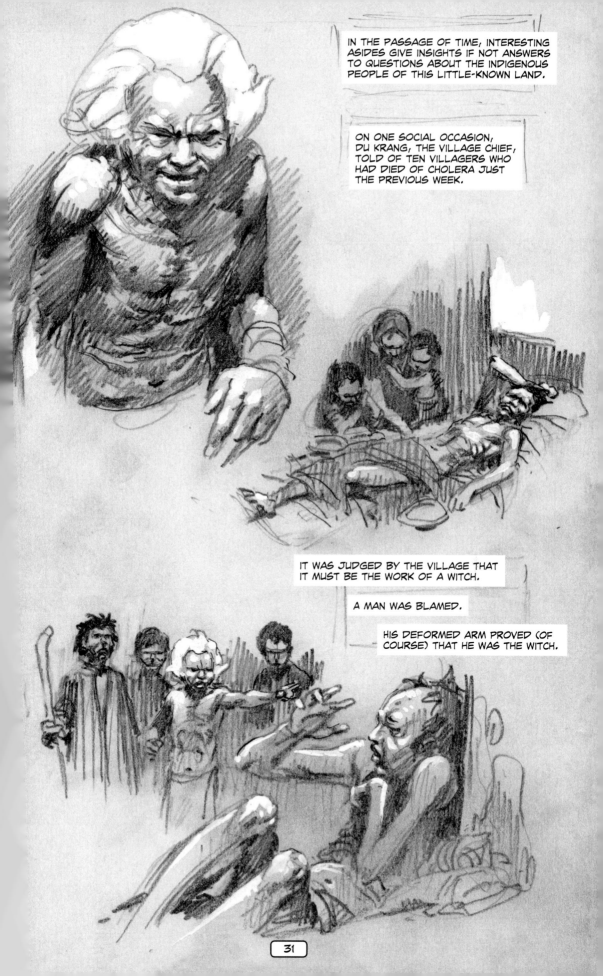

IN THE PASSAGE OF TIME, INTERESTING ASIDES GIVE INSIGHTS IF NOT ANSWERS TO QUESTIONS ABOUT THE INDIGENOUS PEOPLE OF THIS LITTLE-KNOWN LAND.

ON ONE SOCIAL OCCASION, DU KRANG, THE VILLAGE CHIEF, TOLD OF TEN VILLAGERS WHO HAD DIED OF CHOLERA JUST THE PREVIOUS WEEK.

IT WAS JUDGED BY THE VILLAGE THAT IT MUST BE THE WORK OF A WITCH.

A MAN WAS BLAMED.

HIS DEFORMED ARM PROVED (OF COURSE) THAT HE WAS THE WITCH.

THE POOR CRIPPLE DEFENDED HIS INNOCENCE VEHEMENTLY AND DENIED THAT HE WAS A WITCH. BUT HIS PROTESTS WENT FOR NAUGHT.

THERE WAS ONLY ONE SURE WAY TO PROVE HIS GUILT OR INNOCENCE. A TEST MUST BE PERFORMED.

MOLTEN LEAD HAD TO BE POURED INTO THE PALM OF HIS GOOD HAND. IF THE HOT LEAD BURNED THROUGH HIS HAND, HE TRULY WAS A WITCH.

THE TEST NEVER FAILED.

SO THE TEST TOOK PLACE.

THE HOT LEAD DID NOT EAT THROUGH THE MAN'S HAND. BUT, SADLY, THIS WAS NOT THE EXPECTED (OR ACCEPTABLE) OUTCOME.

DESPITE THE TEST'S RESULT OF INNOCENCE -- THE VILLAGERS KILLED THE POOR CRIPPLE.

AFTER WHICH HIS HEAD AND LIMBS WERE SEVERED AND HIS LIVER WAS CUT OUT. ALL WAS THROWN ONTO A GARBAGE HEAP. OR SO THE STORY WENT.

ACCORDING TO THE WITNESSES, THE EVENT SERVED TWO POSITIVE PURPOSES:
   IT SUGGESTED THAT ANYONE WITH PHYSICAL DIFFICULTIES LOOK ELSEWHERE TO RESIDE; AND IT HELPED PROMOTE BETTER VILLAGE SANITATION.

   ANYHOW, THAT'S HOW THE STORY WENT.

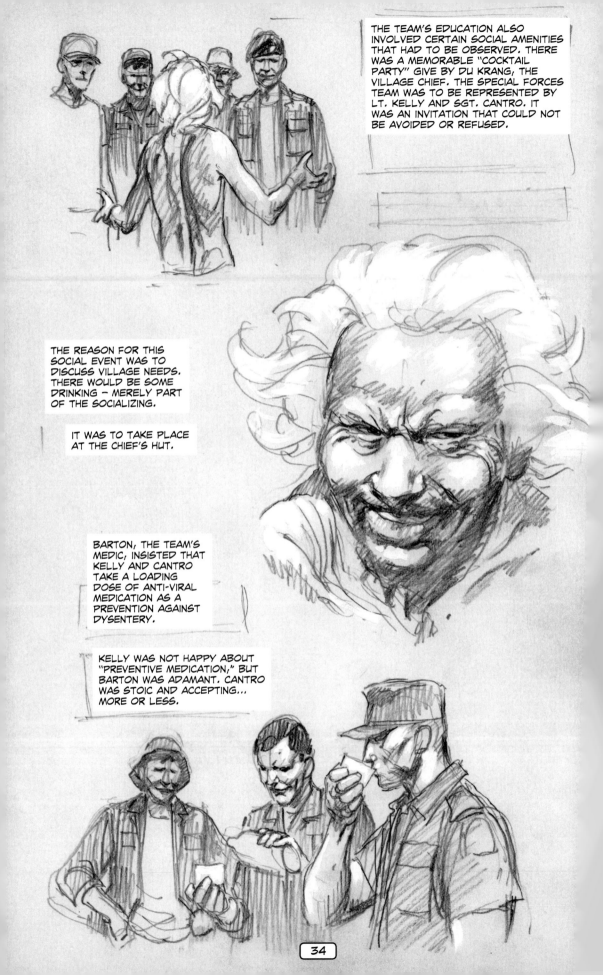

THE TEAM'S EDUCATION ALSO INVOLVED CERTAIN SOCIAL AMENITIES THAT HAD TO BE OBSERVED. THERE WAS A MEMORABLE "COCKTAIL PARTY" GIVE BY DU KRANG, THE VILLAGE CHIEF. THE SPECIAL FORCES TEAM WAS TO BE REPRESENTED BY LT. KELLY AND SGT. CANTRO. IT WAS AN INVITATION THAT COULD NOT BE AVOIDED OR REFUSED.

THE REASON FOR THIS SOCIAL EVENT WAS TO DISCUSS VILLAGE NEEDS. THERE WOULD BE SOME DRINKING – MERELY PART OF THE SOCIALIZING.

IT WAS TO TAKE PLACE AT THE CHIEF'S HUT.

BARTON, THE TEAM'S MEDIC, INSISTED THAT KELLY AND CANTRO TAKE A LOADING DOSE OF ANTI-VIRAL MEDICATION AS A PREVENTION AGAINST DYSENTERY.

KELLY WAS NOT HAPPY ABOUT "PREVENTIVE MEDICATION," BUT BARTON WAS ADAMANT. CANTRO WAS STOIC AND ACCEPTING... MORE OR LESS.

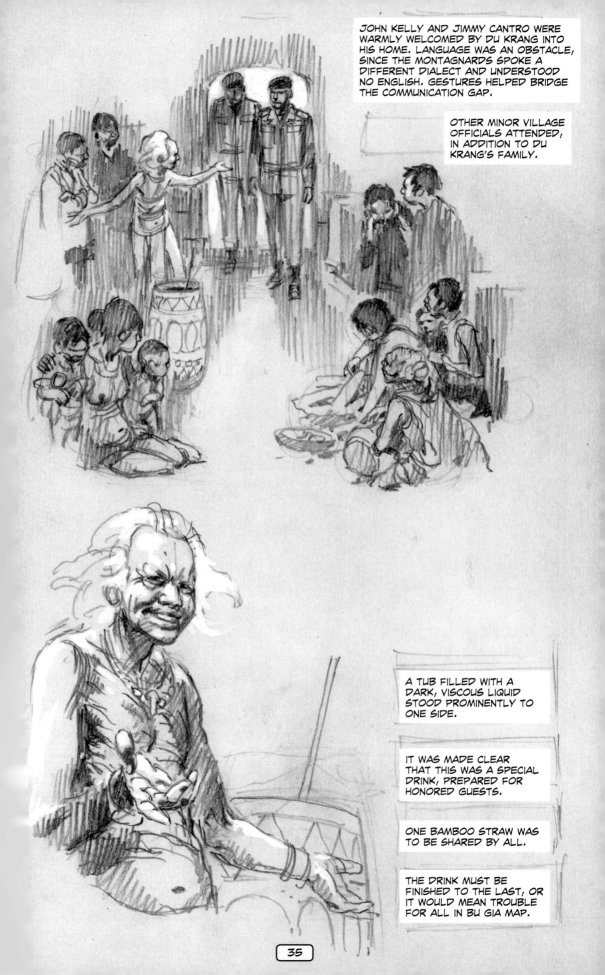

JOHN KELLY AND JIMMY CANTRO WERE WARMLY WELCOMED BY DU KRANG INTO HIS HOME. LANGUAGE WAS AN OBSTACLE, SINCE THE MONTAGNARDS SPOKE A DIFFERENT DIALECT AND UNDERSTOOD NO ENGLISH. GESTURES HELPED BRIDGE THE COMMUNICATION GAP.

OTHER MINOR VILLAGE OFFICIALS ATTENDED, IN ADDITION TO DU KRANG'S FAMILY.

A TUB FILLED WITH A DARK, VISCOUS LIQUID STOOD PROMINENTLY TO ONE SIDE.

IT WAS MADE CLEAR THAT THIS WAS A SPECIAL DRINK, PREPARED FOR HONORED GUESTS.

ONE BAMBOO STRAW WAS TO BE SHARED BY ALL.

THE DRINK MUST BE FINISHED TO THE LAST, OR IT WOULD MEAN TROUBLE FOR ALL IN BU GIA MAP.

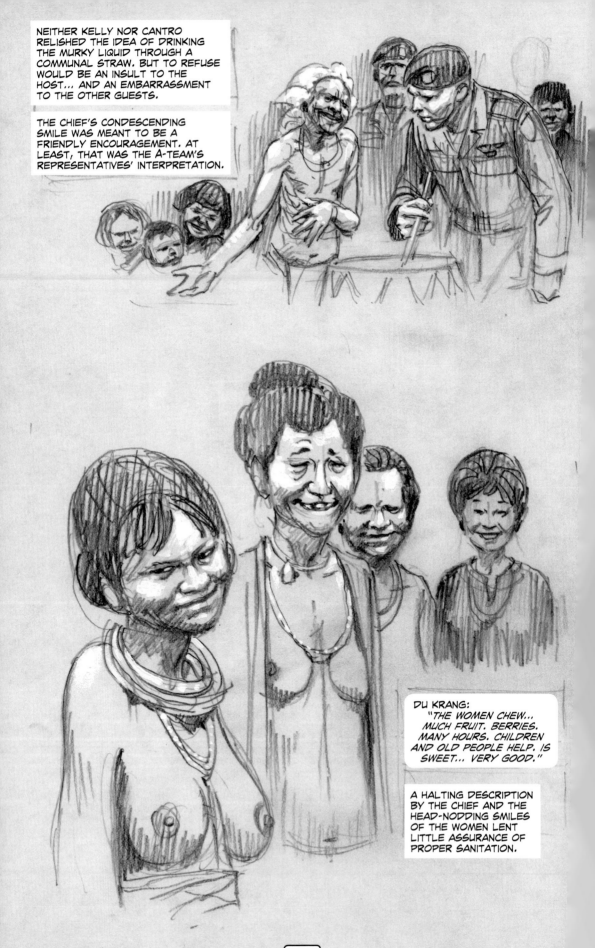

NEITHER KELLY NOR CANTRO RELISHED THE IDEA OF DRINKING THE MURKY LIQUID THROUGH A COMMUNAL STRAW. BUT TO REFUSE WOULD BE AN INSULT TO THE HOST... AND AN EMBARRASSMENT TO THE OTHER GUESTS.

THE CHIEF'S CONDESCENDING SMILE WAS MEANT TO BE A FRIENDLY ENCOURAGEMENT. AT LEAST, THAT WAS THE A-TEAM'S REPRESENTATIVES' INTERPRETATION.

DU KRANG:
"THE WOMEN CHEW... MUCH FRUIT. BERRIES. MANY HOURS. CHILDREN AND OLD PEOPLE HELP. IS SWEET... VERY GOOD."

A HALTING DESCRIPTION BY THE CHIEF AND THE HEAD-NODDING SMILES OF THE WOMEN LENT LITTLE ASSURANCE OF PROPER SANITATION.

WITH A SILENT PRAYER, BOTH KELLY AND CANTRO TOOK THEIR TURN AT THE STRAW REED AGAIN AND AGAIN. THEY FELT FINE... EVEN A BIT EXHILARATED. CASTING CAUTION ASIDE, THEY JOINED IN WITH THE FESTIVITIES. AFTER ALL, IT WAS IMPORTANT TO CEMENT RELATIONSHIPS WITH THESE COMRADES IN ARMS.

EVENTUALLY, THE HUT RESOUNDED WITH SOUNDS AKIN TO MUSIC. WHEN DANCING COMMENCED, THE HOST HAD LITTLE TROUBLE IN CONVINCING KELLY TO JOIN IN.

PERHAPS EMBOLDENED BY THE SWEET DRINK, KELLY SHOWED THEM HOW TO SHAKE A LEG... OR TWO. CANTRO WATCHED IN AWE AND ASTONISHMENT.

THE SOCIALIZING WENT ON LATE INTO THE NIGHT... AND A GOOD TIME WAS HAD BY ALL PARTICIPANTS.

DAWN WITNESSED A RECIPROCAL EXCHANGE OF TOKENS OF FRIENDSHIP. DU KRANG, CHIEF OF THE MONTAGNARDS, GAVE LT. KELLY A BRACELET. A PROTECTION FROM HARM. KELLY GAVE THE CHIEF AN EPISCOPAL MEDALLION HE REMOVED FROM HIS DOGTAG CHAIN... TO SERVE A SIMILAR PURPOSE.

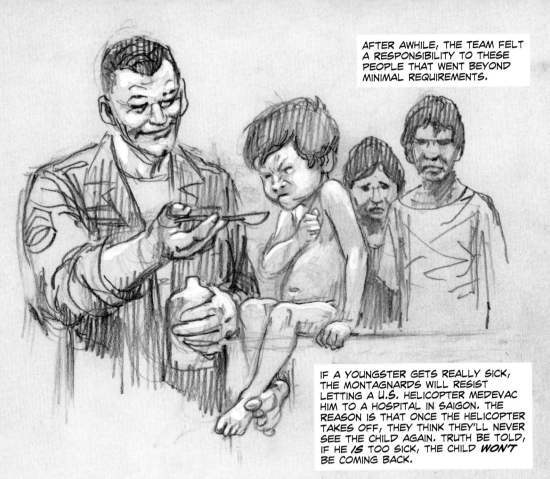

AFTER AWHILE, THE TEAM FELT A RESPONSIBILITY TO THESE PEOPLE THAT WENT BEYOND MINIMAL REQUIREMENTS.

IF A YOUNGSTER GETS REALLY SICK, THE MONTAGNARDS WILL RESIST LETTING A U.S. HELICOPTER MEDEVAC HIM TO A HOSPITAL IN SAIGON. THE REASON IS THAT ONCE THE HELICOPTER TAKES OFF, THEY THINK THEY'LL NEVER SEE THE CHILD AGAIN. TRUTH BE TOLD, IF HE *IS* TOO SICK, THE CHILD *WON'T* BE COMING BACK.

TRAINING THESE PEOPLE IS A CHALLENGE. THEY STILL HAVE A WAYS TO GO TO ENTER THE 20TH CENTURY.

IN ADDITION TO THE PROBLEMS OF ACCLIMATION, PROPER CARE AND MAINTENANCE OF EQUIPMENT IS A CONSTANT CHORE. WEAPONS NEED TO BE KEPT CLEAN AND OILED... READY FOR USE.

TRAINING THE VIETNAMESE TO USE THEM TAKES TIME AND PATIENCE. *LOTS* OF PATIENCE.

IT WAS AT THIS TIME THAT A TEAM LED BY MARTINEZ AND BARTON LEFT BU GIA MAP ON A RECON MISSION VIA HELICOPTER INSERTION.

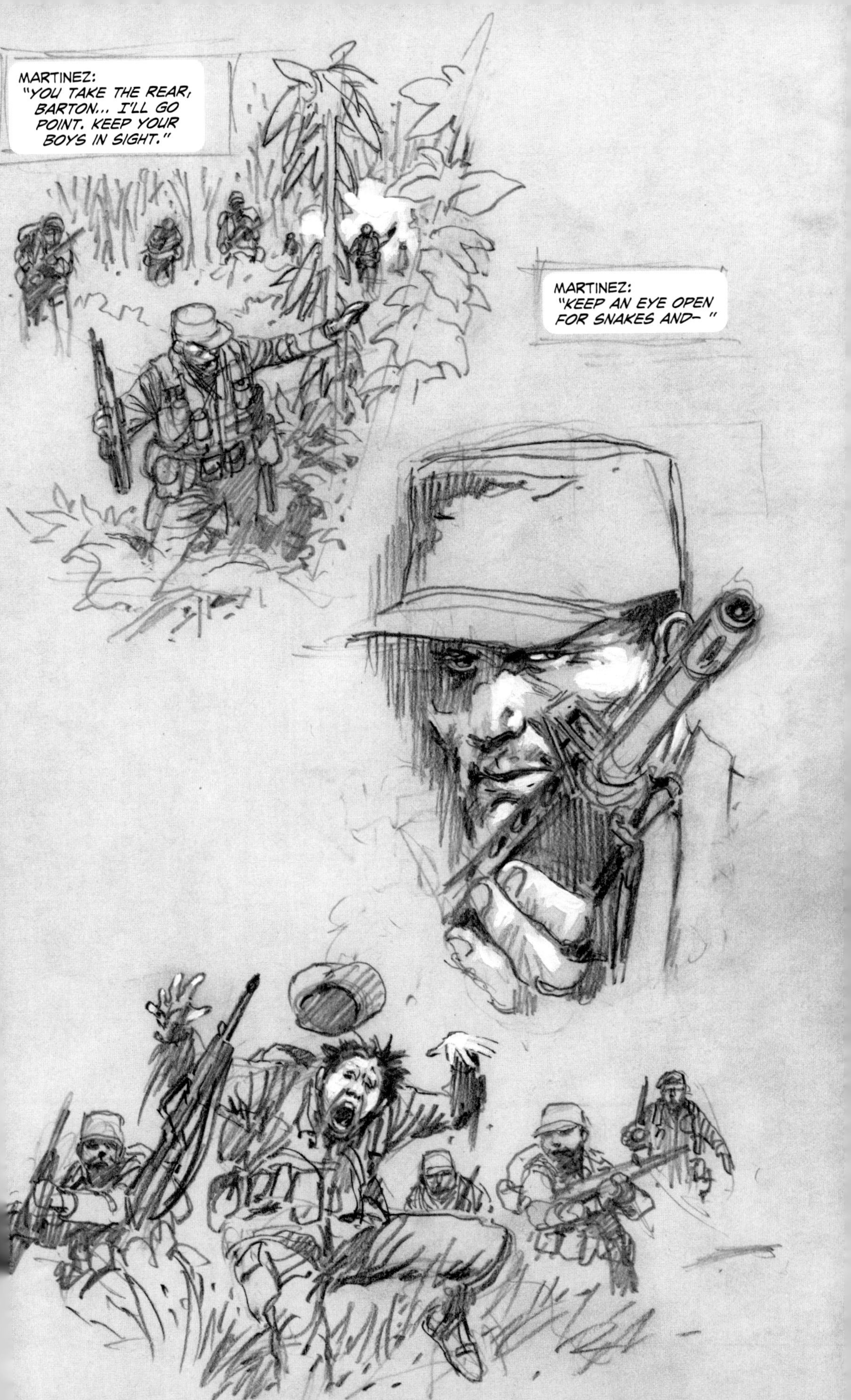
MARTINEZ:
"YOU TAKE THE REAR, BARTON... I'LL GO POINT. KEEP YOUR BOYS IN SIGHT."
MARTINEZ:
"KEEP AN EYE OPEN FOR SNAKES AND– "

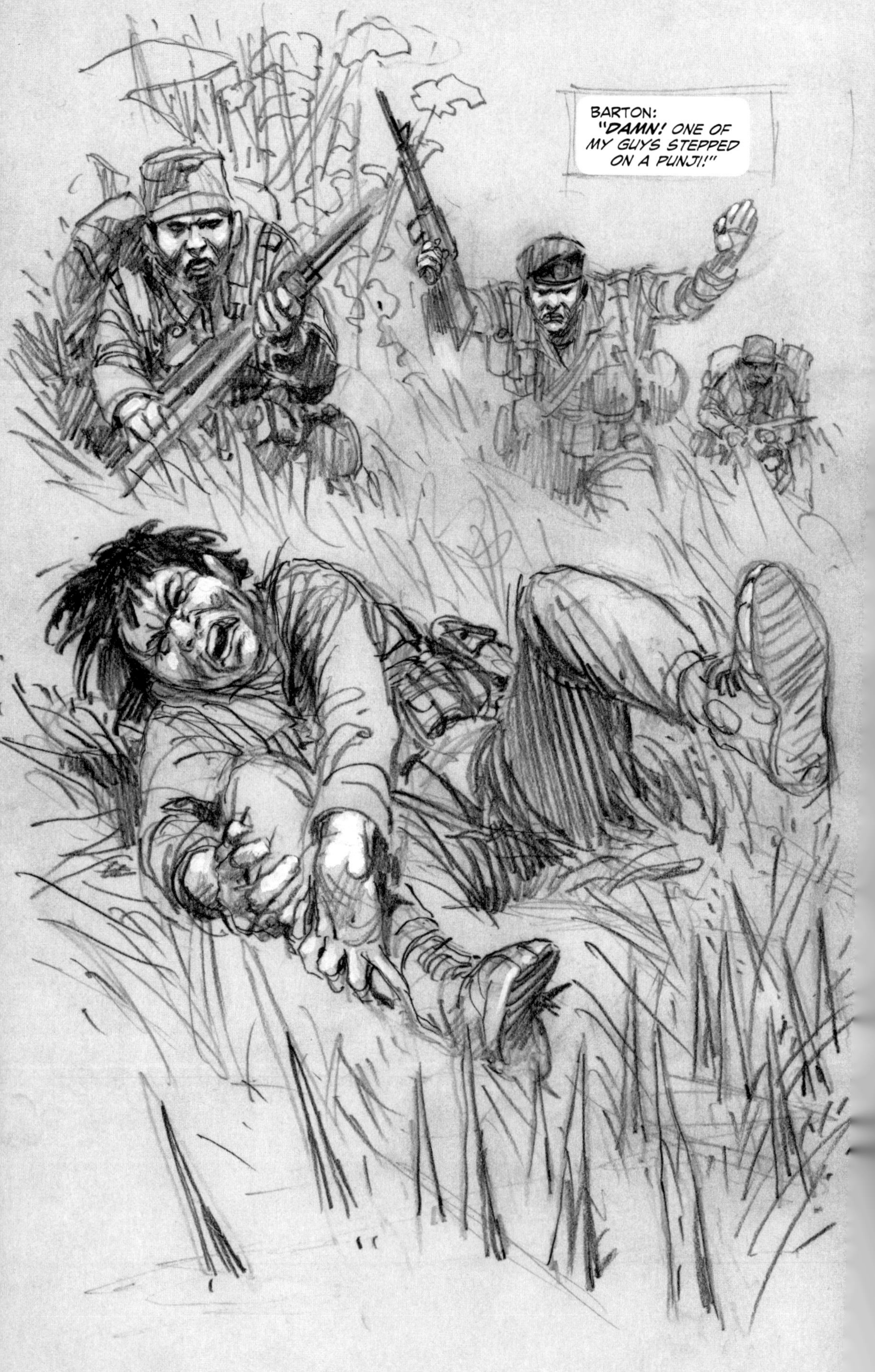
BARTON:
"DAMN! ONE OF MY GUYS STEPPED ON A PUNJI!"

PUNJI STICKS. A FAVORED BOOBY TRAP EMPLOYED BY THE VIETCONG. SHARPENED BAMBOO STAKES... HIDDEN IN GRASS AND SOFT EARTH...TAINTED WITH HUMAN FECES. THE MONTAGNARDS' THIN-SOLED SNEAKER BOOTS AFFORD LITTLE PROTECTION.

QUICKLY, THE WOUND IS CLEANED AND SULFA-POWDERED TO COUNTER THE POISONOUS EFFECTS.

BARTON:
"CAN YOU WALK?"

THE TERSE ANSWER IS A SILENT, POSITIVE NOD.

MARTINEZ:
"HERE... THIS'LL HELP A LITTLE."

BARTON:
"OKAY... WE GOTTA MOVE. CHECK THIS AREA BEFORE IT GETS TOO DARK TO SEE ANYTHING."

NIGHTFALL. THE JUNGLE IS MANTLED IN DARKNESS. SLEEP ELUDES THE RECON GROUP... EXCEPT FOR A FEW SHORT MINUTES AT A TIME. EACH MAN TAKES HIS TURN AT GUARD... LISTENING FOR ANY SOUNDS OF MOVEMENT.
ONLY THE CHITTERING OF MONKEYS AND A NIGHT BIRD'S FLUTTER IS HEARD.

AT LAST, DAWN FILTERS THROUGH THE JUNGLE CANOPY. THE RECON GROUP IS UP AND ALERT AT FIRST LIGHT... SEARCHING FOR FOOTPRINTS AND TRACKS.

BARTON:
"PLENTY OF TRAFFIC THROUGH HERE."

MARTINEZ:
"LOOK AT THESE RUTS. *MUCHO* HEAVY EQUIPMENT MOVIN' THROUGH HERE. A *LOT* OF STUFF. WITHIN THE LAST FEW DAYS."

BARTON:
"WE'LL CHECK AS WIDE AN AREA AS POSSIBLE BEFORE WE REPORT BACK."

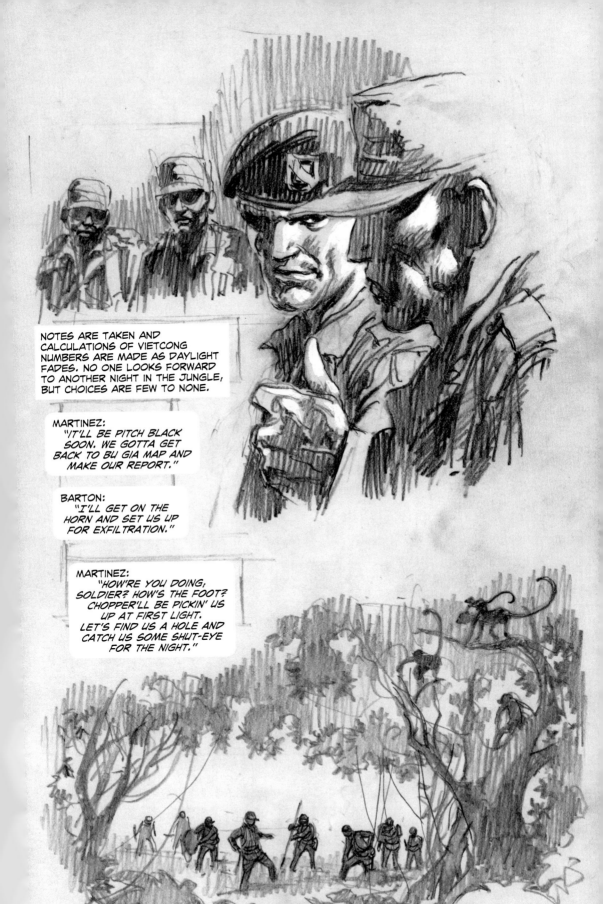

NOTES ARE TAKEN AND
CALCULATIONS OF VIETCONG
NUMBERS ARE MADE AS DAYLIGHT
FADES. NO ONE LOOKS FORWARD
TO ANOTHER NIGHT IN THE JUNGLE,
BUT CHOICES ARE FEW TO NONE.

MARTINEZ:
"IT'LL BE PITCH BLACK
SOON. WE GOTTA GET
BACK TO BU GIA MAP AND
MAKE OUR REPORT."

BARTON:
"I'LL GET ON THE
HORN AND SET US UP
FOR EXFILTRATION."

MARTINEZ:
"HOW'RE YOU DOING,
SOLDIER? HOW'S THE FOOT?
CHOPPER'LL BE PICKIN' US
UP AT FIRST LIGHT.
LET'S FIND US A HOLE AND
CATCH US SOME SHUT-EYE
FOR THE NIGHT."

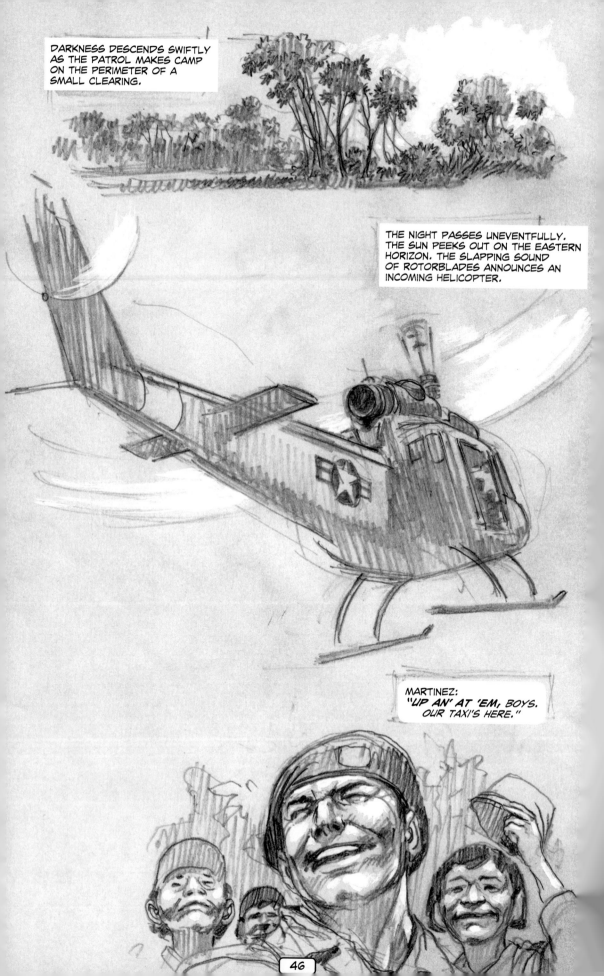

DARKNESS DESCENDS SWIFTLY AS THE PATROL MAKES CAMP ON THE PERIMETER OF A SMALL CLEARING.

THE NIGHT PASSES UNEVENTFULLY. THE SUN PEEKS OUT ON THE EASTERN HORIZON. THE SLAPPING SOUND OF ROTORBLADES ANNOUNCES AN INCOMING HELICOPTER.

MARTINEZ:
"UP AN' AT 'EM, BOYS. OUR TAXI'S HERE."

EQUIPMENT IS QUICKLY PACKED AND SECURED AS THE GROUP MAKES READY TO MOUNT THE HOVERING TRANSPORT.

BARTON:
"LIFT HIM EASY... LOOKS LIKE HIS LEG IS SWOLLEN."

MARTINEZ:
"DON'T WORRY... THEY'LL TAKE CARE OF YOU SOON'S WE GET BACK TO BU GIA MAP."

CAREFULLY, THE WOUNDED SOLDIER IS PLACED ABOARD AND MADE COMFORTABLE.

BARTON:
"OKAY...LET'S GO... LET'S GO! BEFORE WE ATTRACT ANY UNWELCOME COMPANY."

BARTON:
"THERE'S BU GIA MAP BELOW. WE'LL HAVE YOU IN THE INFIRMARY IN A COUPLE OF MINUTES, SOLDIER."

BARTON:
"HEY, ALLISON... WHERE'S CAP'N KEANE? WE'VE GOT SOME STUFF COMING DOWN."

MARTINEZ:
"OUR RECON SHOWS A LOT OF TRAFFIC. MOVEMENT OF HEAVY EQUIPMENT AND NUMEROUS V.C. PERSONNEL..."

STARK:
"KEANE IS AT A PLACE CALLED DONG XOAI. HE'S PREP'N FOR US TO FOLLOW HIM THERE."

STARK:
"NEW ORDERS CALL FOR OUR TEAM TO BE DEPLOYED AT DONG XOAI. THAT'LL BE OUR NEW BASE FOR OPERATIONS AND TRAINING. LOOK HERE..."

STARK:
"DONG XOAI IS THE DISTRICT H.Q. FOR THE PROVINCE OF PHUOC LONG. BU GIA MAP IS LOCATED HERE... NEAR THE BORDER OF CAMBODIA. DONG XOAI IS WELL SOUTH OF BU GIA MAP. IT'S IMPORTANT BECAUSE SEVERAL CRITICAL ROADS INTERSECT NEAR DONG XOAI. ROADS THAT MOVE MEN AND MATERIAL BETWEEN WAR ZONES.

THAT MAKES DONG XOAI OF MAJOR INTEREST TO THE VIET CONG, AS WELL AS TO OUR GUYS."

CAMBODIA

BU GIA MAP

VIETNAM

NHA TRA

DONG XOAI

SAIGON

SOUTH CHINA SEA

IN SHORT ORDER, DETACHMENT A-342 IS HELICOPTERED TO THEIR NEW LOCATION ADJACENT TO THE VILLAGE OF DONG XOAI. AL KEANE, CAPTAIN AND TEAM LEADER, TAKES CHARGE OF ORIENTATION AND INFORMATION.

MILITARY COMPOUNDS

ROADS

VILLAGE

KEANE:
"AN ASSESSMENT TEAM HAS ALREADY SCOPED THE VILLAGE AND THE ADJACENT CAMP AREA. A SEABEE SUPPORT TEAM WILL ASSIST US IN OUR MISSION."

BARTON:
"THAT COINCIDES WITH INFO WE OBTAINED ON OUR RECON OUTSIDE BU GIA MAP. LOTS OF MOVEMENT TO THE SOUTHEAST..."
KEANE:
"DONG XOAI WAS HIT BY V.C. MORTARS LAST MONTH. MAYBE A DOZEN ROUNDS. MINIMAL CASUALTIES. NOTHING'S HAPPENED SINCE."

KEANE:
"OKAY, GUYS...LET'S GO OVER THIS ONE MORE TIME. WE'VE BEEN CHARGED WITH THREE PRIMARY MISSIONS HERE IN DONG XOAI.

FIRST, WE'RE ADVISORS. WE DISSEMINATE INFORMATION AND ADVISE SUBSECTOR PERSONNEL.

SECOND, WE WORK WITH DISTRICT CHIEFS AND VIETNAMESE SPECIAL FORCES. ALSO, WITH CIVILIAN IRREGULAR DEFENSE GROUP FORCES.

THIRD... AND EQUALLY IMPORTANT... WE CONDUCT OPERATIONS AGAINST INCURSIONS OF WAR ZONES ABUTTING DONG XOAI."

INDOCTRINATION BEGINS
IMMEDIATELY FOR THE A-TEAM,
AND FULL REALIZATION OF
NEEDS BECOMES APPARENT.

McCABE:
"NO AIRSTRIP... JUST AN
UNPAVED ROAD. MEANS NO
BIG BOYS CAN LAND HERE."

KELLY:
"RIGHT, CAP'N. MAYBE
C-7 CARIBOUS OR C-123
CARGO AIRCRAFT...
MAYBE."

ALLISON:
"CHOPPERS'LL MAKE IT IN.
NO PROBLEM."

KELLY:
"OKAY, GENTLEMEN...
WE'RE SET TO MEET OUR
LOCAL COUNTERPARTS
IN TEN MINUTES. SO —
LET'S GET MOVING."

AFTER THE NEWCOMERS STOW THEIR PERSONAL GEAR AT THEIR BILLETS, CAPT. AL KEANE, SFC. ED SMITH AND SSGT. DAN ALLISON HEAD FOR THEIR MEETING WITH THE DISTRICT MILITARY CHIEF, CAPT. CON, TO EXCHANGE INTEL INFO.

CON:
"MY MEN HAVE HAD SIGHTINGS OF V.C. NEAR OUR ENCAMPMENT... COMING FROM THE NORTHEAST. WE HERE IN DONG XOAI HAVE RECEIVED INTERMITTENT MORTAR FIRE. SPORADIC. NOT SUSTAINED. ONE MAN WAS KILLED.

SONG BE CAMP IS FIFTEEN MILES NORTH OF US. IT WAS ATTACKED A FEW DAYS AGO. I AM SORRY TO SAY THAT OUR ARVN FORCES WITHDREW – DESPITE THE FACT THAT THE V.C. NEVER ATTEMPTED TO ACTUALLY OCCUPY THE CAMP. THE U.S. ADVISORS DID REMAIN.
V.C. HAVE BEEN REPORTED TO BE PREPARING AN ATTACK HERE – ON DONG XOAI."

CON:
"WITH THE HELP OF YOUR ADVISOR COMRADES, SONG BE IS HELD. SUPPLIES WERE BROUGHT IN BY YOUR AIR FORCE... AND MEDEVACS TRANSPORTED THE BADLY WOUNDED.

THERE HAS BEEN SUBSTANTIAL V.C. MOVEMENT AROUND DONG XOAI. THERE IS LITTLE DOUBT THAT WE ARE VULNERABLE TO AN ATTACK. NOT IF — THE ONLY QUESTION IS — WHEN?"

KEANE:
"THANK YOU, CAPT. CON. MY MEN AND I WILL CHECK DONG XOAI'S DEFENSE POSTURE. WE WILL MAKE YOU AWARE OF THE RESULTS IMMEDIATELY."

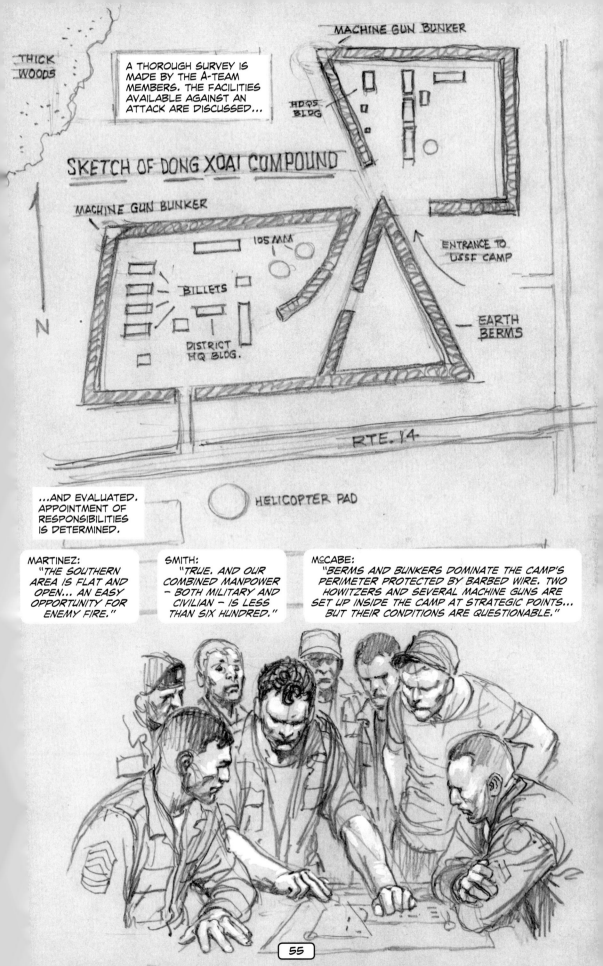

THICK WOODS

MACHINE GUN BUNKER

A THOROUGH SURVEY IS MADE BY THE A-TEAM MEMBERS. THE FACILITIES AVAILABLE AGAINST AN ATTACK ARE DISCUSSED...

HDQS BLDG

SKETCH OF DONG XOAI COMPOUND

MACHINE GUN BUNKER

105 MM

BILLETS

ENTRANCE TO USSF CAMP

N

EARTH BERMS

DISTRICT HQ BLDG.

RTE. 14

...AND EVALUATED. APPOINTMENT OF RESPONSIBILITIES IS DETERMINED.

HELICOPTER PAD

MARTINEZ:
"THE SOUTHERN AREA IS FLAT AND OPEN... AN EASY OPPORTUNITY FOR ENEMY FIRE."

SMITH:
"TRUE. AND OUR COMBINED MANPOWER – BOTH MILITARY AND CIVILIAN – IS LESS THAN SIX HUNDRED."

McCABE:
"BERMS AND BUNKERS DOMINATE THE CAMP'S PERIMETER PROTECTED BY BARBED WIRE. TWO HOWITZERS AND SEVERAL MACHINE GUNS ARE SET UP INSIDE THE CAMP AT STRATEGIC POINTS... BUT THEIR CONDITIONS ARE QUESTIONABLE."

THE A-TEAM KNOWS IT HAS ITS WORK CUT OUT FOR IT. A LOT TO BE DONE AND A SHORT TIME IN WHICH TO DO IT. ARVN SOLDIERS ARE ASSIGNED TO PATCHING BUNKERS AND SHORING UP BERMS.

CIDG TROOPS HAVE THE RESPONSIBILITY TO CHECK AND RESTRING BARBED WIRE AROUND THE CAMP'S PERIMETER.

FLARES MUST BE PLACED IN STRATEGIC SPOTS AND PROPERLY CONCEALED. WORKING ALONGSIDE THEIR VIETNAMESE COUNTERPARTS, THE USSF MEN KNOW THAT THE ONLY CURE FOR NERVOUS ANTICIPATION IS CAREFUL PREPARATION.

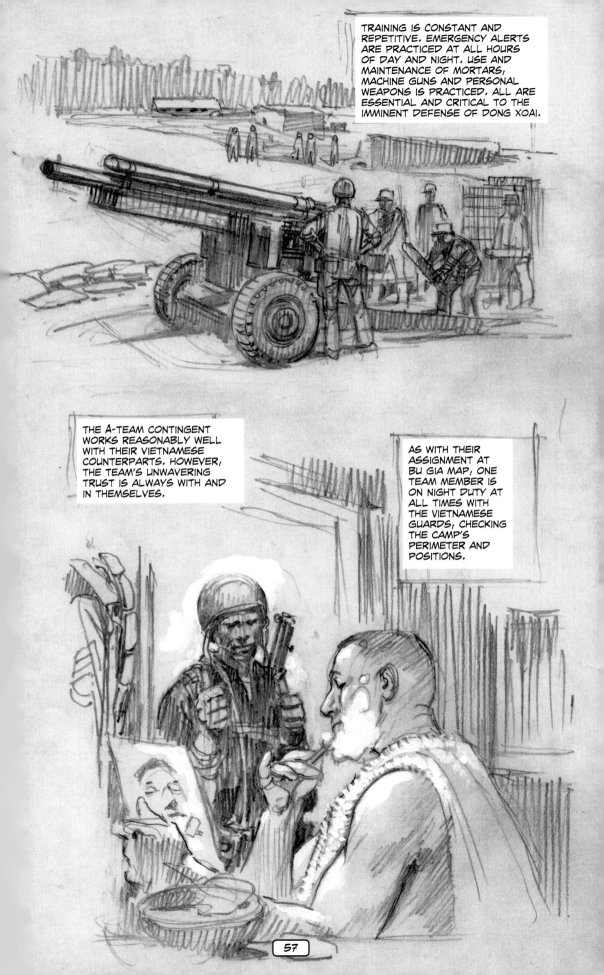

TRAINING IS CONSTANT AND REPETITIVE. EMERGENCY ALERTS ARE PRACTICED AT ALL HOURS OF DAY AND NIGHT. USE AND MAINTENANCE OF MORTARS, MACHINE GUNS AND PERSONAL WEAPONS IS PRACTICED. ALL ARE ESSENTIAL AND CRITICAL TO THE IMMINENT DEFENSE OF DONG XOAI.

THE A-TEAM CONTINGENT WORKS REASONABLY WELL WITH THEIR VIETNAMESE COUNTERPARTS. HOWEVER, THE TEAM'S UNWAVERING TRUST IS ALWAYS WITH AND IN THEMSELVES.

AS WITH THEIR ASSIGNMENT AT BU GIA MAP, ONE TEAM MEMBER IS ON NIGHT DUTY AT ALL TIMES WITH THE VIETNAMESE GUARDS, CHECKING THE CAMP'S PERIMETER AND POSITIONS.

STEADY EVIDENCE MOUNTS TO
CORROBORATE THE FACT THAT
THE V.C. ARE IN CLOSE PROXIMITY
TO DONG XOAI. MORE FREQUENT
PATROLS ARE ORDERED TO
DETERMINE SUSPICIONS THAT DONG
XOAI IS SLATED FOR AN ONSLAUGHT
IN THE VERY NEAR FUTURE.

SHEER:
"THESE'RE FRESH TRACKS...
ONLY A STONE'S THROW
FROM THE CAMP.
V.C.... NO DOUBT."

SHEER:
"TAKE HALF THE PATROL.
SPREAD THE MEN OUT.
COVER THE AREA NORTH... N
MORE'N TWO K'S, STAY ALER
– WATCH FOR TRAPS."

ALLISON:
"WILL DO. WE'LL MEET BACK
AT CAMP."

STAYING IN SHADOWS FORMED BY THE JUNGLE FOLIAGE, SSGT. DAN ALLISON LED HIS GROUP IN SILENCE... INSTRUCTING THEM BY PHYSICAL SIGNALS.

CHECKING AND ANALYZING ANY UNUSUAL SIGNS OF PREVIOUS PASSAGE, ALLISON LEADS HIS CREW TO NAVIGATE A NARROW LOG SPANNING A SHALLOW STREAM.

IMPATIENTLY, THE SPECIAL FORCES NONCOM MOTIONS HIS MEN TO INCREASE THEIR PACE ACROSS THE SWAYING BRIDGE.

SSGT. DAN ALLISON'S URGING IS REWARDED WITH A LOSS OF BALANCE...

...FOLLOWED BY AN UNEXPECTED BATH IN WATER LESS THAN CLEAN...

...ACCOMPANIED BY MUFFLED LAUGHTER.

ALLISON:
"YEAH... GO AHEAD AN' LAUGH. BUT IF I HAD MONKEY-TOES LIKE YOU GUYS, I'D'A WALKED ACROSS THAT LOG WITH NO PROBLEM."

AT THE MOMENT SSGT. DAN ALLISON WAS REMOVING LEECHES FROM HIS BACK AND SHOULDERS, SGT. JOE SHEER WAS APPROACHING THE VILLAGE OF DAK O... SOME TWO OR THREE KILOMETERS DISTANT.

BLACK SMUDGES OF SMOKE WAFTING INTO A CLEAR SKY FORETELL A DARK EVENT.

SHEER:
"THIS PLACE HAS BEEN HIT BAD. BUT... WHERE'D EVERYONE GO? NO BODIES... NOTHING. ONLY BURNT HUTS AND GUTTED BUILDINGS. EVERYONE MUST'VE RUN OFF... SCARED OFF BY THE V.C. I'D BETTER GET BACK TO DONG XOAI AND MAKE MY REPORT IN PERSON. ALLISON SHOULD BE ON HIS WAY BACK, TOO."

BOTH SHEER AND ALLISON RETURN TO DONG XOAI – THEIR PATROLS INTACT EXCEPT FOR ALLISON'S DUNKING – WITHIN A SHORT TIME OF EACH OTHER'S ARRIVAL. THE A-TEAM GATHERS FOR A REPORT...

ALLISON:
"THERE'S NO DOUBT THAT THE V.C. ARE CLOSE – AND CHECKING US OUT. TRACKS SHOW THEM USING HEAVY EQUIPMENT. IT'S ONLY A MATTER OF TIME BEFORE THEY MAKE THEIR MOVE."

DONG XOAI

ALLISON:
"THE V.C. CAN'T ACTIVATE A MEANINGFUL OFFENSIVE IN THIS WHOLE AREA UNLESS DONG XOAI IS KNOCKED OUT OF THE PICTURE. WE CAN GIVE THEM TROUBLE – IF THEY DON'T NEUTRALIZE US. AND TIME IS OF THE ESSENCE FOR THEM... AND US."

KEANE:
"WE'RE GOING TO NEED MORE SUPPLIES AND FIREPOWER. WE'RE ALSO SHORT ON FOOD... MEDICAL SUPPLIES..."

KELLY:
"REPORTS HAVE COME IN OF V.C. TROOP SIGHTINGS NORTH OF DONG XOAI. WE'LL NEED TO —"

DISCUSSIONS ARE CUT SHORT BY THE UNMISTAKABLE SOUND OF MORTAR SHELLS ERUPTING WITHIN THE CAMP'S PERIMETER.

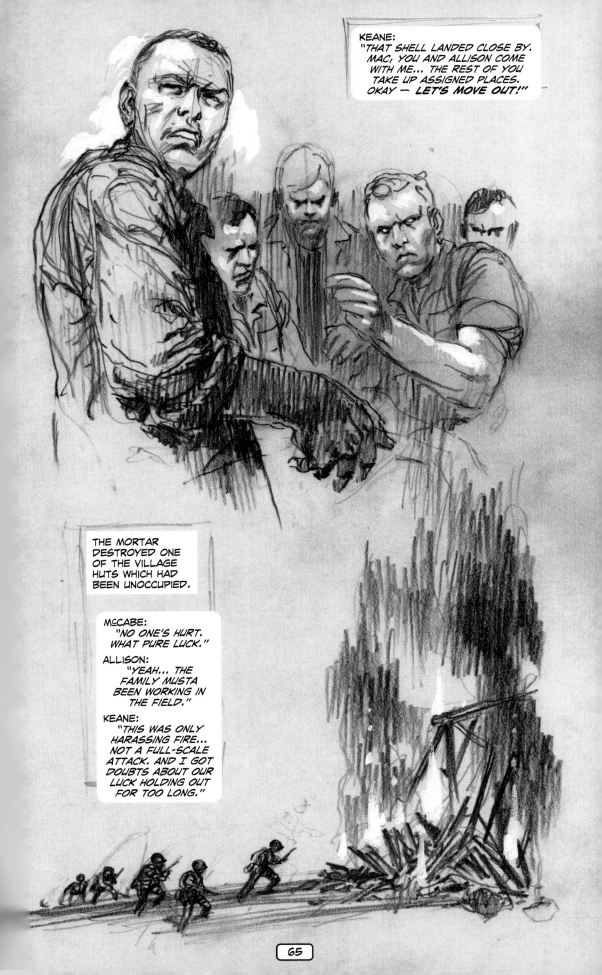

KEANE:
"THAT SHELL LANDED CLOSE BY. MAC, YOU AND ALLISON COME WITH ME... THE REST OF YOU TAKE UP ASSIGNED PLACES. OKAY — LET'S MOVE OUT!"

THE MORTAR DESTROYED ONE OF THE VILLAGE HUTS WHICH HAD BEEN UNOCCUPIED.

McCABE:
"NO ONE'S HURT. WHAT PURE LUCK."

ALLISON:
"YEAH... THE FAMILY MUSTA BEEN WORKING IN THE FIELD."

KEANE:
"THIS WAS ONLY HARASSING FIRE... NOT A FULL-SCALE ATTACK. AND I GOT DOUBTS ABOUT OUR LUCK HOLDING OUT FOR TOO LONG."

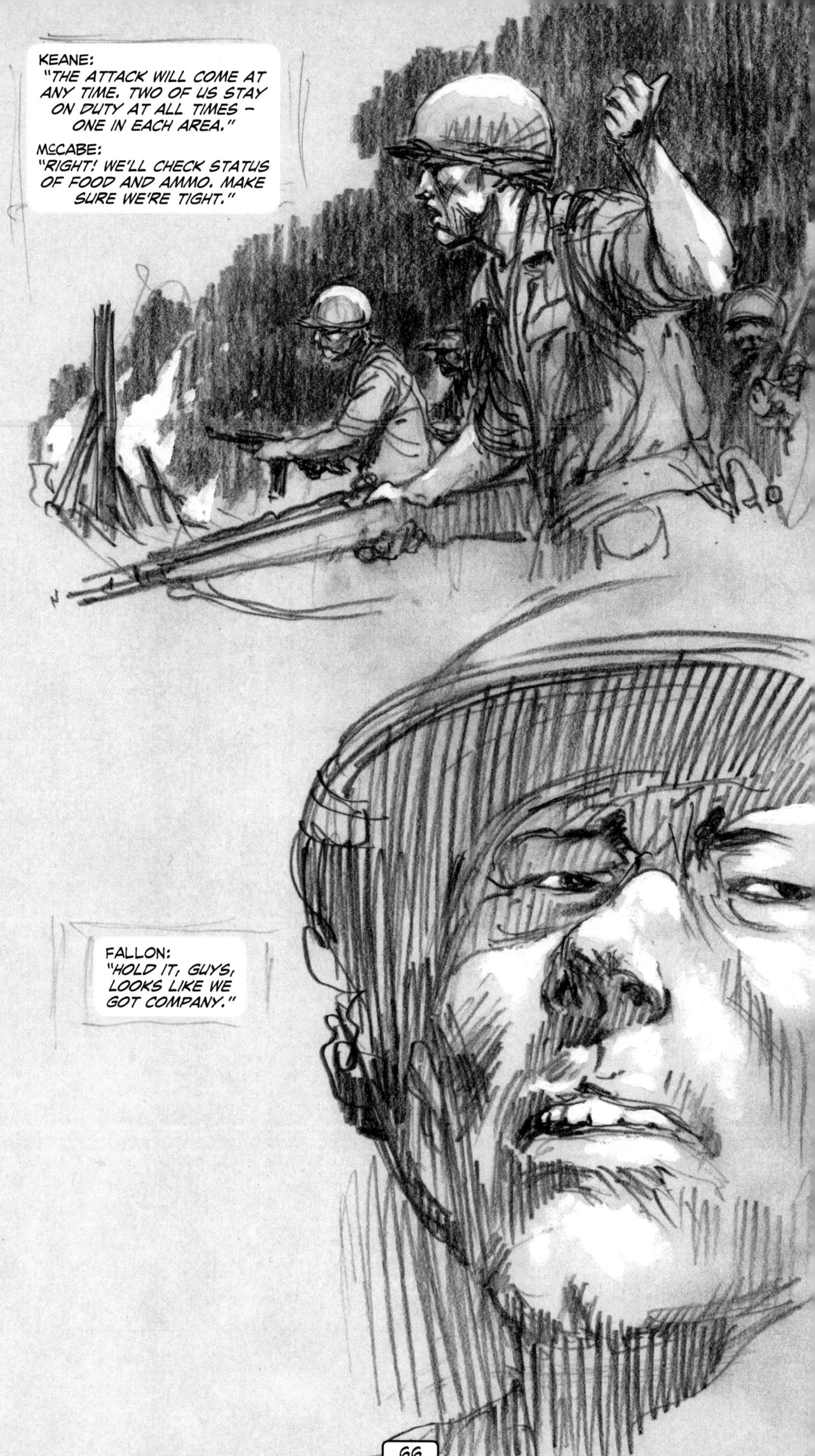
KEANE:
"THE ATTACK WILL COME AT ANY TIME. TWO OF US STAY ON DUTY AT ALL TIMES – ONE IN EACH AREA."
McCABE:
"RIGHT! WE'LL CHECK STATUS OF FOOD AND AMMO. MAKE SURE WE'RE TIGHT."
FALLON:
"HOLD IT, GUYS, LOOKS LIKE WE GOT COMPANY."

BALASCO:
"CAP'N KEANE? I'M BALASCO. WE'RE THE ANSWER TO YOUR REQUEST FOR ADDITIONAL PERSONNEL. ASSIGNED TO YOUR S.F. GROUP."

STEWART:
"WE'RE HERE TO BUILD YOU GUYS SOME PROTECTION. LOOKS LIKE WE JUST MISSED OUR WELCOMING COMMITTEE."

KEANE:
"WE'RE SURE GLAD TO SEE YOU SEABEES. WE CAN USE SOME MORE HANDS... AS YOU CAN NOTICE."

HASEN:
"WE CARRY NO HEAVY EQUIPMENT, BUT, YEAH... LOOKS LIKE WE GOT HERE AT A GOOD TIME. A NICE WARM HELLO — JUST FOR US."

AS NIGHT FALLS, THE SEABEES ARE MADE AWARE OF THE ENCAMPMENT'S CONDITIONS AND ITS DEFENSES.

KELLY:
"TOO BAD YOU SEABEES COULDN'T CARRY IN A COUPLE OF 'DOZERS... OR MAYBE A TANK OR TWO."

ADAMS:
"WE THOUGHT THIS WAS GONNA BE A *VACATION.*"

BALASCO:
"YEAH. THEY DIDN'T TELL US THERE WAS A WAR GOIN' ON."

ADAMS:
"SERIOUSLY, LIEUTENANT KELLY... AFTER WHAT WE'VE SEEN OF DONG XOAI, IF THE V.C. GET IT INTO THEIR HEADS TO MAKE A CONCERTED ATTACK... YOU GOT A *PROBLEM.*"

KELLY:
"NO, ADAMS. *WE* GOT A PROBLEM."

KELLY:
"YOU KNOW WHAT THE SITUATION IS, BALASCO. YOU SEABEES ARE PART OF THE TEAM NOW. ONE OF US STANDS GUARD AT ALL TIMES – IN EACH AREA."

BALASCO:
"UNDERSTOOD. ANY V.C. MOVES, WE WANNA BE THE FIRST ONES TO KNOW."

KELLY:
"NOT MUCH LEFT OF THE NIGHT. GOTTA BE READY FOR TOMORROW. IT'S BEEN A LONG DAY. LET'S GET SOME SHUT-EYE."

BUT THAT NIGHT SLEEP WOULD NOT COME TO THE TEAM OF MEN IN THE DONG XOAI ENCAMPMENT. V.C. MORTAR SHELLS MADE SURE OF THAT.

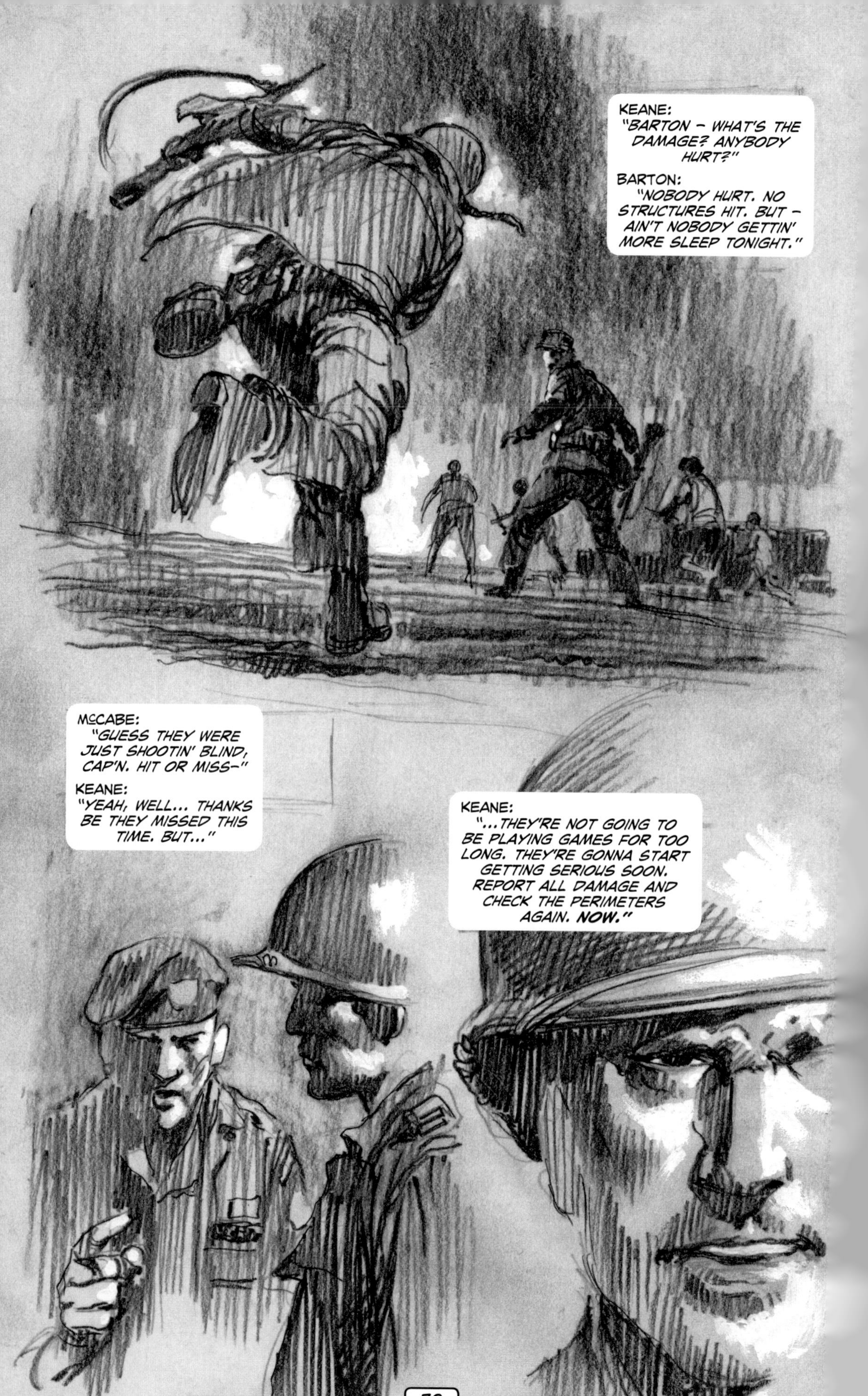
KEANE:
"BARTON – WHAT'S THE DAMAGE? ANYBODY HURT?"
BARTON:
"NOBODY HURT. NO STRUCTURES HIT. BUT – AIN'T NOBODY GETTIN' MORE SLEEP TONIGHT."
McCABE:
"GUESS THEY WERE JUST SHOOTIN' BLIND, CAP'N. HIT OR MISS–"
KEANE:
"YEAH, WELL... THANKS BE THEY MISSED THIS TIME. BUT..."
KEANE:
"...THEY'RE NOT GOING TO BE PLAYING GAMES FOR TOO LONG. THEY'RE GONNA START GETTING SERIOUS SOON. REPORT ALL DAMAGE AND CHECK THE PERIMETERS AGAIN. **NOW.**"

McCABE:
"DAYLIGHT'S COMING UP...
ANOTHER DAY IN VEET-NAM.
NO CASUALTIES THIS TIME.
LUCKY..."

KEANE:
"I DON'T THINK WE CAN
TRUST OUR LUCK TO LAST
MUCH LONGER, MAC. DONG
XOAI IS TOO IMPORTANT FOR
THE V.C. TO PASS UP."

BARTON:
"YEAH, AL. THEY CAN'T
AFFORD TO LET THIS
STEPPING STONE TO THE
SOUTH TRIP 'EM UP."

KEANE:
"WE'VE GOT TO
KEEP TIGHTENING
OUR DEFENSES
WITH MATERIALS
ON HAND. AND
MAKE SURE THAT
ALL PERSONNEL –
INCLUDING OUR
VIETNAMESE
COUNTERPARTS –
ARE ALL ON THE
SAME PAGE."

ALL THOUGHTS OF SLEEP ARE GONE AS CAPT. KEANE CALLS A MEETING WITH ALL U.S. PERSONNEL.

KEANE:
"I WANT ALL YOU GUYS TO GET CLOSE TO YOUR VIETNAM COUNTERPARTS. THEY HAVE TO TRUST *US* — SO *WE* CAN TRUST *THEM* UNDER EXTREME CONDITIONS."

MARTINEZ:
"THAT MEANS THE HEAD OF THE MILITIA, AS WELL AS THE DISTRICT CHIEF, RIGHT?"
KEANE:
"RIGHT. I DON'T HAVE TO TELL YOU ALL THAT WE'RE IN AN EXTREMELY SENSITIVE SITUATION. WE'RE ADVISORS. WE'VE GOT TO *FOLLOW* AND *LEAD* — AT THE SAME TIME."

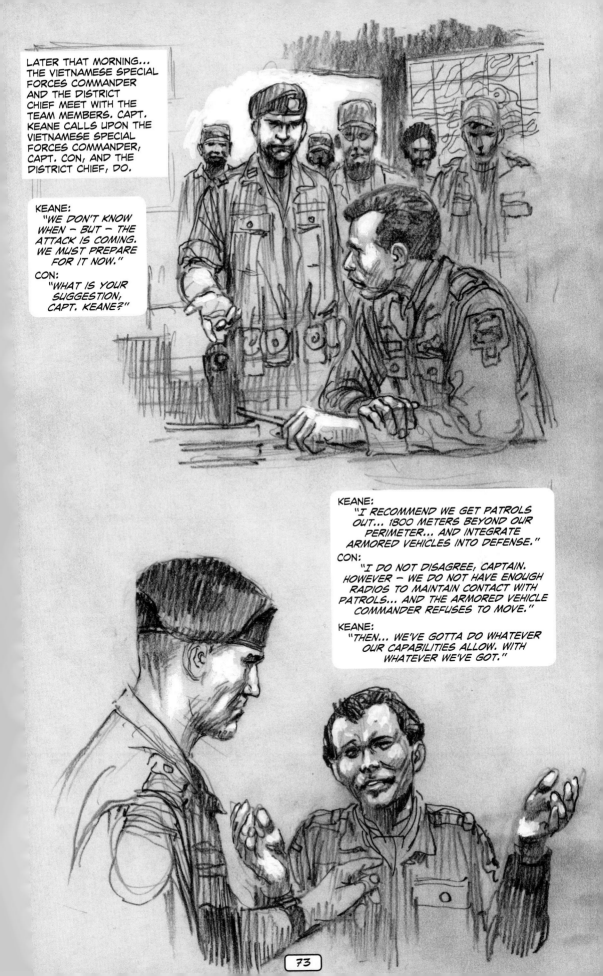

LATER THAT MORNING...
THE VIETNAMESE SPECIAL
FORCES COMMANDER
AND THE DISTRICT
CHIEF MEET WITH THE
TEAM MEMBERS. CAPT.
KEANE CALLS UPON THE
VIETNAMESE SPECIAL
FORCES COMMANDER,
CAPT. CON, AND THE
DISTRICT CHIEF, DO.

KEANE:
"WE DON'T KNOW
WHEN — BUT — THE
ATTACK IS COMING.
WE MUST PREPARE
FOR IT NOW."
CON:
"WHAT IS YOUR
SUGGESTION,
CAPT. KEANE?"

KEANE:
"I RECOMMEND WE GET PATROLS
OUT... 1800 METERS BEYOND OUR
PERIMETER... AND INTEGRATE
ARMORED VEHICLES INTO DEFENSE."
CON:
"I DO NOT DISAGREE, CAPTAIN.
HOWEVER — WE DO NOT HAVE ENOUGH
RADIOS TO MAINTAIN CONTACT WITH
PATROLS... AND THE ARMORED VEHICLE
COMMANDER REFUSES TO MOVE."
KEANE:
"THEN... WE'VE GOTTA DO WHATEVER
OUR CAPABILITIES ALLOW. WITH
WHATEVER WE'VE GOT."

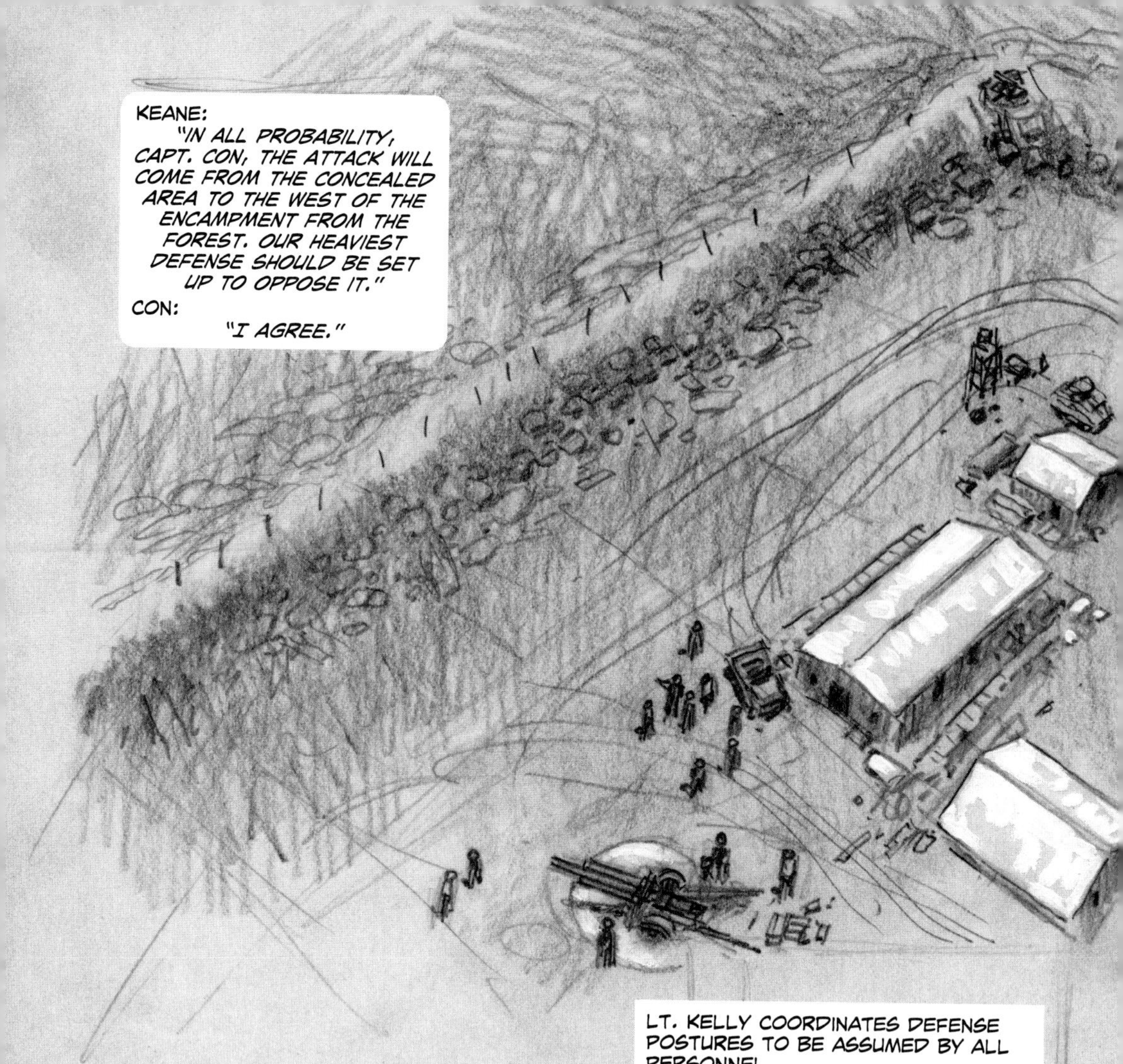
KEANE:
"IN ALL PROBABILITY, CAPT. CON, THE ATTACK WILL COME FROM THE CONCEALED AREA TO THE WEST OF THE ENCAMPMENT FROM THE FOREST. OUR HEAVIEST DEFENSE SHOULD BE SET UP TO OPPOSE IT."
CON:
"I AGREE."

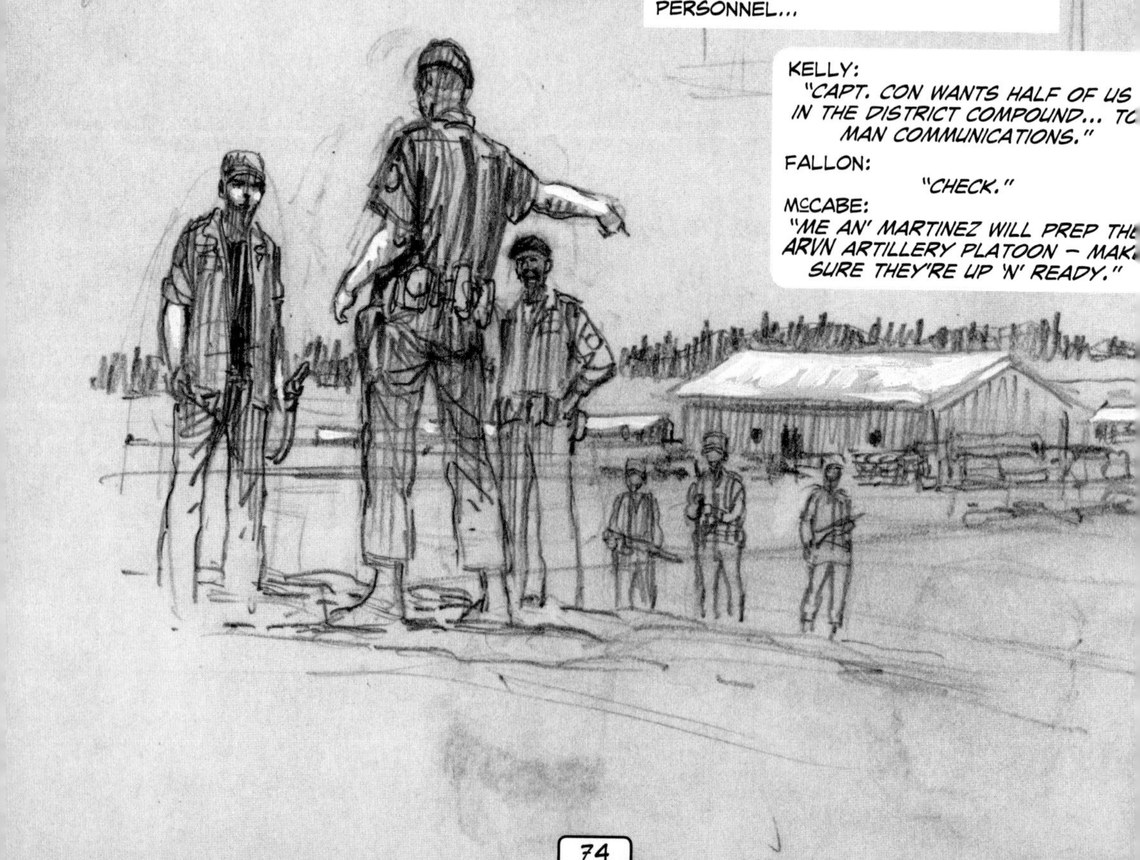
LT. KELLY COORDINATES DEFENSE POSTURES TO BE ASSUMED BY ALL PERSONNEL...
KELLY:
"CAPT. CON WANTS HALF OF US IN THE DISTRICT COMPOUND... TO MAN COMMUNICATIONS."
FALLON:
"CHECK."
McCABE:
"ME AN' MARTINEZ WILL PREP THE ARVN ARTILLERY PLATOON – MAKE SURE THEY'RE UP 'N' READY."

1 JUNE, 1965

REPORTS BY LOCALS ON THE OUTSKIRTS OF DONG XOAI TELL OF V.C. PROBES. ALSO, SIGHTINGS OF HEAVY EQUIPMENT AND AN INCREASE OF MILITARY MANPOWER.

SMITH:
"YOU KNOW THIS INFORMATION TO BE TRUE?"

MONTAGNARD:
"YES. THEY COME WITH MANY SOLDIERS FROM THE NORTH... SONG BE TO PHU RIENG."

MONTAGNARD:
"THEY ASK MANY QUESTIONS. TAKE FOOD. THEY SAY THEY COME TO DONG XOAI. THEY STRONG. THEY BRING MUCH BOMBS."

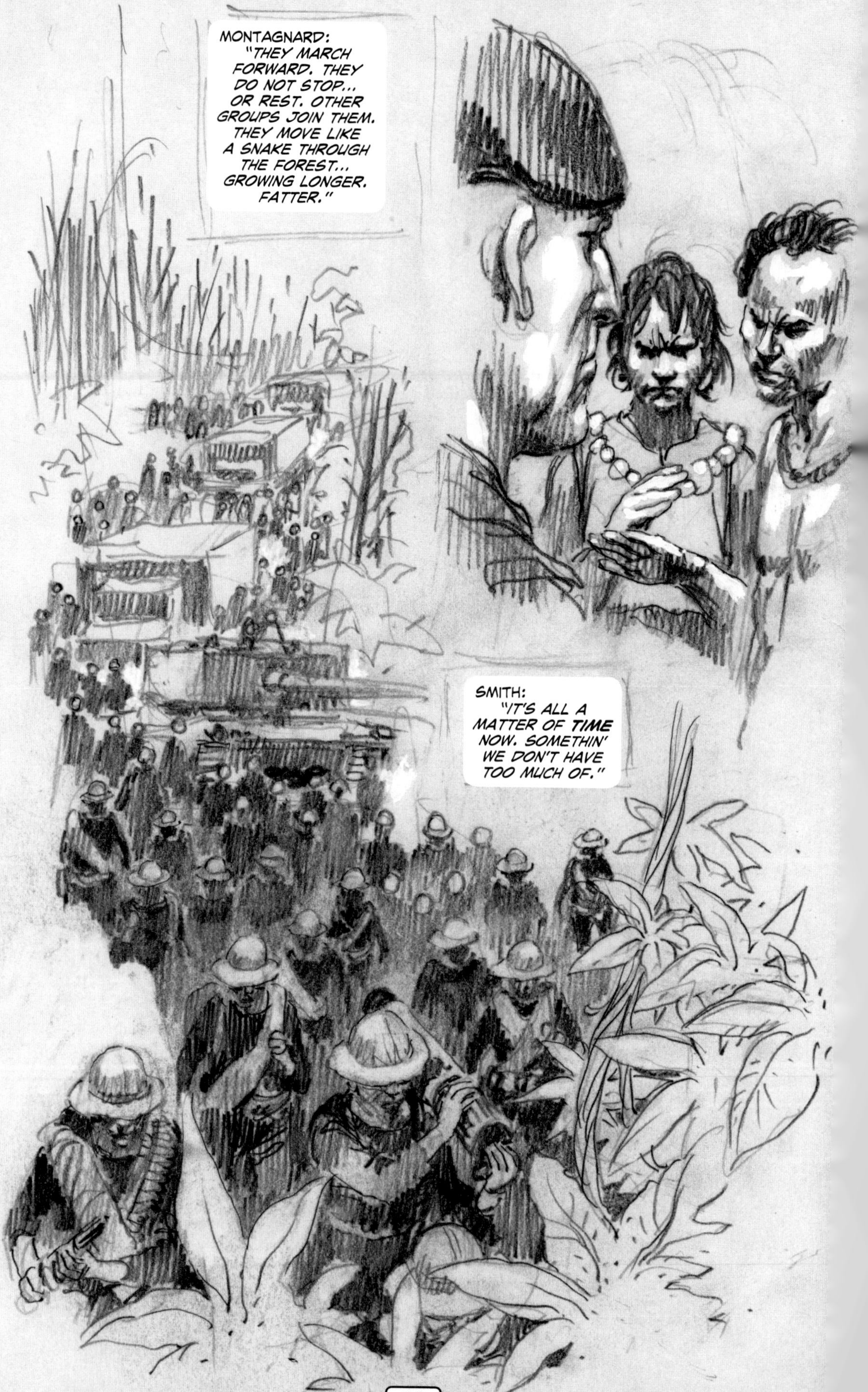
MONTAGNARD:
"THEY MARCH FORWARD. THEY DO NOT STOP... OR REST. OTHER GROUPS JOIN THEM. THEY MOVE LIKE A SNAKE THROUGH THE FOREST... GROWING LONGER. FATTER."
SMITH:
"IT'S ALL A MATTER OF TIME NOW. SOMETHIN' WE DON'T HAVE TOO MUCH OF."

6 JUNE, 1965

THE DAYS PASS QUICKLY. DONG XOAI IS ON ALERT, AND DEFENSES ARE REVIEWED. THE LACK OF MATERIAL IS A RECOGNIZED DEFICIT... ONE WITH WHICH THE ENCAMPMENT DEFENDERS MUST LIVE.

A V.C. SPY HAS BEEN CAUGHT AND BROUGHT IN FOR QUESTIONING.

GUARD:
"WE FOUND HIM IN THE FOREST — JUST OUTSIDE THE CAMP."

SMITH:
"AND YOU WALKED HIM THROUGH THE COMPOUND WITHOUT A BLINDFOLD? WHY NOT JUST SHOW HIM THE PLANS FOR THE WHOLE CAMP? COME ON, WE'LL BRING HIM TO CAPT. KEANE."

KEANE:
"HAS HE TOLD US ANYTHING ABOUT THE V.C. NUMBERS? WHERE THEY ARE — HOW FAR FROM US?"

GUARD:
"NO."

THERE HAVE BEEN MANY
ACCUSATIONS OF MALTREATMENT
OF PRISONERS DURING THE
VIETNAMESE CONFLICT. BOTH
THE SOUTH AND THE NORTH
SHARED THE GUILT. IN 1965,
THE U.S. PERSONNEL WERE IN A
POSITION OF ADVISORS AND HAD
NO DIRECT INVOLVEMENT IN THE
QUESTIONING PROCESS.

THE PRISONER WAS RESTRAINED
AND REMOVED TO A SHED
ON THE FAR SIDE OF THE
ENCAMPMENT.

NO INFORMATION WAS
GAINED AS A RESULT OF
HIS INTERROGATION.

UNDER THE CIRCUMSTANCES, THE TEAM MEMBERS AVOID THE QUESTIONING EPISODE AND CONCENTRATE ON THEIR RESPONSIBILITIES.

FALLON:
"WHATEVER INFO THEY GET — OR *DON'T* GET — IT WON'T CHANGE ANYTHING."

SMITH:
"RIGHT."

KEANE:
"CATCHING THAT SPY IS ONLY ANOTHER INDICATION OF HOW CLOSELY DONG XOAI HAS BEEN MONITORED BY THE V.C., AND NO MATTER WHAT — WE WILL HANDLE THIS DEAL WITH THE CARDS WE'VE BEEN DEALT — LIKE WE ALWAYS DO."

CON:
"PARDON, CAPT. KEANE.
MAY I SPEAK?"

KEANE:
"OF COURSE, CAPT. CON."

CON:
"WE WERE UNABLE TO
RETRIEVE ANY CREDIBLE
INFORMATION FROM THE SPY.
NEVERTHELESS, THE V.C.
ARE INDEED MOUNTING
A MASSIVE OFFENSIVE.
WE HERE AT DONG XOAI ARE
THEIR FIRST OBSTACLE —
FIRST TO BE ELIMINATED."

CON:
"WE SIT ON A CRITICAL
CROSSROADS — BETWEEN
THEM AND SAIGON."

CON:
"THEY CANNOT ALLOW
US TO REMAIN AS A
DETERRENT."

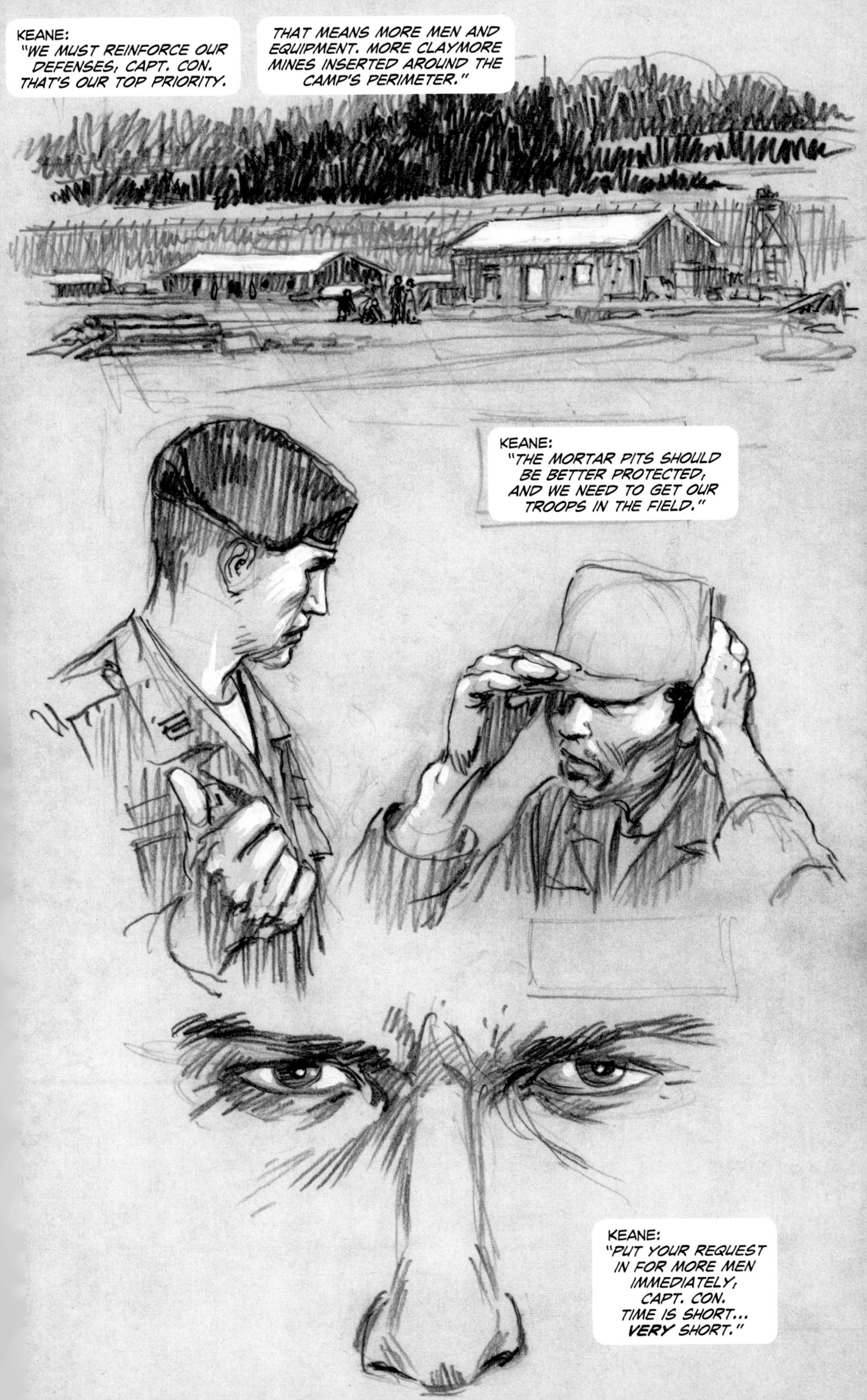
KEANE: "WE MUST REINFORCE OUR DEFENSES, CAPT. CON. THAT'S OUR TOP PRIORITY.
THAT MEANS MORE MEN AND EQUIPMENT. MORE CLAYMORE MINES INSERTED AROUND THE CAMP'S PERIMETER."
KEANE: "THE MORTAR PITS SHOULD BE BETTER PROTECTED, AND WE NEED TO GET OUR TROOPS IN THE FIELD."
KEANE: "PUT YOUR REQUEST IN FOR MORE MEN IMMEDIATELY, CAPT. CON. TIME IS SHORT... **VERY** SHORT."

CON:
"CALL IN YOUR AIR POWER, CAPT. KEANE. AN AIR STRIKE—"

KEANE:
"NOT FEASIBLE. THE V.C. WON'T MASS UNTIL THEY'RE READY TO ATTACK — AND WE DON'T KNOW WHEN THAT WILL BE. IT'D BE LIKE TRYING TO HIT A BEE WITH A CANNON VOLLEY."

CON:
"WE HAVE ASKED FOR RECONNAISSANCE FLIGHTS AND MORE GROUND PATROLS. BUT WE HAVE HAD NO RESPONSE."

THE ANSWER TO THE REQUEST FOR ADDITIONAL MEN COMES THE NEXT MORNING... IN THE FORM OF AN ARVN HELICOPTER CARRYING A SMALL CONTINGENT OF SOLDIERS.

SUNG:
"I AM LT. SUNG. I HAVE BEEN SENT TO DETERMINE CONDITIONS AND YOUR NEEDS."

A SHORT TIME LATER...

SUNG:
"I DO NOT AGREE WITH YOUR ESTIMATE OF DANGER, CAPT. CON. CERTAINLY, THERE ARE SIGNS OF V.C. IN THE VICINITY — BUT NO EVIDENCE OF AN IMMINENT ATTACK."

SUNG:
"MY MEN AND I WILL RETURN TO OUR HEADQUARTERS IMMEDIATELY. MY RECOMMENDATION WILL BE FOR YOU TO PROCEED WITH YOUR PREPARATIONS WITH MATERIALS ON HAND."

KELLY:
"I HOPE THESE GUYS KNOW WHAT THEY'RE DOING, AL."

KEANE:
"SO DO I, JOHN. NOTHING FOR US TO DO BUT THE BEST WE CAN. AND SLEEP WITH OUR CLOTHES ON."

THAT NIGHT DONG XOAI IS HIT ONCE MORE BY TWO MORTAR SHELLS LAUNCHED FROM THE FOREST WEST OF THE ENCAMPMENT.

FALLON:
"TOO BAD SUNG LEFT SO SOON. MAYBE THOSE MORTAR BURSTS WOULD'VE CHANGED HIS SITUATION ASSESSMENT."

KEANE:
"YEAH, WELL... WOULD'VE AND COULD'VE DON'T WIN DISCUSSIONS, FALLON."

CON:
"FIRST, WE WILL CHECK FOR ANY DAMAGE OR WOUNDED. THEN WE WILL DO MORE THAN CONJECTURE, CAPT. KEANE."

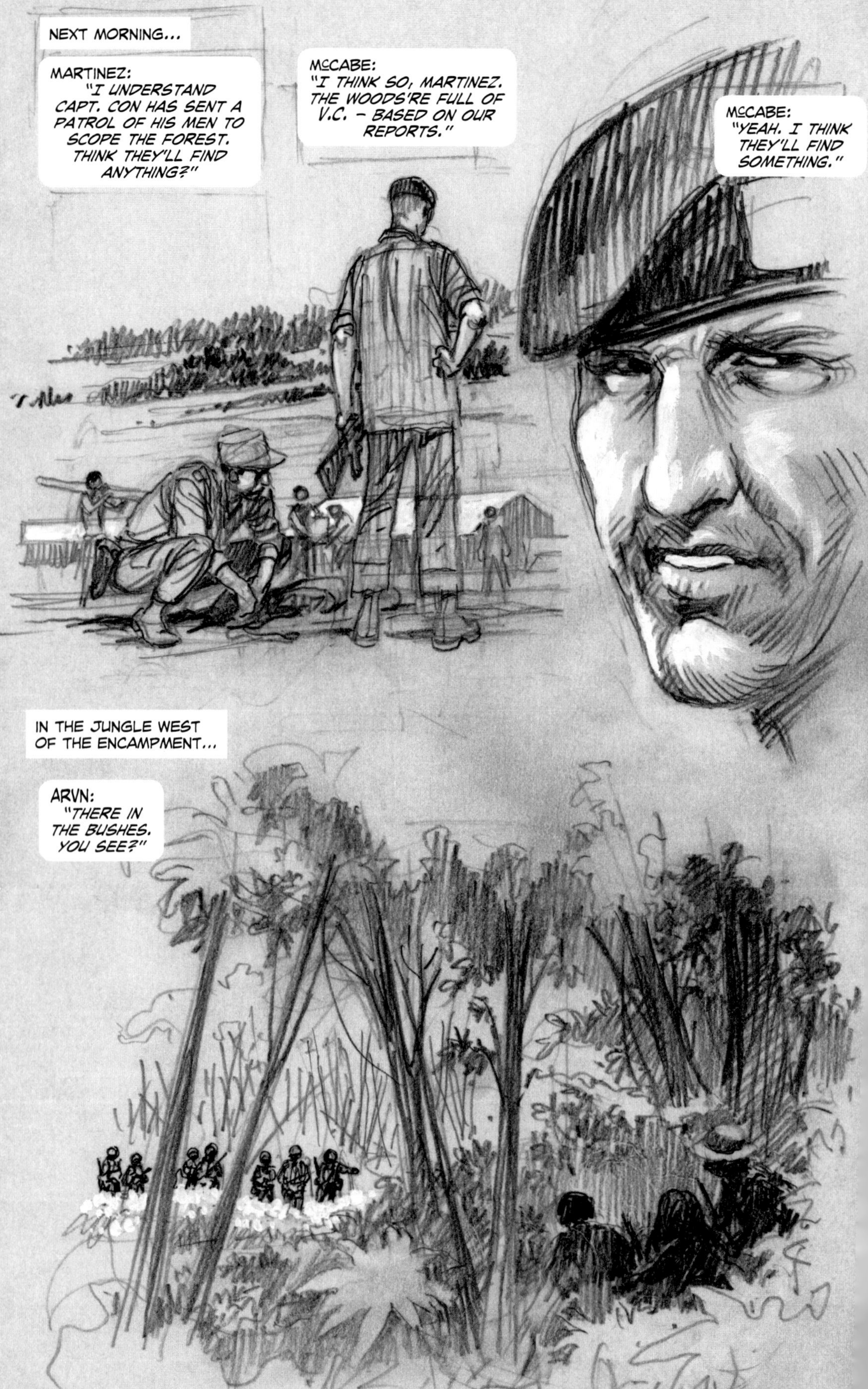
NEXT MORNING...
MARTINEZ: "I UNDERSTAND CAPT. CON HAS SENT A PATROL OF HIS MEN TO SCOPE THE FOREST. THINK THEY'LL FIND ANYTHING?"
McCABE: "I THINK SO, MARTINEZ. THE WOODS'RE FULL OF V.C. – BASED ON OUR REPORTS."
McCABE: "YEAH. I THINK THEY'LL FIND SOMETHING."
IN THE JUNGLE WEST OF THE ENCAMPMENT...
ARVN: "THERE IN THE BUSHES. YOU SEE?"

THE ARVN SQUAD LEADER SHOUTS AN ORDER...

"OPEN FIRE!"

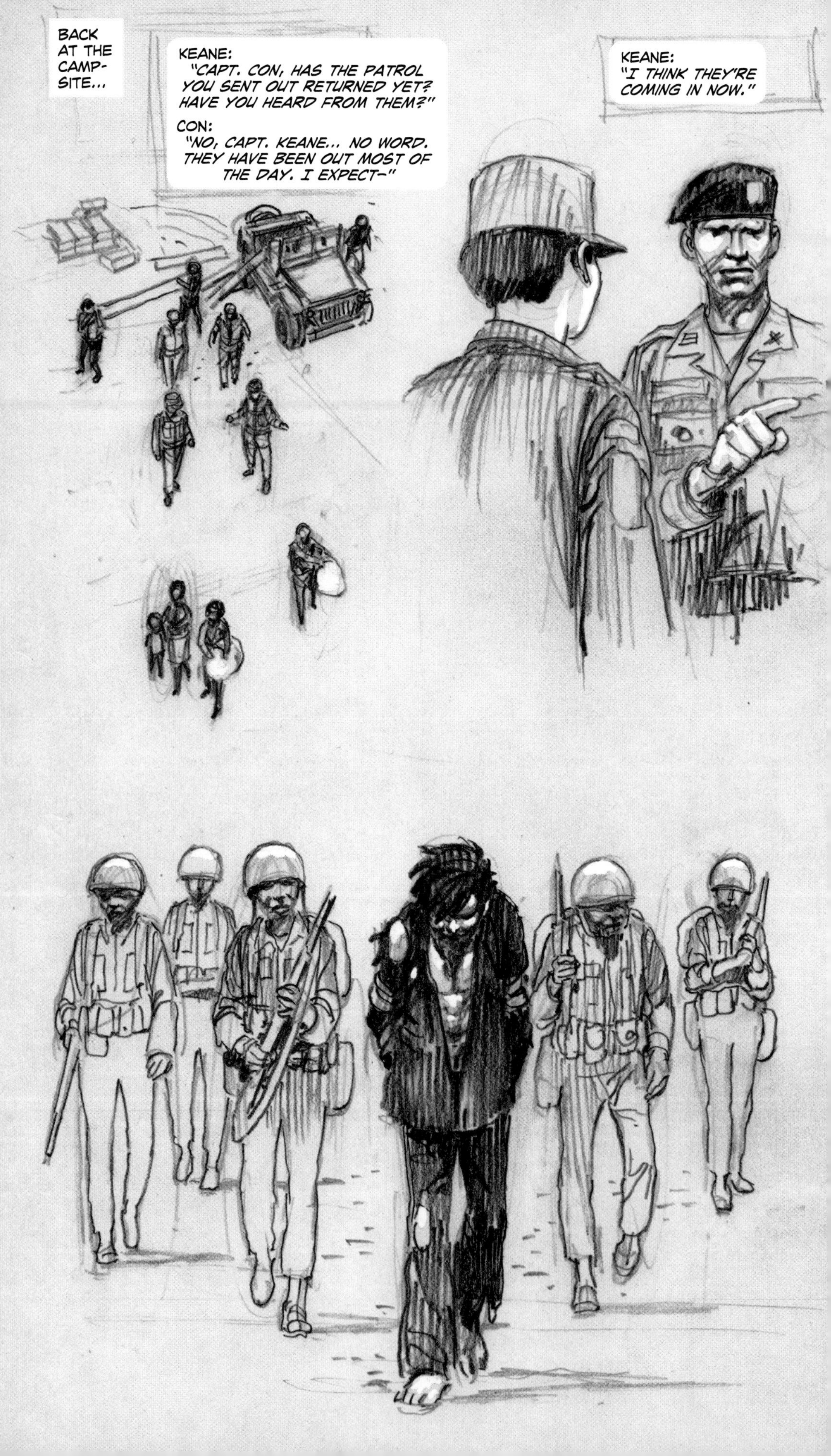

BACK AT THE CAMP-SITE...
KEANE: "CAPT. CON, HAS THE PATROL YOU SENT OUT RETURNED YET? HAVE YOU HEARD FROM THEM?"
CON: "NO, CAPT. KEANE... NO WORD. THEY HAVE BEEN OUT MOST OF THE DAY. I EXPECT-"
KEANE: "I THINK THEY'RE COMING IN NOW."

ARVN GUARD:
"WE FOUND THREE
HIDING IN THE
WOODS. THE OTHER
TWO ARE DEAD."

CON:
"WE WILL QUESTION THE PRISONER
– BUT I DO NOT EXPECT ANY
NEW REVELATIONS."
KEANE:
"YOU LET US KNOW AS SOON AS
POSSIBLE IF YOU DO GET ANY
NEW INFORMATION, CAPT. CON?"

CON:
"THESE VIETCONG
ARE A STUBBORN
LOT, CAPT. KEANE.
BUT – I WILL DO
AS YOU ASK."

WASTING NO TIME, CAPT. KEANE CALLS A MEETING WITH HIS A-TEAM AND THE SUPPORTING SEABEE TEAM.

KEANE:
"AS YOU MEN KNOW, DONG XOAI IS THE DISTRICT H.Q. FOR DON LUAN DISTRICT OF PHUOC LONG PROVINCE. FROM A MILITARY POINT OF VIEW, WE SIT ASTRIDE CRITICAL GROUND ROUTES."

KEANE:
"OUR TEAM, A-342, HAS THREE PRIMARY MISSIONS. ONE — TO SERVE AS ADVISORS TO DON LUAN DISTRICT. TWO — ADVISORS TO THE VIETNAMESE MILITARY AND CIVILIAN FORCES. THREE — TO CONDUCT OPERATIONS AGAINST WAR ZONES."

ALLISON:
"RIGHT. BUT, AS HEAV WEAPONS NCO, OUR GU ARE LACKING WEIGHT AND EQUIPMENT. HOW ABOUT YOU, ED?

SMITH:
"MY JOB'S INTELLIGEN(NCO, AND TO ME IT CONTINUES TO LOOK LII WE'RE IN DEEP UP TO OUR KNEES."

KEANE:
"TRUE. IT IS WHAT IT IS

KEANE:
"WE'VE GOT TO CONTINUE STRENGTHENING THOSE AREAS MOST APT TO BE HIT IN THE EVENT OF AN ATTACK. CHECK ALL DEFENSES IN AND AROUND THE BERM PERIMETER."

SMITH:
"THEY'RE GONNA COME FROM THE WEST — THE FOREST. THAT'LL BE COVER FOR THEM WHEN THEY MOUNT THEIR ATTACK."

KEANE:
"OKAY, ED. IT'S UP TO US TO BE READY WITH WHATEVER WE GOT."

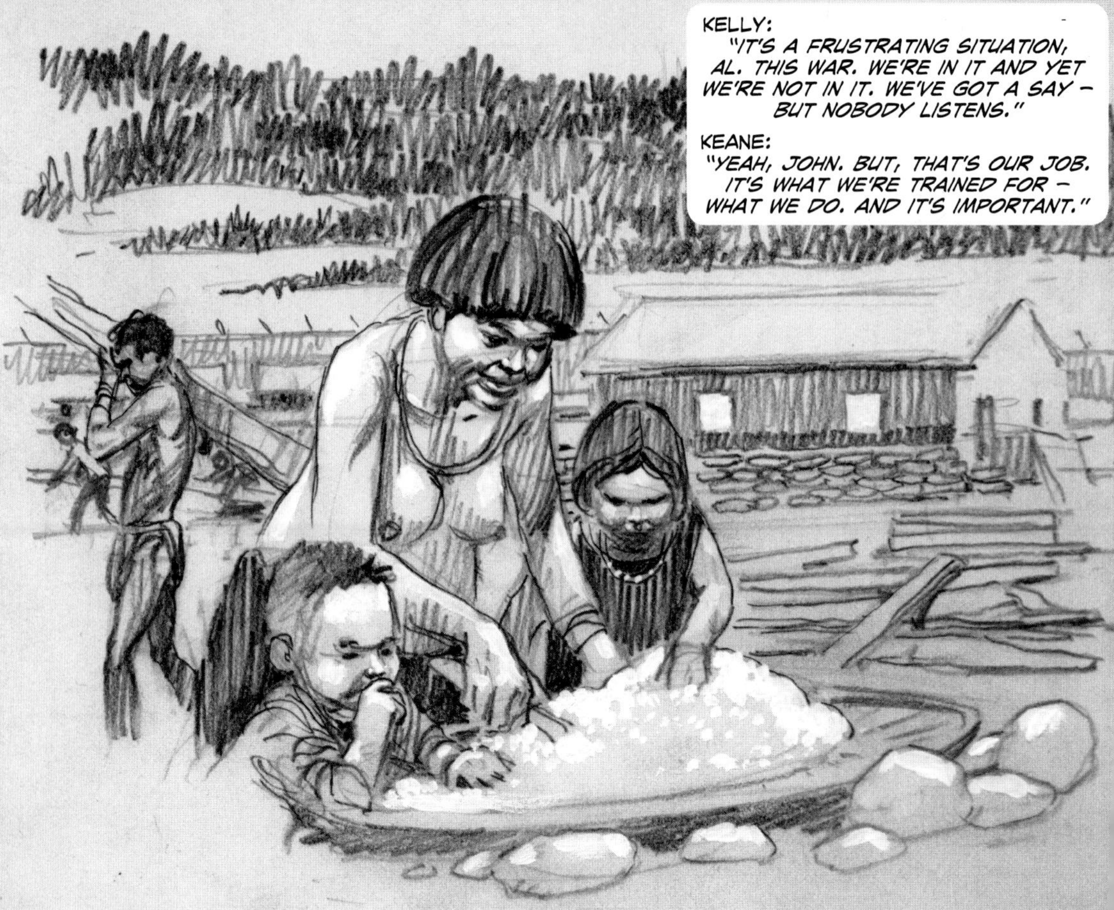
KELLY:
"IT'S A FRUSTRATING SITUATION, AL. THIS WAR. WE'RE IN IT AND YET WE'RE NOT IN IT. WE'VE GOT A SAY – BUT NOBODY LISTENS."
KEANE:
"YEAH, JOHN. BUT, THAT'S OUR JOB. IT'S WHAT WE'RE TRAINED FOR – WHAT WE DO. AND IT'S IMPORTANT."

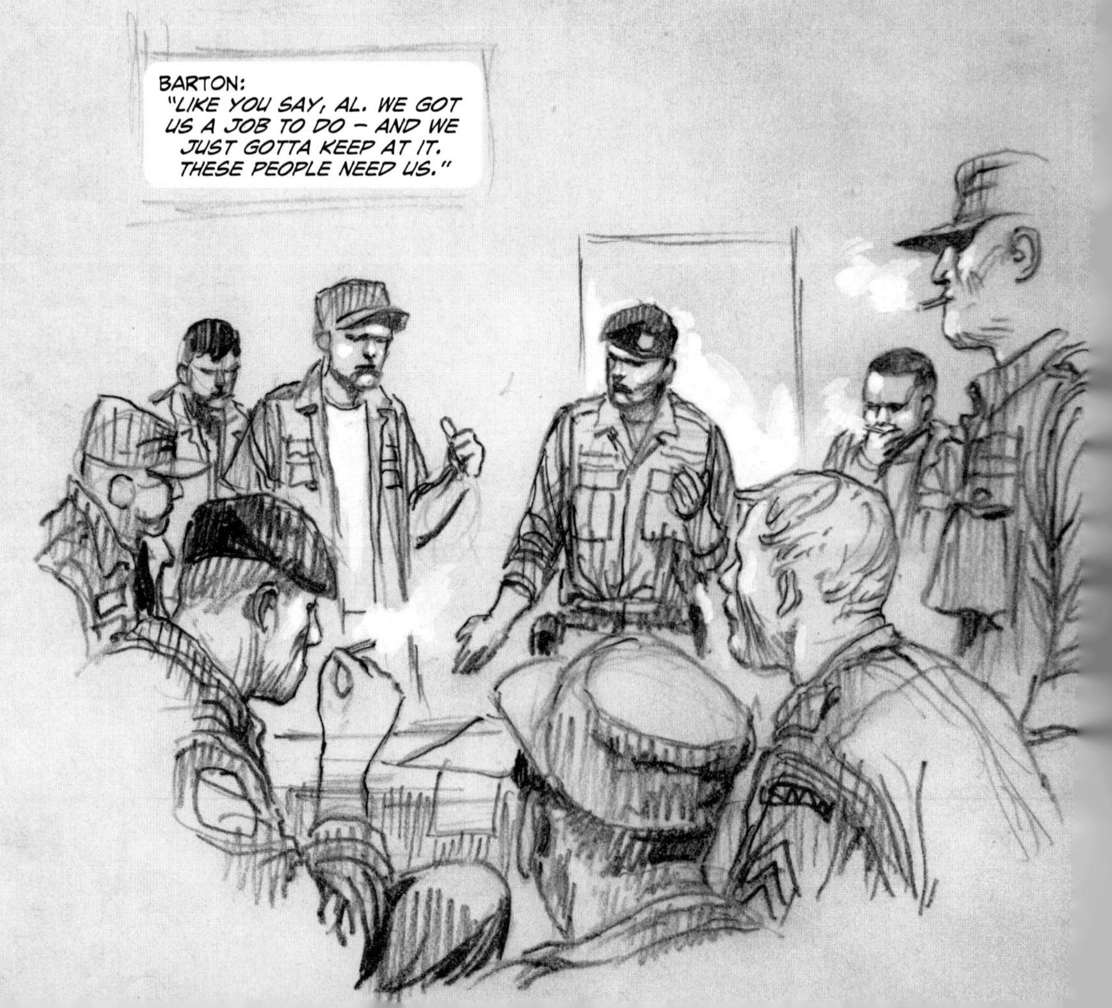
BARTON:
"LIKE YOU SAY, AL. WE GOT US A JOB TO DO – AND WE JUST GOTTA KEEP AT IT. THESE PEOPLE NEED US."

9 JUNE 1965

THAT NIGHT THE RAIN POURED DOWN IN A STEADY STREAM... DRUMMING A TATTOO ON THE CORRUGATED METAL ROOFS.

THE GROUND BECAME A SEA OF ANKLE-DEEP MUD.

A THICK GROUND FOG AROSE FROM THE MIX OF COOL RAIN SUCKED INTO THE WARM EARTH.

DONG XOAI CAMP SENTINELS STARE INTO THE OVERCAST, BUT MIST AND RAIN OBSCURES THE LANDSCAPE. LITTLE CAN BE SEEN THROUGH THE STEADY DOWNPOUR.

UNSEEN FROM THE ENCAMPMENT, IN THE THICK MASS OF TREES AND FOLIAGE THERE IS MOVEMENT... LIKE A CARPET OF CRAWLING ANTS.

NOT MORE THAN 500 YARDS FROM THE CAMP'S PERIMETER, THE ENEMY ENCIRCLES AND IS CLOSING IN ON DONG XOAI.

FROM THE DARK, WET SHADOWS OF THE FOREST THE ENEMY APPROACHES... ONTO THE HIGH GROUND OVERLOOKING THE CAMP. THEY NUMBER IN THE HUNDREDS OR MORE AND ARE WELL ARMED.

THEY CARRY 75 MM HOWITZERS – FLAME THROWERS – POLE CHARGES – HAND GRENADES – SMALL ARMS – RECOILLESS RIFLES – ROCKET-PROPELLED GRENADES – MACHINE GUNS.

THE VIET CONG HAVE CUT ALL ROADS AROUND DONG XOAI. NO ONE CAN LEAVE OR ENTER THE IMMEDIATE AREA.

IGNORING THE RAIN, FIGURES IN BLACK PAJAMA-LIKE UNIFORMS ASSEMBLE AND MOUNT HOWITZERS... SNOUTS AIMED AT THE CAMP BUILDINGS.

SILENTLY... SWIFTLY, THE ATTACK IS READY TO BE ACTIVATED.

THE FIRST VOLLEY OF MORTAR SHELLS HITS THEIR PRIMARY TARGETS: THE CAMP'S MASONRY BUILDINGS.

APPARENTLY, THE V.C. KNEW WHICH STRUCTURE HELD THE COMMAND POST AND WHICH WERE THE BILLET BUILDINGS. THE STRIKES HIT WITH A CONSISTENT EARTH-SHAKING RHYTHM.

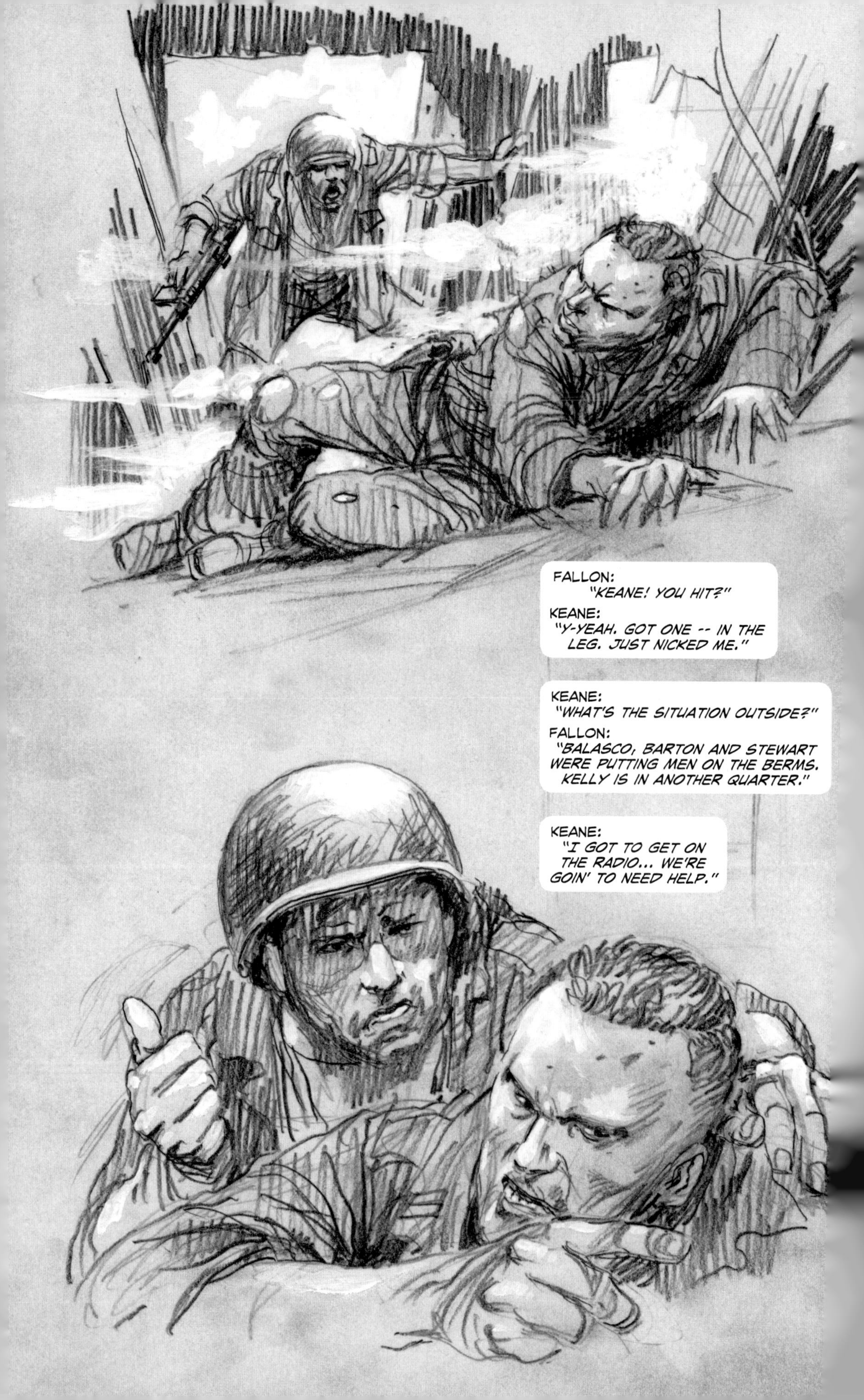
FALLON: "KEANE! YOU HIT?"
KEANE: "Y-YEAH. GOT ONE -- IN THE LEG. JUST NICKED ME."
KEANE: "WHAT'S THE SITUATION OUTSIDE?"
FALLON: "BALASCO, BARTON AND STEWART WERE PUTTING MEN ON THE BERMS. KELLY IS IN ANOTHER QUARTER."
KEANE: "I GOT TO GET ON THE RADIO... WE'RE GOIN' TO NEED HELP."

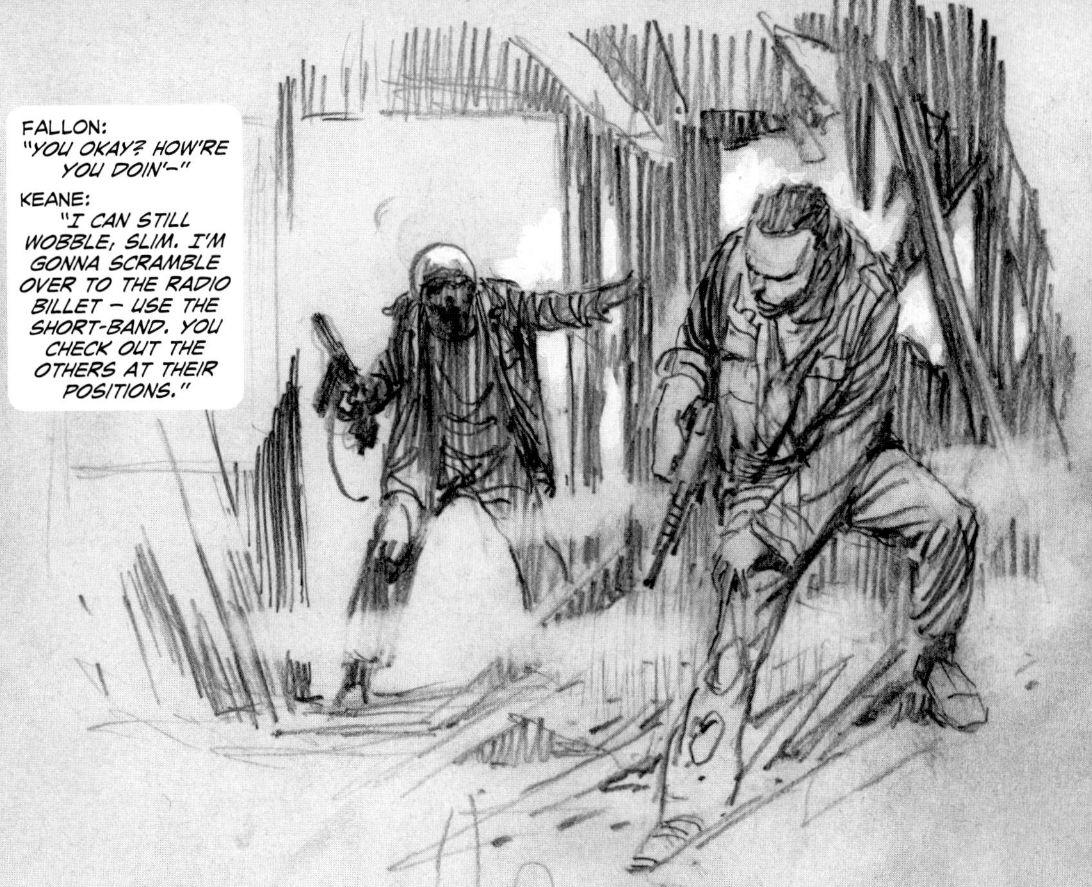
FALLON: "YOU OKAY? HOW'RE YOU DOIN'–"
KEANE: "I CAN STILL WOBBLE, SLIM. I'M GONNA SCRAMBLE OVER TO THE RADIO BILLET – USE THE SHORT-BAND. YOU CHECK OUT THE OTHERS AT THEIR POSITIONS."

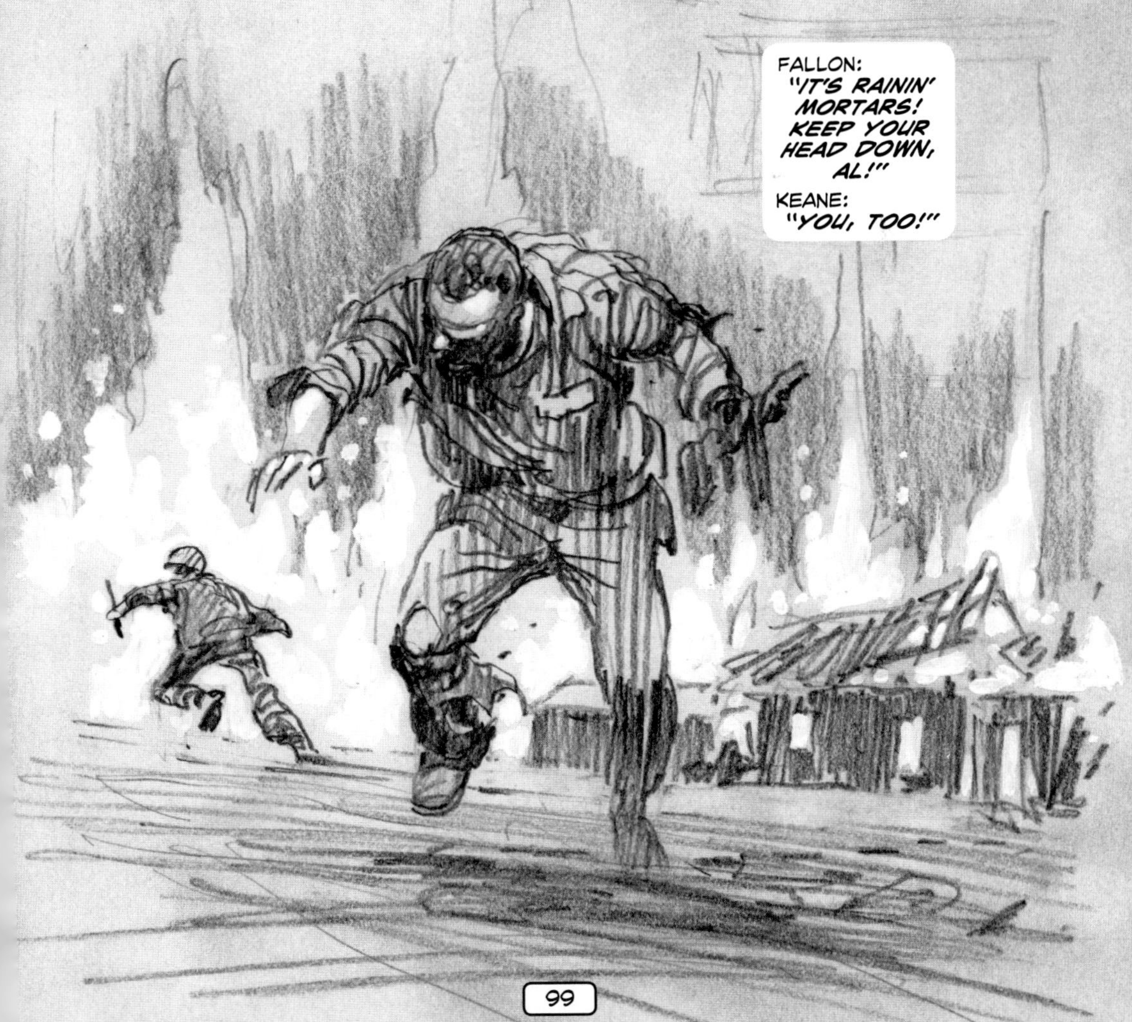
FALLON: "IT'S RAININ' MORTARS! KEEP YOUR HEAD DOWN, AL!"
KEANE: "YOU, TOO!"

THE RADIO BILLET HAD BEEN HIT BUT IS STILL STANDING...

CARTER:
"HI, CAP'N. C'MON IN OUTTA THE RAIN."

KEANE:
"IS THE RADIO STILL WORKING? WHERE'S THE REST OF THE TEAM?"

CARTER:
"ME AN' MAC HAVE BEEN COVERING HERE... WORKIN' ON THE RADIO. WIRE'S BEEN CUT."

McCABE:
"ALLISON AND HARRISON ARE WITH THE CIDG — STIFFENING THE TROOPS. SHEER IS PUSHING MORTAR ROUNDS. RUSSELL'S BEEN HIT."

CONVERSATION IN THE BILLET COMES TO A SUDDEN HALT...

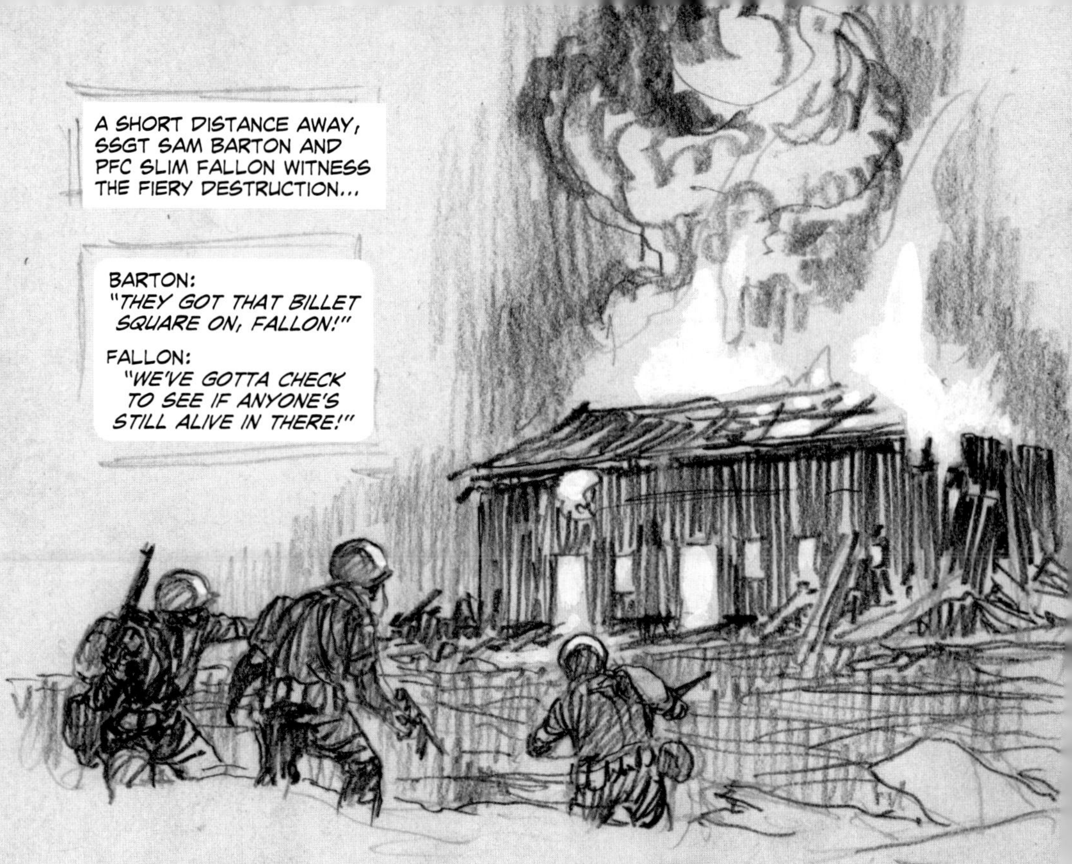
A SHORT DISTANCE AWAY, SSGT SAM BARTON AND PFC SLIM FALLON WITNESS THE FIERY DESTRUCTION...
BARTON: "THEY GOT THAT BILLET SQUARE ON, FALLON!"
FALLON: "WE'VE GOTTA CHECK TO SEE IF ANYONE'S STILL ALIVE IN THERE!"

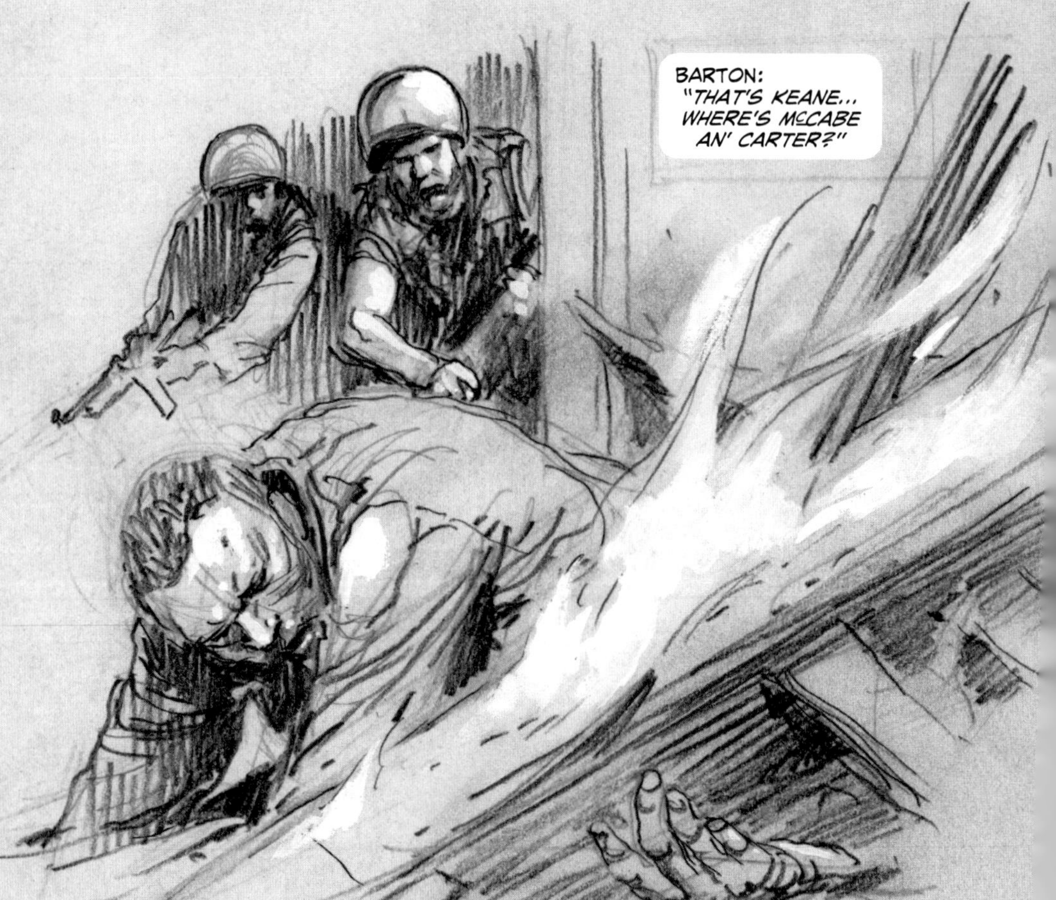
BARTON: "THAT'S KEANE... WHERE'S McCABE AN' CARTER?"

BARTON:
"KEANE — ARE YOU OKAY?"

KEANE:
"M-MY LEGS... CAN'T STAND UP. SHRAPNEL."

FALLON:
"THE OTHERS—?"

BARTON:
"HELP ME STAND HIM UP, SLIM. GET HIM OVER TO THE BERM."

BARTON:
"WE GOTTA GET YOU OUT OF HERE, KEANE—"

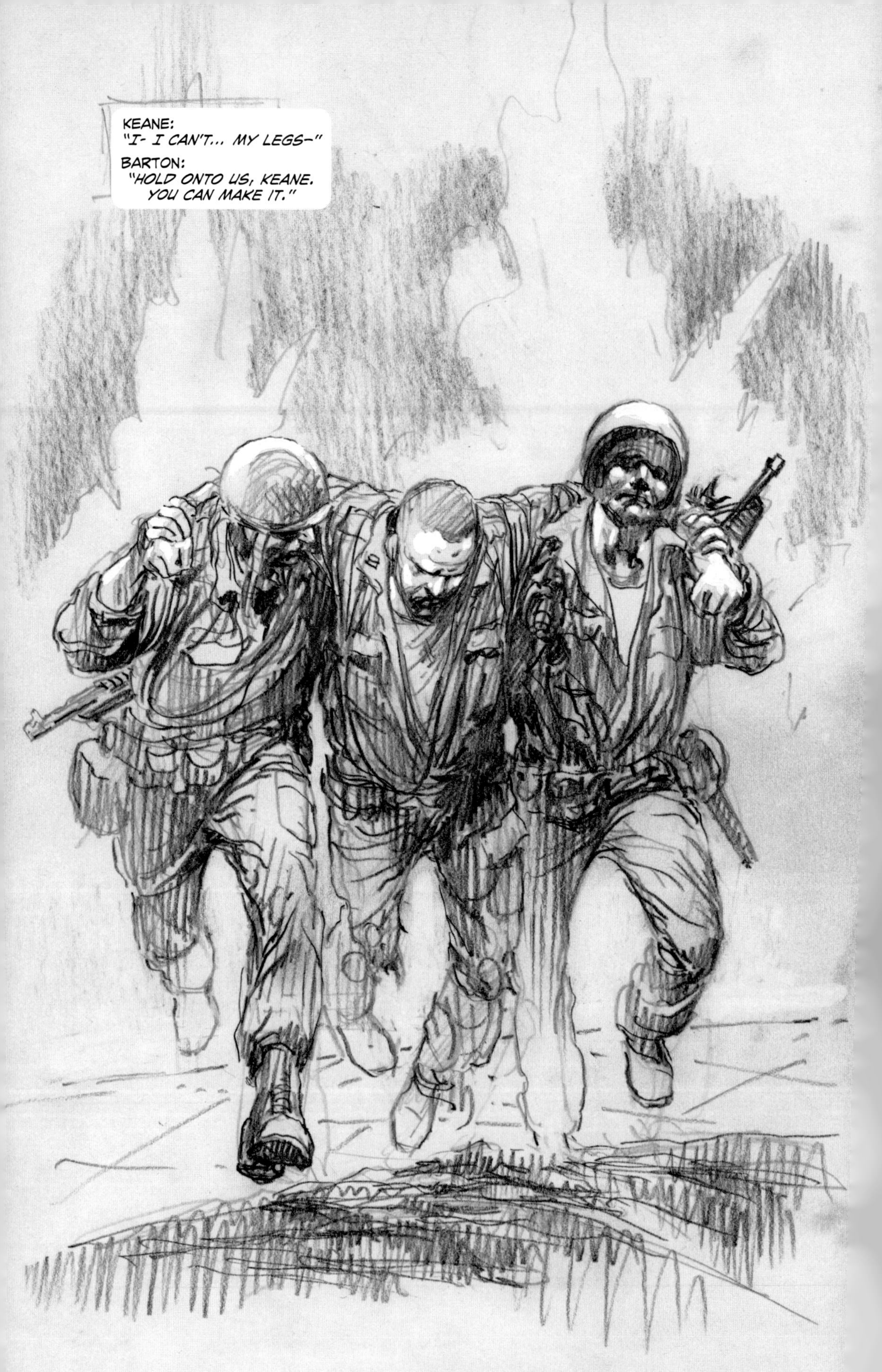
KEANE:
"I- I CAN'T... MY LEGS-"
BARTON:
"HOLD ONTO US, KEANE. YOU CAN MAKE IT."

THE CONSISTENT EXPLOSIONS OF MORTAR SHELLS AND GROUND TREMORS NEVER STOP...

...AS KEANE IS FINALLY SET DOWN NEAR A MACHINE GUN PLACEMENT.

BARTON:
"YOU'LL BE OKAY HERE, KEANE... FOR AWHILE."

FALLON:
"HERE'S A LAUNCHER AND A FEW ROUNDS. FOR COMPANY. AND YOU'RE IN LUCK... IT STOPPED RAINING."

KEANE:
"YEAH, YEAH. OKAY... I'M SET HERE. YOU TWO GET BACK AND CHECK OUR LINES... KEEP OUR BOYS RETURNING FIRE. AND WE GOTTA TRY TO COMMUNICATE OUR STATUS HERE – OUTSIDE."

KEANE:
"SOON AS THE V.C. LAY OFF LOBBING MORTAR SHELLS – THEY'LL ATTACK IN FORCE."

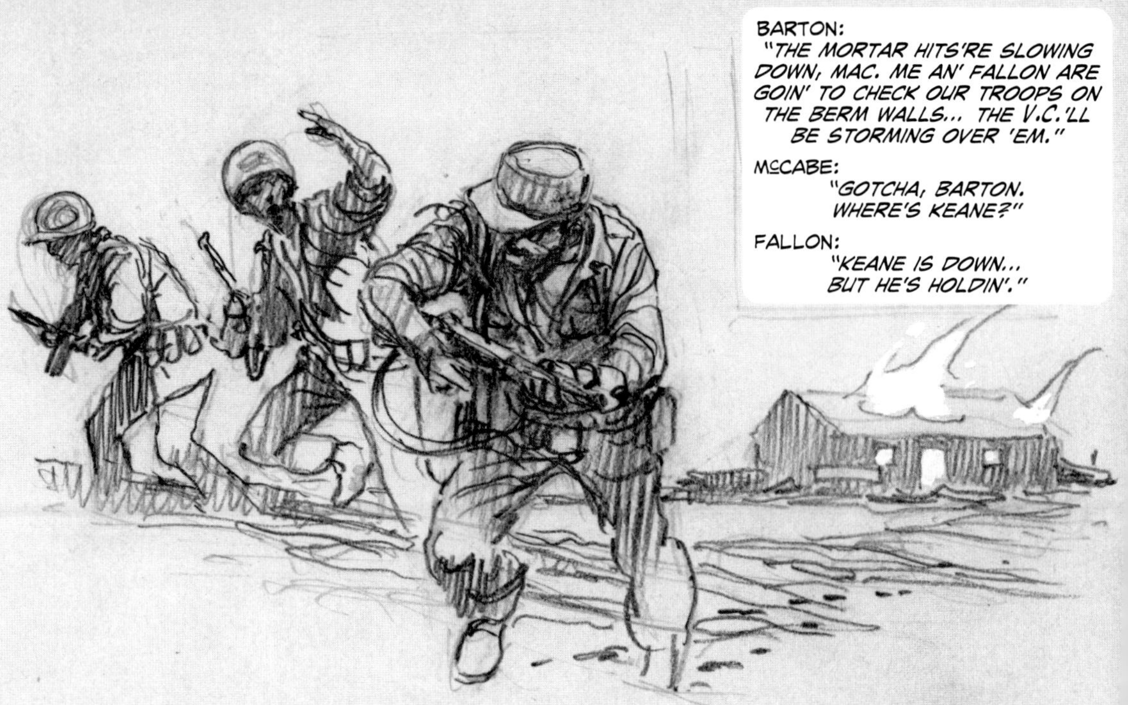
BARTON:
"THE MORTAR HITS'RE SLOWING DOWN, MAC. ME AN' FALLON ARE GOIN' TO CHECK OUR TROOPS ON THE BERM WALLS... THE V.C.'LL BE STORMING OVER 'EM."
McCABE:
"GOTCHA, BARTON. WHERE'S KEANE?"
FALLON:
"KEANE IS DOWN... BUT HE'S HOLDIN'."

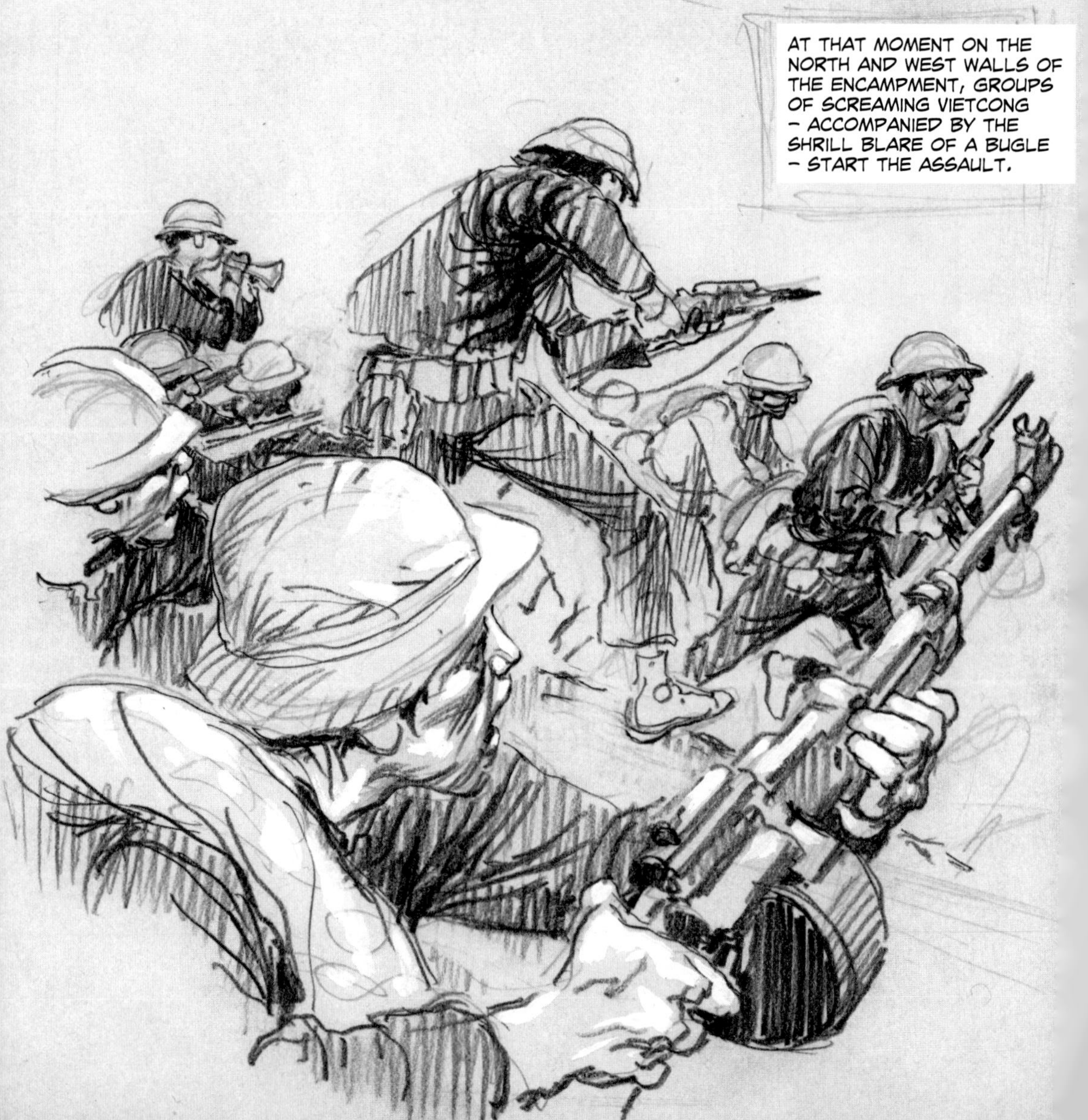
AT THAT MOMENT ON THE NORTH AND WEST WALLS OF THE ENCAMPMENT, GROUPS OF SCREAMING VIETCONG – ACCOMPANIED BY THE SHRILL BLARE OF A BUGLE – START THE ASSAULT.

ATOP THE BERM WALL IN THE NORTHWEST CORNER, SGT. DAN ALLISON HAS TAKEN HIS POSITION — SHOUTING ENCOURAGEMENT TO THE TROOPS.

IGNORING THE WILD YELLING OF THE V.C. PUNCTUATED BY WHINING BULLETS, HE CONCENTRATES ON KEEPING THE BARREL OF HIS MG HOT AND SMOKING.

ALLISON IS HIT — SUSTAINING WOUNDS IN HIS HEAD AND CHEST. STILL HE CONTINUES TO FIRE AT THE ADVANCING HORDE.

WITNESSING ALLISON'S STAND IN SPITE OF CRITICAL WOUNDS, HIS MEN MOUNT SUPPORT FIRE AS THE FIGHTING GOES ON UNABATED.

CAUGHT IN HIS BILLET
JUST PRIOR TO THE
V.C. CHARGE, SEABEE
HARRISON IS HIT
DURING THE INITIAL
MORTAR BARRAGE.

HURT... BLEEDING... HARRISON
MAKES IT OUT OF HIS BATTERED
MASONRY BUILDING TO FACE
THE ONCOMING HORDE.

SEABEE TOM
HARRISON FOUGHT
TO THE END.

SGT. JOE SHEER MANNED THE 81 MM MORTAR ALONE — BY HIMSELF — FROM THE OUTSET OF THE ATTACK.

ALTHOUGH HE WAS IN AN EXPOSED POSITION UNDER FIRE...

...HE CONTINUED HIS COUNTERFIRE OF MORTAR SHELLS AGAINST THE ADVANCING V.C.

SGT. JOE SHEER DIED
IN THE EARLY MORNING
HOURS OF 10 JUNE 1965
— IN A DARKNESS LIT BY
EXPLODING SHELLS AND
SCREAMING BULLETS.
HE FELL, KILLED AT HIS
GUN AS THE BATTLE OF
DONG XOAI RAGED ON.

ONCE MORE THE BLARE OF A BUGLE ADDS TO THE EAR-SPLITTING CACOPHONY OF BULLETS, GRENADES AND MORTARS...

...HERALDING AN INTENSIFIED ATTACK FROM THE NORTHWEST SECTOR OF THE CIDG COMPOUND.

THEN A HUGE WAVE — A SURGING MASS OF ENEMY FORCES — POURS OVER THE BERMS AND PAST THE SANDBAG SECURITIES.

BECAUSE OF THE MULTIPLE NUMBERS OF VIETCONG ATTACK UNITS, THEY HAVE BEEN GIVEN DISTINCTIVE GARMENTS FOR RECOGNITION PURPOSES AMONG THEIR OWN.

ONE GROUP WEARS BRIGHT COLORED ARM BANDS...

,,,WHILE ANOTHER HAS A CHECKERED CLOTH WRAPPED AROUND THE WAIST.

POLE CHARGES

GRENADES

SOME WEAR SHIRTS THAT EXPOSE ONE SHOULDER...

MACHINE GUNS

FLAME THROWERS

...SO THAT WHEN ATTACKING IN GROUPS AND IN BATTLE CONTACT, COMRADES CAN BE DISTINGUISHED FROM FOES.

IN THE MIDST OF FLAMES AND ERUPTING GRENADES, SGT. SAM BARTON – IGNORING HIS OWN SAFETY – DIRECTS HIS MEN TO HOLD DEFENSIVE POSITIONS.

HE LOWERS HIS THOMPSON ONLY TO TEND THE WOUNDED AND TO DISTRIBUTE AMMUNITION. HE'S EVERYWHERE AT ONCE.

SILHOUETTED AGAINST THE SPREADING FLAMES, BARTON STANDS LIKE A BEACON – URGING HIS GROUP TO FIGHT ON AGAINST OVERWHELMING ENEMY FORCES.

MIRACULOUSLY, HE CONTINUES TO STAND.

NOT FAR FROM BARTON, CAPT. KEANE IS HELPLESS TO MOVE – SHRAPNEL IN HIS LEGS – HE IS PREPARED TO DEFEND HIS GROUND.

KEANE, DESPITE HIS HANDICAP OF IMMOBILITY, USES HIS .30 CALIBER AUTOMATIC EFFECTIVELY — BUT SPARINGLY. ONLY A FEW BULLETS REMAIN IN HIS GUN'S CLIP.

AT THE NORTHWEST PERIMETER, A V.C. FLAMETHROWER HAS PENETRATED THE CAMP'S DEFENSES.

IT WAS THEN THAT THE V.C. CRESTED THE NORTHWEST WALL. MANY FALL — BUT MORE POUR OVER THEIR FALLEN COMRADES.

SEABEES STEWART AND BALASCO BECOME SEPARATED FROM THE OTHERS. BOTH MEN HAVE SUSTAINED WOUNDS, BUT ARE ABLE TO AVOID THE V.C. AND MAKE IT TO THE OUTSIDE OF THE CAMP. THEY SEPARATE — HOPING THAT EACH ALONE WOULD STAND A BETTER CHANCE OF SURVIVAL.

SSGT. DAN ALLISON IS DOWN — WOUNDED — CAUGHT IN THE LINE OF ENEMY FIRE. MANY OF THE VIETNAMESE CIDG DEFENDERS ARE DEAD OR SLIPPING OUT OF THE EMBATTLED CAMP TO PROTECT THEIR FAMILIES IN THE VILLAGE.

WITH MOST OF THE CIDG GONE, ONLY A HANDFUL OF SPECIAL FORCES AND SEABEE PERSONNEL ARE LEFT STANDING AGAINST THE ONCOMING V.C. HORDE. SEABEES GALLO AND ADAMS STAND THEIR GROUND WITH BARTON.

ADAMS

BARTON

GALLO

IT WAS DURING THIS ASSAULT THAT SSGT. DAN ALLISON WAS FATALLY STRUCK DOWN.

SLOWLY... STUBBORNLY... THE REMAINING AMERICAN DEFENDERS MOVE FROM THE NORTHWEST CORNER TOWARDS THE DISTRICT H.Q.

NO MAN LEAVES UNSCATHED. THEY LIMP TO THE REAR... PRESSI ON OPEN WOUNDS... HELPING ONE ANOTHER. COVERING THEIR RETRE. WITH SMALL ARMS FIRE

BARTON:
"KEEP MOVIN'... KEEP MOVIN'! WE GOTTA FIRM UP OUR LINES... GET OUR GUYS BACK UP AGAIN!"

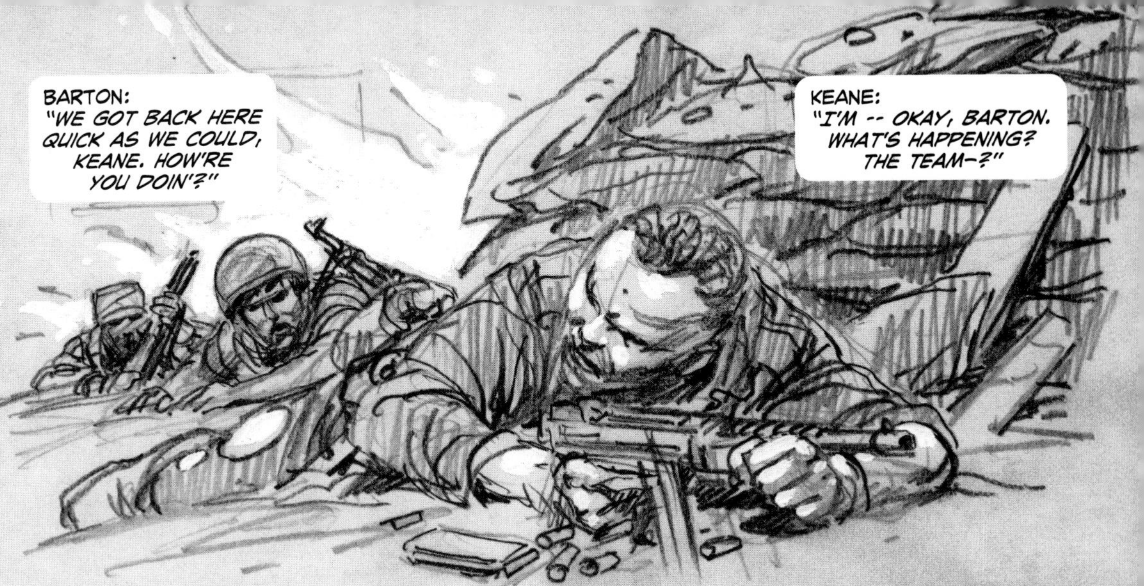
BARTON: "WE GOT BACK HERE QUICK AS WE COULD, KEANE. HOW'RE YOU DOIN'?"
KEANE: "I'M -- OKAY, BARTON. WHAT'S HAPPENING? THE TEAM-?"

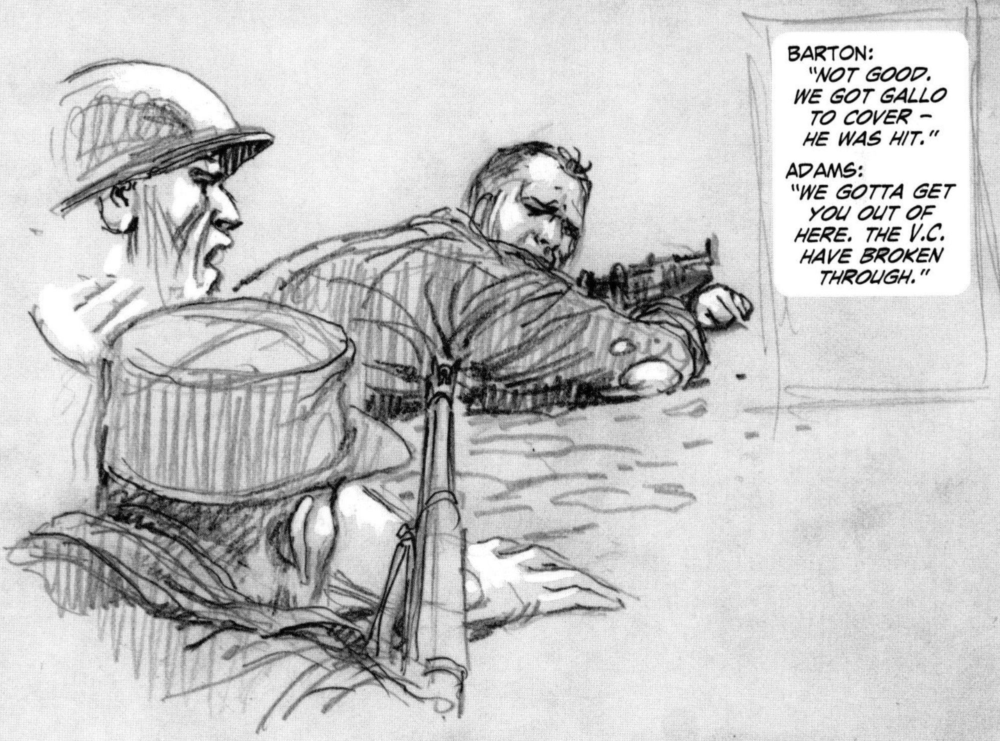
BARTON: "NOT GOOD. WE GOT GALLO TO COVER - HE WAS HIT."
ADAMS: "WE GOTTA GET YOU OUT OF HERE. THE V.C. HAVE BROKEN THROUGH."

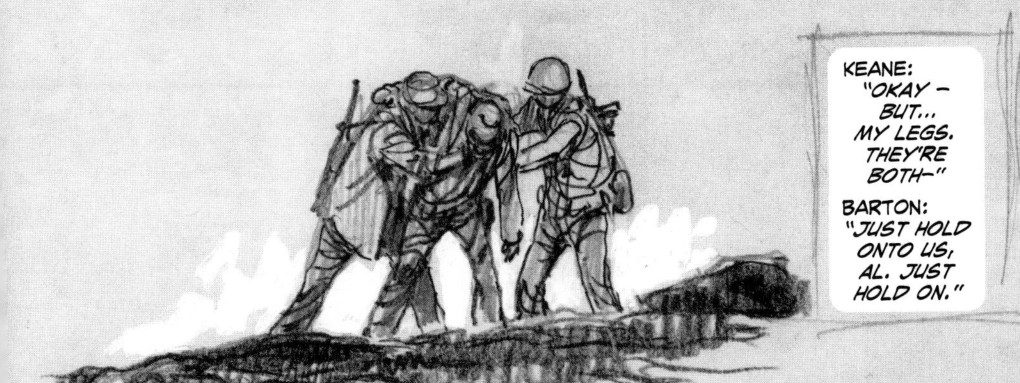
KEANE: "OKAY - BUT... MY LEGS. THEY'RE BOTH-"
BARTON: "JUST HOLD ONTO US, AL. JUST HOLD ON."

HIS LEGS USELESS, AL KEANE'S LIMBS DANGLE AS HE'S HOISTED AND CARRIED ON HIS COMRADES' BACKS.

ADAMS:
"WE GOTTA GET HIM OVER TO THE H.Q. BUILDING."

BARTON:
"OR WHAT'S *LEFT* OF IT."

KEANE:
"UNH—MY LEGS."

BARTON:
"*YOU GOT HIT, ADAMS.*"

ADAMS:
"I—I'M OKAY. *KEEP GOING'. GET HIM INSIDE. I—I'LL CATCH UP.*"

THERE IS NO CESSATION OF ERUPTING GRENADES OR FLYING SHRAPNEL, AS SAM BARTON CARRIES JIM KEANE INTO THE DECIMATED H.Q. BUILDING.

INSIDE THE BATTERED
BUILDING, BARTON
TENDS KEANE'S WOUNDS
AS BEST HE CAN.

BARTON:
"MAYBE THAT SPLINT
I PUT ON YOUR LEG'LL
HELP A LITTLE. ANY
MORPHINE-?"

FALLON:
"MORPHINE'S GONE,
AL. ALL OUT-"

KEANE:
"TELL KELLY HE'S -- IN
CHARGE. JUST -- JUST
KEEP ME POSTED."

BARTON:
"OKAY, AL - KEEP
YOUR BUTT DOWN.
WE'LL BE BACK."

BY THE TIME BARTON AND FALLON STEP INTO THE COMPOUND, THE V.C. FLAME-THROWERS WERE COOKING A SWATH THROUGH THE CAMP.

THE WHOLE AREA IS ABLAZE.

NOW THE PERIMETER HAS BEEN PENETRATED IN SEVERAL PLACES AND THE ASSAULT IS COMING FROM ALL DIRECTIONS. THE BERM IS NO OBSTACLE.

THE BLACK-CLAD ATTACKERS COME — A SEEMINGLY ENDLESS OCEAN OF BODIES. AS ONE DROPS, TWO MORE TAKE HIS PLACE IN THE INTERMINABLE FLOW.

SILHOUETTED AGAINST THE CRACKLING
FLAMES, THE A-TEAM SURVIVORS RUN
ALONG THE BERM EXCHANGING FIRE
WITH THE ATTACKERS... EXHORTING
THEIR VIETNAMESE COUNTERPARTS
NOT TO GIVE IN... NOT TO GIVE UP.

VASTLY OUTNUMBERED BY
THE OPPOSING FORCES, THE
DEFENDERS FIGHT ON...

IT IS ONLY LATER THAT THE TEAM
LEARNS THAT SEABEE HARRISON
– WOUNDED DURING THE INITIAL
ATTACK – WAS KILLED IN THE EARLY
MORNING OF TUESDAY, JUNE 10.

SOME OF THE REMAINING ARVN ARTILLERY STILL STANDING FIRED THEIR LAST ROUNDS OUT OF AN 81 MM BEFORE THEY WERE OVERRUN.

AGAIN AND AGAIN THE V.C. CAME ON. NOT ENOUGH MEN OR AMMUNITION FOR THE DEFENDERS TO STOP THEM. THE ENEMY CONTINUED TO GAIN MOMENTUM WITH EACH ADVANCING STEP.

AT 1:20 A.M., THE SOUND OF A BUGLE ONCE MORE HERALDED A CONCENTRATED ATTACK. ANOTHER V.C. ASSAULT ON THE CAMP'S NORTHWEST CORNER OVER THE BERM.

YELLING AND SCREAMING TO FURTHER DIMINISH THE DEFENDERS' RESOLVE, THE ATTACKING FORCES ARE EVERYWHERE TAKING A BLOODY TOLL.

AMID A STACCATO OF AUTOMATIC RIFLE FIRE, EXPLODING GRENADES AND THE HIGH-PITCHED WHINE OF SHRAPNEL, THE FIGHTING CONTINUES WITH UNDIMINISHED FURY.

NOW THE ATTACKERS WHO HAVE ALTERED THEIR BLACK PAJAMA-LIKE UNIFORMS FOR RECOGNITION PURPOSES BREACH THE REMAINING DEFENSIVE LINES.

THE OBVIOUS ALTERATIONS IN DRESS LEND AN IRONIC IF NOT HUMOROUS NOTE TO THE BLOOD-LETTING. BUT — NONE OF THOSE INVOLVED ARE GIVEN TO LEVITY.

INSTEAD OF LAUGHTER, THE AIR IS FILLED WITH THE UNENDING COUGH OF GUNFIRE. AND THE TREMOR OF EXPLODING MISSILES MINGLES WITH THE CRIES OF THE WOUNDED AND DYING.

ON THE ENCAMPMENT'S BERM, SSGT. SAM BARTON CONVEYS ORDERS BY DEMONSTRATION.

BARTON:
"STAY WITH ME, MEN! DON'T LET 'EM PUSH US OFF!"

SHOULDER TO SHOULDER HE STANDS WITH HIS ARVN COUNTERPARTS — AN IMMOVABLE OBJECT IN A CONSTANTLY SHIFTING LANDSCAPE.

BARTON:
"MAKE 'EM PAY! MAKE 'EM PAY!"

NOT FAR FROM BARTON, SEABEE PAUL ADAMS LENDS SUPPORT AND REASON FOR THE ARVN TROOPS TO STAY AND CONTINUE FIGHTING...

...UNTIL A BULLET SHATTERS HIS KNEE.

UNABLE TO WALK, ADAMS IS CARRIED TO COVER BY PFC. SLIM FALLON AND SEABEE HASEN.

FALLON:
"WE DIN'T KNOW YOU WAS THERE! WHY'N'T YOU YELL OR SOMETHING, ADAMS?"

ADAMS:
"I... KNEW YOU GUYS'D... SHOW UP... EVENTUALLY."

CARTER:
"WHAT'S WRONG WITH ADAMS?"

FALLON:
"LEG'S CHOPPED UP."

HASEN:
"ANY LUCK WITH THE RADIO, CARTER?"

CARTER:
"YES AND NO. I GOT THROUGH — BUT — WE GOTTA WAIT FOR FULL WEATHER CLEARANCE BEFORE THEY'LL FLY."

FALLON:
"NOT GOOD. AMMO RUNNIN' OUT — ARVN LEAVING TO TAKE CARE OF THEIR OWN FAMILIES — AND OUR TEAM'S TAKING A LOT OF HITS."

HASEN:
"HOW'S THE LEG, ADAMS? ANOTHER SHOT OF MORPHINE?"

ADAMS:
"I'M... OKAY. THEY NEED YOU OUTSIDE..."

KEANE:
"LOOKS LIKE IT'S FINALLY GETTING DAYLIGHT, FALLON. MAYBE THEY'LL FLY–"

FALLON:
"I DON'T THINK SO. FOG'S COVERING THE AREA – THICK AS GRAVY."

PLANES MAY NOT FLY, BUT MORNING FOG IS NO DETERRENT FOR THE V.C. SHELLS, AND THE BARRAGE NEVER STOPS RIPPING MEN AND DEFENSES.

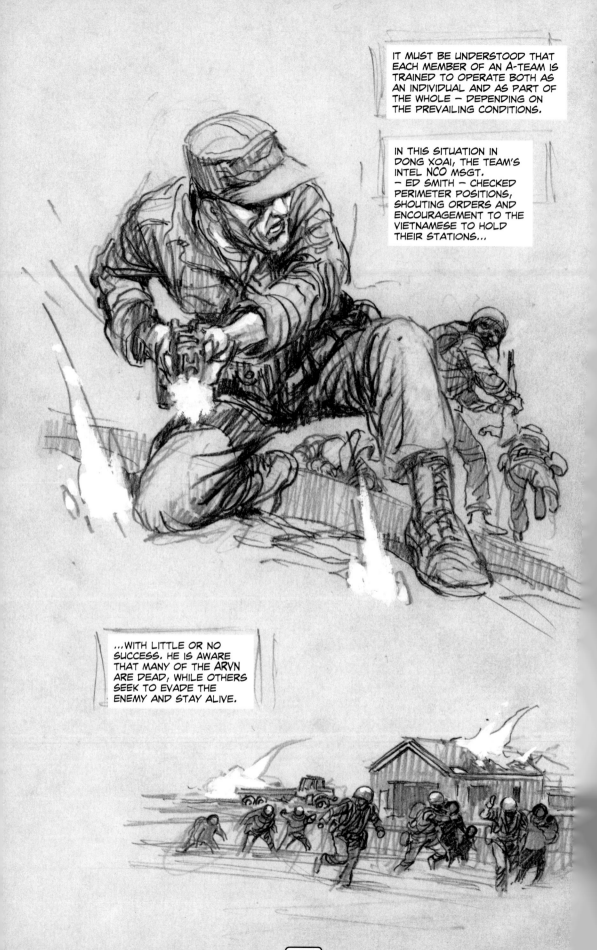

IT MUST BE UNDERSTOOD THAT EACH MEMBER OF AN A-TEAM IS TRAINED TO OPERATE BOTH AS AN INDIVIDUAL AND AS PART OF THE WHOLE — DEPENDING ON THE PREVAILING CONDITIONS.

IN THIS SITUATION IN DONG XOAI, THE TEAM'S INTEL NCO MSGT. — ED SMITH — CHECKED PERIMETER POSITIONS, SHOUTING ORDERS AND ENCOURAGEMENT TO THE VIETNAMESE TO HOLD THEIR STATIONS...

...WITH LITTLE OR NO SUCCESS. HE IS AWARE THAT MANY OF THE ARVN ARE DEAD, WHILE OTHERS SEEK TO EVADE THE ENEMY AND STAY ALIVE.

FOGGY DAYLIGHT... AND DONG XOAI'S REMAINING DEFENSIVE FORCES ARE COMPRESSED AND DRIVEN TO TAKE REFUGE IN THE REMAINING BATTERED MASONRY BUILDINGS.

THE DEFENDERS' NUMBERS HAVE BEEN DRASTICALLY DEPLETED. THOSE LEFT ARE MOSTLY SPECIAL FORCES PERSONNEL. ALMOST ALL OF THEM HAVE SUSTAINED CRITICAL OR MORTAL WOUNDS.

IN THE MIST THAT ENSHROUDS THEM, MORE AND MORE OF THE ARVN ABANDON THE COMPOUND AND RUN FROM THE MURDEROUS POUNDING. ONLY THE AMERICANS REMAIN AT THEIR POSTS.

THE MOMENTUM OF THE ATTACK CONTINUES. EVEN THE BARBED WIRE SURROUNDING THE CAMP'S INNER PERIMETER IS NO DETERRENT, AS THE V.C. OFFICERS COMMAND THEIR MEN TO LIE DOWN ON IT SO THEIR COMRADES MAY SAFELY CROSS OVER.

IN ONE OF THE SHELL-POCKED BUILDINGS THAT REMAIN STANDING, THE DEFENDERS USE THE HOLES IN THE WALLS AS GUN PORTS TO KEEP THE V.C. AT BAY. IT WORKS – BUT ONLY FOR A MOMENT.

CARTER RECEIVES
A HEARTENING
RADIO MESSAGE...

CARTER:
"LOOKS LIKE THE FOG'S
LIFTING! THEY'RE SENDING
OUT AIRCRAFT!"

HASEN:
"I'M HOPIN'
THEY'LL GET
HERE IN TIME!"

CARTER:
"IF THE FOG'S NOT
GONE, HASEN, AIR'S
NOT GOING TO BE ABLE
TO SPOT TARGETS."

FALLON:
"IF THEY DON'T GET HERE
SOON, THE FOG WON'T
MAKE ANY DIFFERENCE
– FOR ANY OF US."

10 JUNE 1965, 6:30 A.M.

TWO USAF B-57'S AND A HELICOPTER GUNSHIP HIT THE AREA NORTH OF DONG XOAI WITH FRAGMENTATION BOMBS AND ROCKETS. THEIR TARGETS ARE STILL PARTIALLY CONCEALED IN LIGHT MIST.

DESPITE THE LACK OF OPPORTUNITY FOR CLEAR SIGHTING, THE BOMB-DROPS ACT AS A RESPITE FOR THE BELEAGUERED MEN WITHIN THE COMPOUND.

IN ANOTHER BATTERED BUILDING, McCABE AND KELLY REESTIMATE THEIR SITUATION WITH OTHER TEAM MEMBERS.

McCABE:
"THE FOG'S CLEARIN', JOHN. MAYBE — WITH A LITTLE MORE LUCK—"

SUDDENLY, THE CLATTER OF MACHINE GUN FIRE PUNCTUATES KELLY'S REMARKS AS SLUGS RIP INTO THE INTERIOR WALLS.

KELLY:
"DOWN! GET DOWN! ANYONE SEE WHERE IT'S COMIN' FROM? STAY ONNA FLOOR!"

HALEY:
"OVER THERE! IN THE OLD SCHOOL BUILDING. SOUNDS LIKE THAT'S A .51 CALIBER TRAINED ON US!"

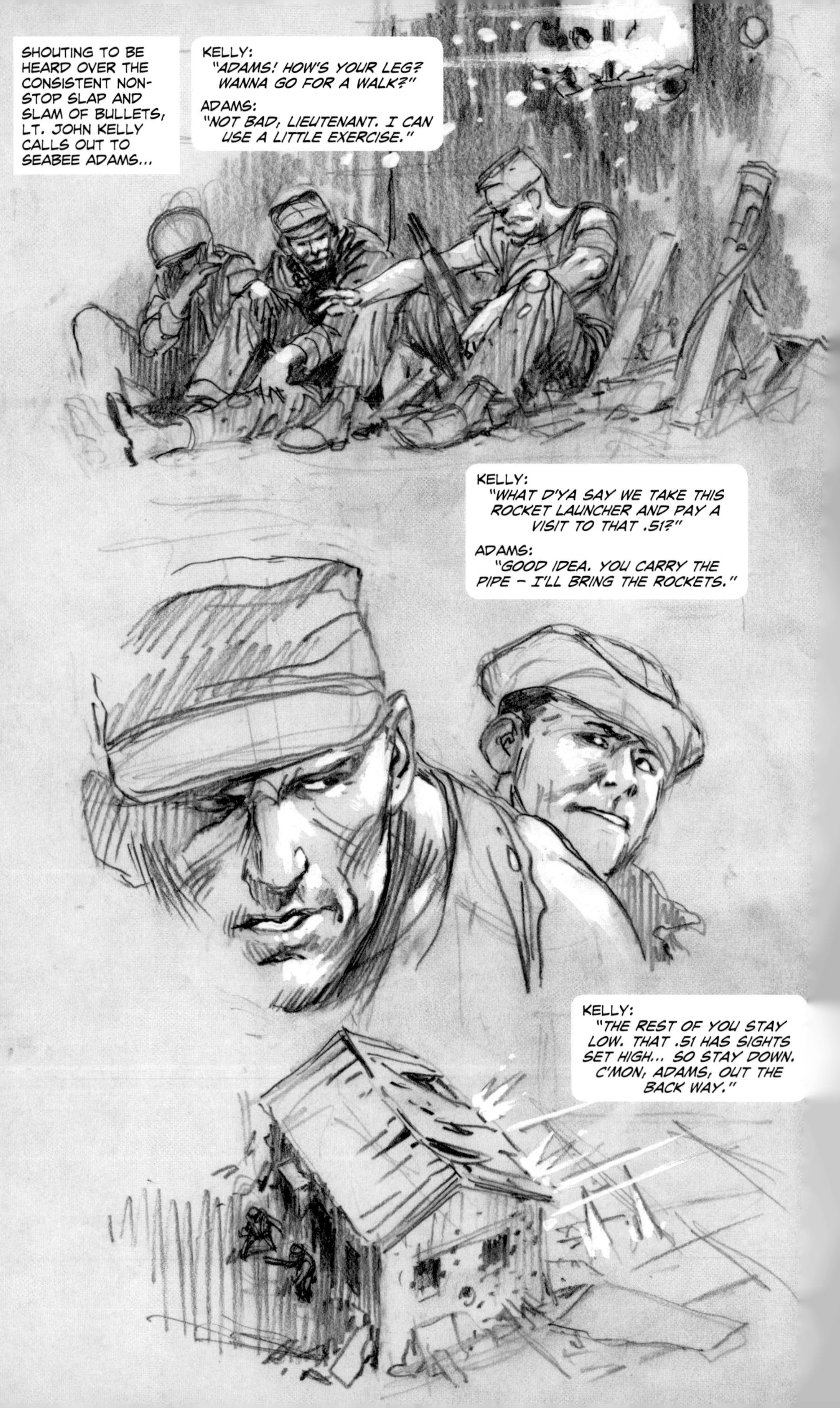
SHOUTING TO BE HEARD OVER THE CONSISTENT NON-STOP SLAP AND SLAM OF BULLETS, LT. JOHN KELLY CALLS OUT TO SEABEE ADAMS...
KELLY: "ADAMS! HOW'S YOUR LEG? WANNA GO FOR A WALK?"
ADAMS: "NOT BAD, LIEUTENANT. I CAN USE A LITTLE EXERCISE."
KELLY: "WHAT D'YA SAY WE TAKE THIS ROCKET LAUNCHER AND PAY A VISIT TO THAT .51?"
ADAMS: "GOOD IDEA. YOU CARRY THE PIPE – I'LL BRING THE ROCKETS."
KELLY: "THE REST OF YOU STAY LOW. THAT .51 HAS SIGHTS SET HIGH... SO STAY DOWN. C'MON, ADAMS, OUT THE BACK WAY."

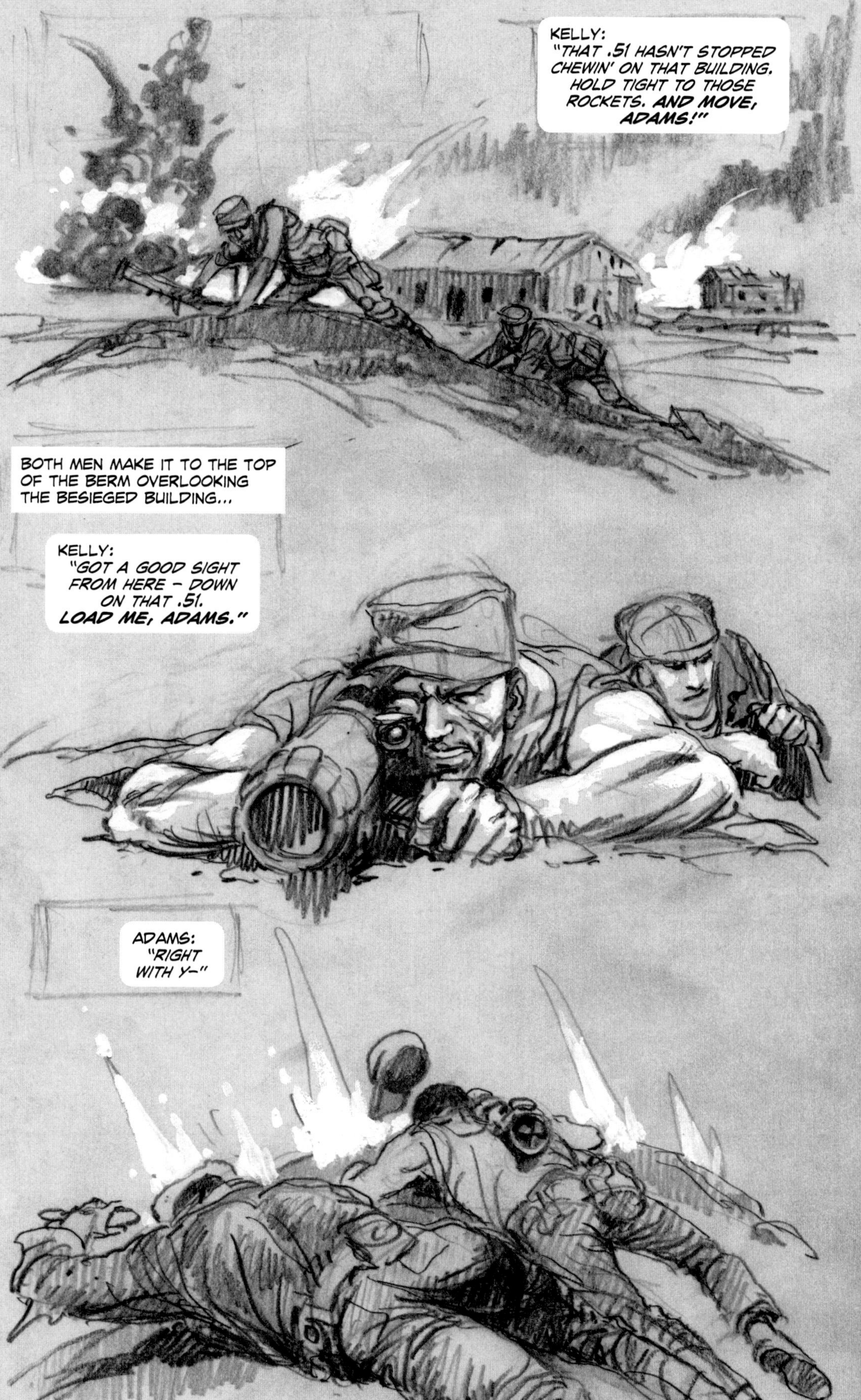
KELLY:
"THAT .51 HASN'T STOPPED CHEWIN' ON THAT BUILDING. HOLD TIGHT TO THOSE ROCKETS. AND MOVE, ADAMS!"
BOTH MEN MAKE IT TO THE TOP OF THE BERM OVERLOOKING THE BESIEGED BUILDING...
KELLY:
"GOT A GOOD SIGHT FROM HERE - DOWN ON THAT .51. LOAD ME, ADAMS."
ADAMS:
"RIGHT WITH Y-"

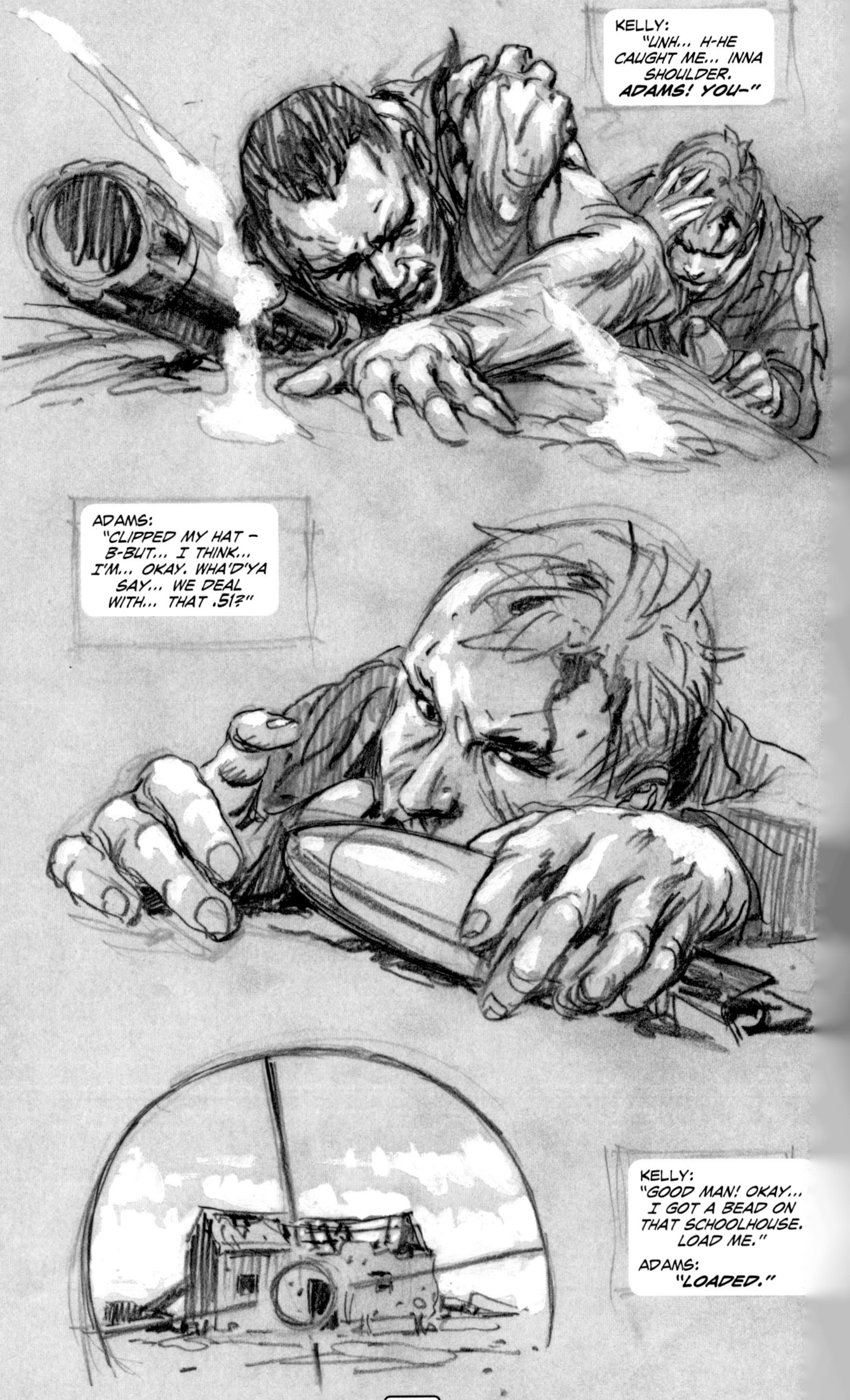
KELLY: "UNH... H-HE CAUGHT ME... INNA SHOULDER. ADAMS! YOU-"
ADAMS: "CLIPPED MY HAT – B-BUT... I THINK... I'M... OKAY. WHA'D'YA SAY... WE DEAL WITH... THAT .51?"
KELLY: "GOOD MAN! OKAY... I GOT A BEAD ON THAT SCHOOLHOUSE. LOAD ME."
ADAMS: "LOADED."

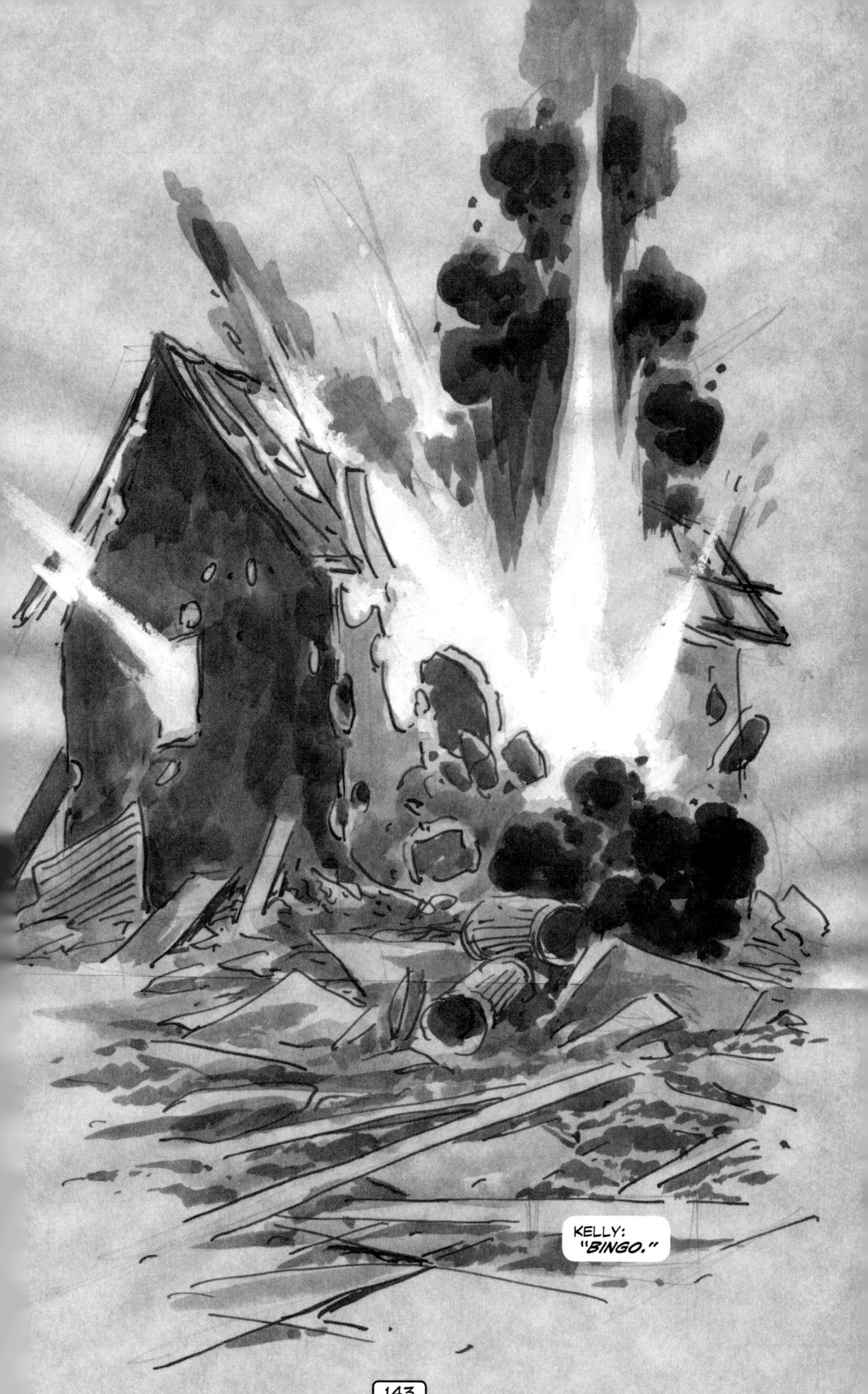
KELLY:
"BINGO."

KELLY:
"WE GOT
'EM, ADAMS!
ADAMS—"

UNABLE TO ASSIST HIS
INERT COMRADE, KELLY
CALLS FOR HELP TO
THE OTHERS IN THE
NEARBY BUILDING.

KELLY:
"HANDLE HIM
EASY — BUT —
RUN LIKE HELL."

FALLON:
"WE'LL GET HIM
TO COVER."

HALEY:
"YOU DON'T LOOK
SO GOOD EITHER,
LIEUTENANT."

AT A CLEARING NOT FAR FROM THE DEVASTATION IN DONG XOAI, A VIETNAMESE FORCE MEANT TO HELP THE TRAPPED ENCAMPMENT IS DROPPED FROM THE HOVERING HELICOPTERS...

...ONLY TO BE MET BY HIDDEN VIETCONG TROOPS AWAITING THEIR ARRIVAL. THE RESULT IS A COMPLETE MISSION FAILURE.

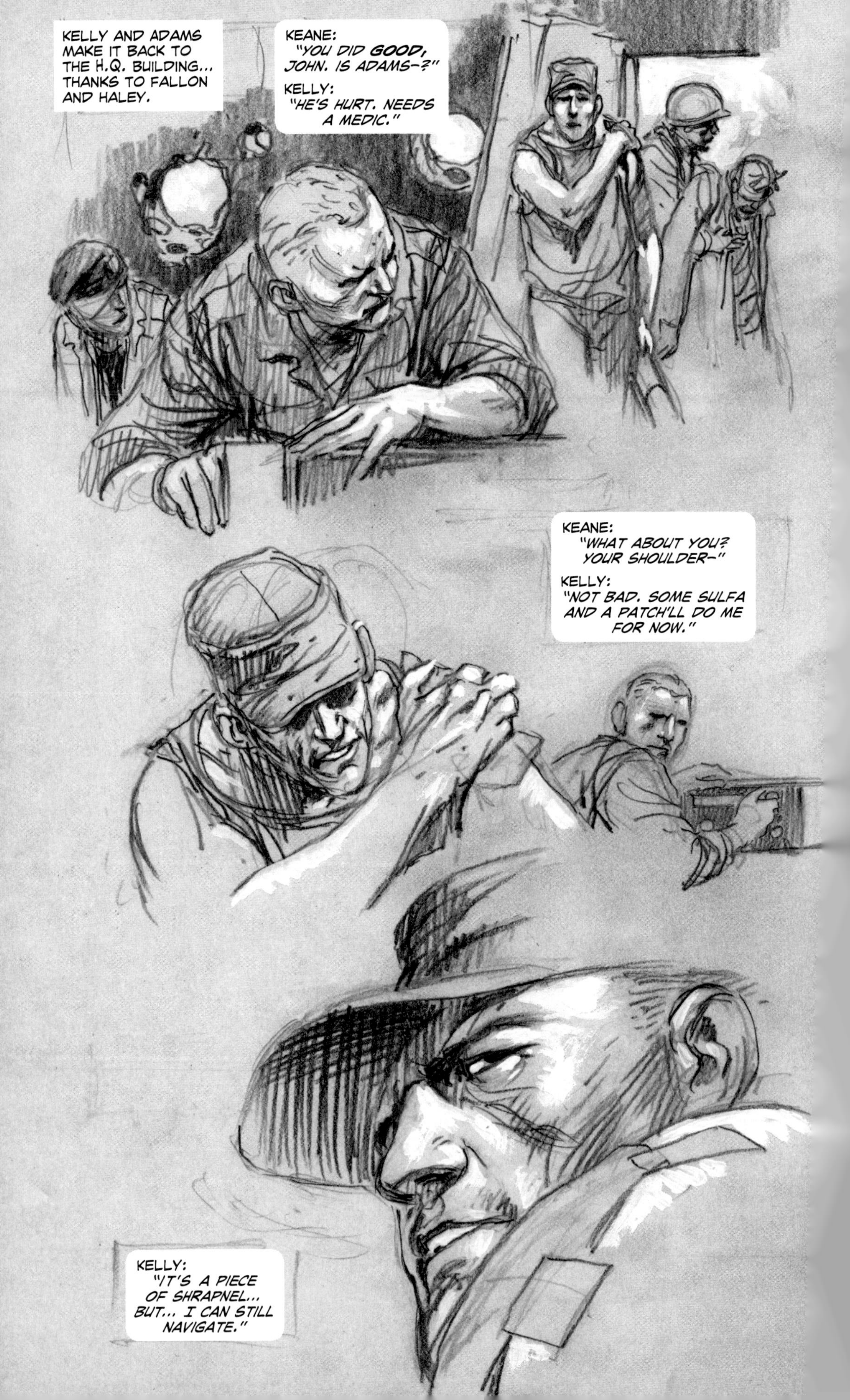
KELLY AND ADAMS MAKE IT BACK TO THE H.Q. BUILDING... THANKS TO FALLON AND HALEY.
KEANE: "YOU DID GOOD, JOHN. IS ADAMS-?"
KELLY: "HE'S HURT. NEEDS A MEDIC."
KEANE: "WHAT ABOUT YOU? YOUR SHOULDER-"
KELLY: "NOT BAD. SOME SULFA AND A PATCH'LL DO ME FOR NOW."
KELLY: "IT'S A PIECE OF SHRAPNEL... BUT... I CAN STILL NAVIGATE."

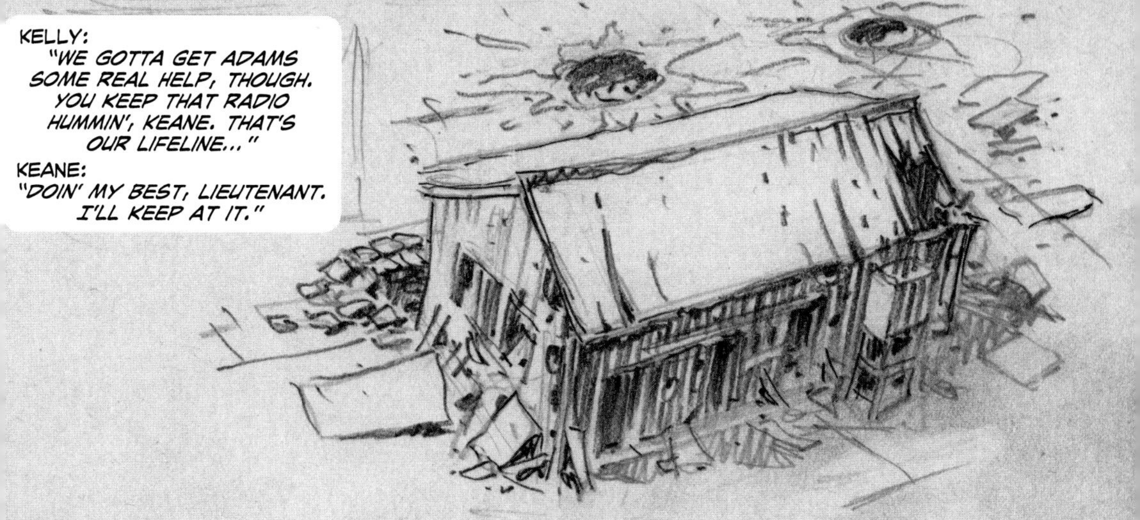
KELLY: "WE GOTTA GET ADAMS SOME REAL HELP, THOUGH. YOU KEEP THAT RADIO HUMMIN', KEANE. THAT'S OUR LIFELINE..."
KEANE: "DOIN' MY BEST, LIEUTENANT. I'LL KEEP AT IT."

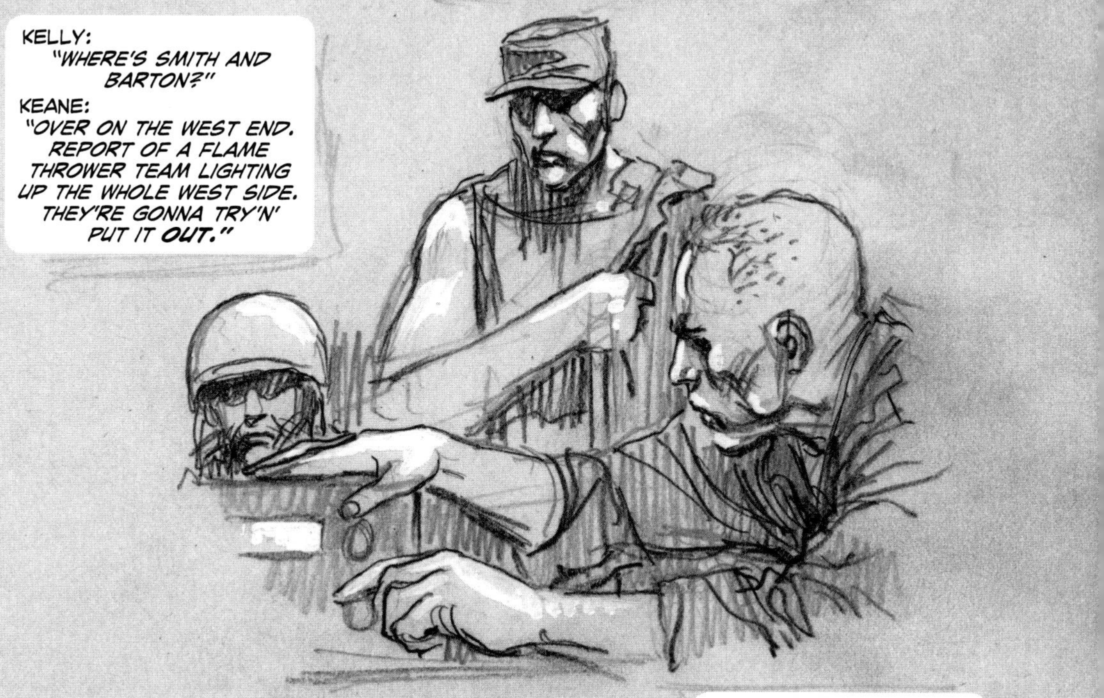
KELLY: "WHERE'S SMITH AND BARTON?"
KEANE: "OVER ON THE WEST END. REPORT OF A FLAME THROWER TEAM LIGHTING UP THE WHOLE WEST SIDE. THEY'RE GONNA TRY'N' PUT IT OUT."

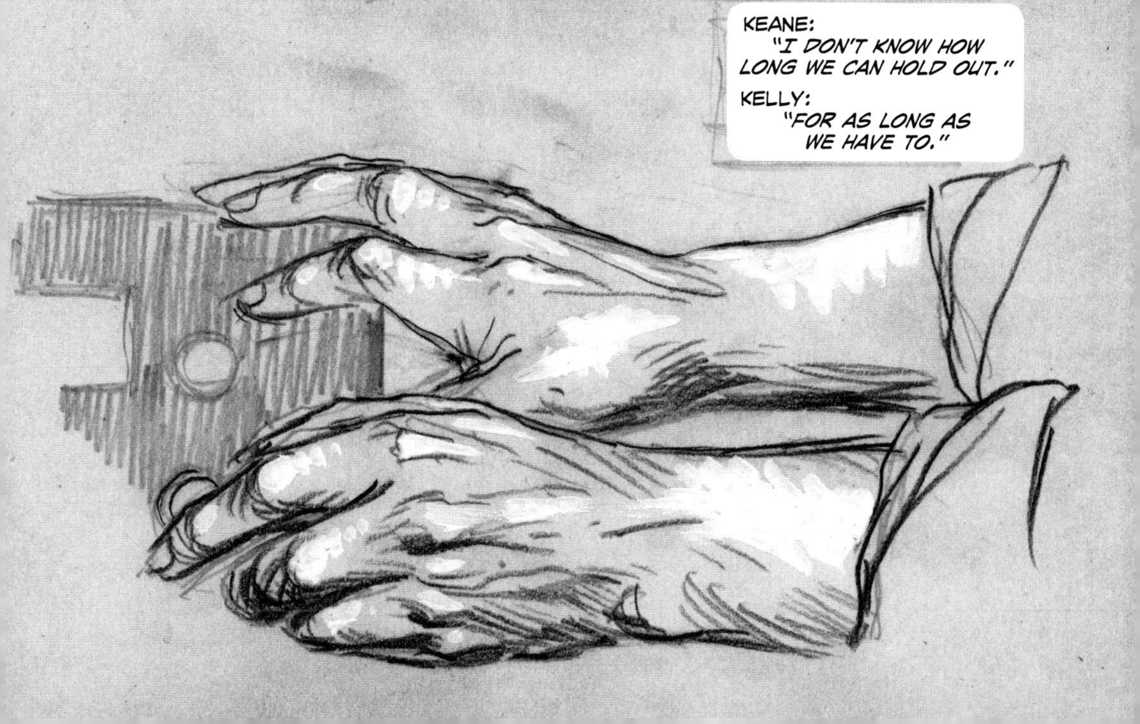
KEANE: "I DON'T KNOW HOW LONG WE CAN HOLD OUT."
KELLY: "FOR AS LONG AS WE HAVE TO."

AT THAT MOMENT — IN THE FAR WEST END OF THE COMPOUND...

BARTON:
"THAT FLAMETHROWER HAS ALREADY TAKEN DOWN SOME BUILDINGS, ED."

SMITH:
"YEAH, SAM — THEY'RE SURE BUSY LITTLE FIREBUGS."

BARTON:
"THEY GOT PLENTY OF COMPANY WITH 'EM. D'YOU THINK WE CAN TAKE 'EM?"

SMITH:
"LET'S FIND OUT IF WE CAN PUT THEIR LIGHTS OUT."

BARTON:
"CHECK AND DOUBLE CHECK, ED."

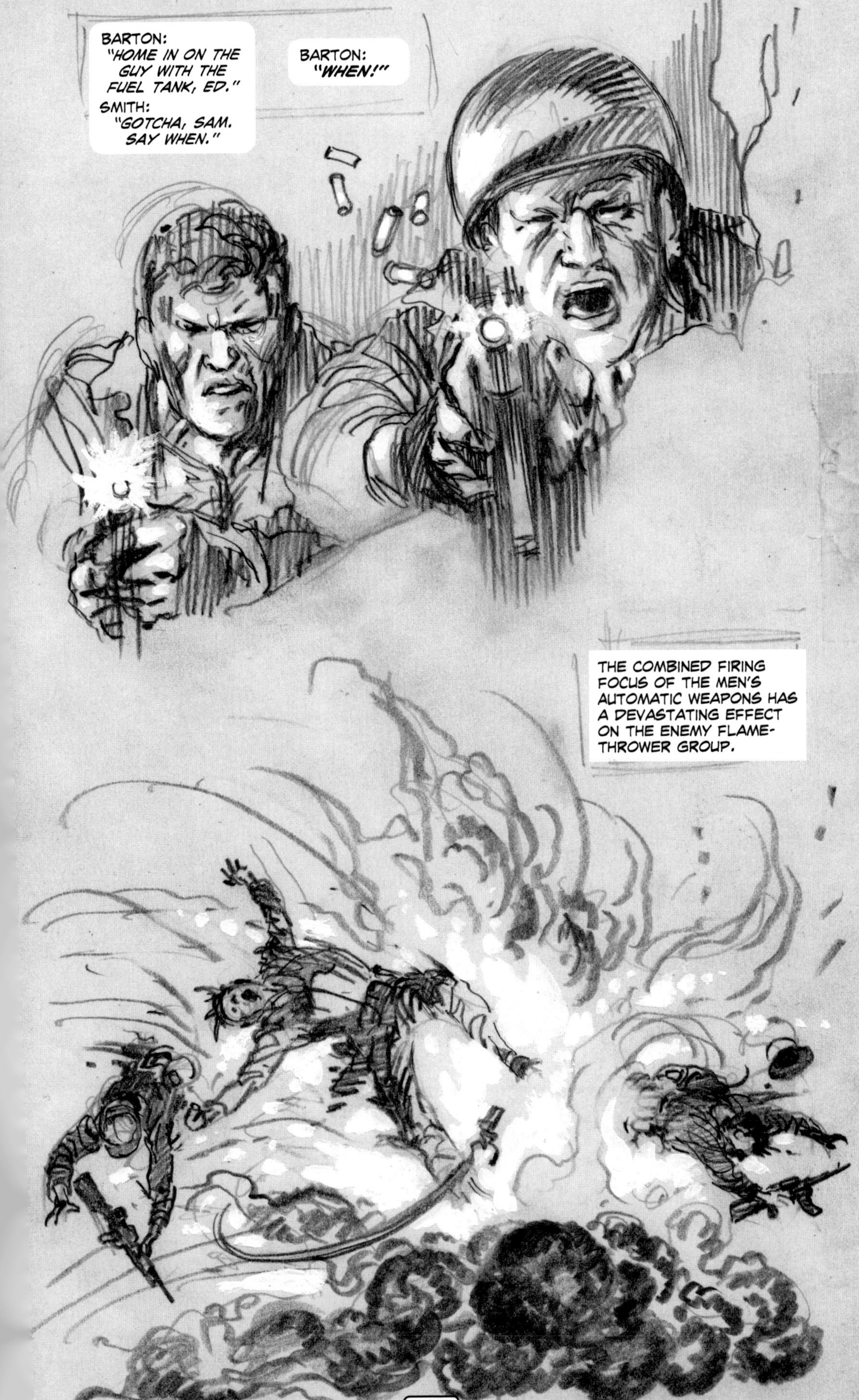
BARTON: "HOME IN ON THE GUY WITH THE FUEL TANK, ED."
SMITH: "GOTCHA, SAM. SAY WHEN."
BARTON: "WHEN!"
THE COMBINED FIRING FOCUS OF THE MEN'S AUTOMATIC WEAPONS HAS A DEVASTATING EFFECT ON THE ENEMY FLAME-THROWER GROUP.

THE UNCONTROLLED SWATH OF LIQUID FIRE IGNITES THE AREA, AND THE ACRID SMELL OF BURNING FLESH IS PERVASIVE.

BARTON:
"LUCKY SHOT — HITTING THAT TANK."

SMITH:
"YOURS OR MINE, SAM?"

BARTON:
"NOBODY'S HANDIN' OUT SHARPSHOOTER MEDALS, ED... SO LET'S GET BACK TO THE OTHERS."

SMITH:
"RIGHT."

IN ANOTHER PART OF THE
DISTRESSED ENCAMPMENT, THE
REMAINING U.S. MEMBERS...
USING THEIR RAPIDLY DEPLETING
AMMUNITION SPARINGLY AND
ACCURATELY... ARE SLOWLY
FORCED TO GATHER INTO TIGHT,
SELF-PROTECTING UNITS.

McCABE:
"WE CAN'T HOLD 'EM HERE,
SLIM — LET'S GO BACK TO
THE H.Q. BUILDING."

FALLON:
"RIGHT, MAC... IF IT'S
STILL THERE."

BACK AT THE SHELL-RIDDLED STRUCTURE, THE SERIOUSLY WOUNDED KEANE AND ADAMS ARE IN NEED OF IMMEDIATE MEDICAL ATTENTION, BUT EVAC HELICOPTERS CANNOT LAND IN THIS MELEE.

TENSION IS THICK IN THE BUILDING'S CONFINEMENT, HEIGHTENED BY THE ERUPTING SHELLS AND SCREAMING METAL SHARDS OUTSIDE. KEANE SHOUTS INTO THE RADIO, HOPING TO BE HEARD ABOVE THE NOISE.

CARTER:
"...AND WE'RE RUNNING OUT OF AMMO. ONLY A COUPLE OF CLIPS FOR RIFLES — AND ONE OR TWO GRENADES. THAT'S *IT!* EXTRACTION IS IMPERATIVE! *NOW!*"

KEANE:
"THINGS MUST BE... GETTIN' HOT. CARTER IS WEARIN' HIS... IRON POT."

KEANE:
"WE CAN'T STAY IN HERE. THEY'RE GOING TO KNOCK DOWN THE WALLS ON US."

KELLY:
"RIGHT, AL — WE GOTTA MOVE OUT... INTO THE HOWITZER PITS."

CARTER:
"LET'S GET THE WOUNDED OUT FIRST."

KELLY:
"HELP THE MEN OUT AND GRAB WHATEVER AMMO IS LEFT — AND — KEEP YOUR HEADS DOWN. LET'S GO—"

UNKNOWN TO THE SURVIVORS, HARRISON, ALLISON AND SHEER HAD DIED OF WOUNDS IN ANOTHER PART OF THE COMPOUND.

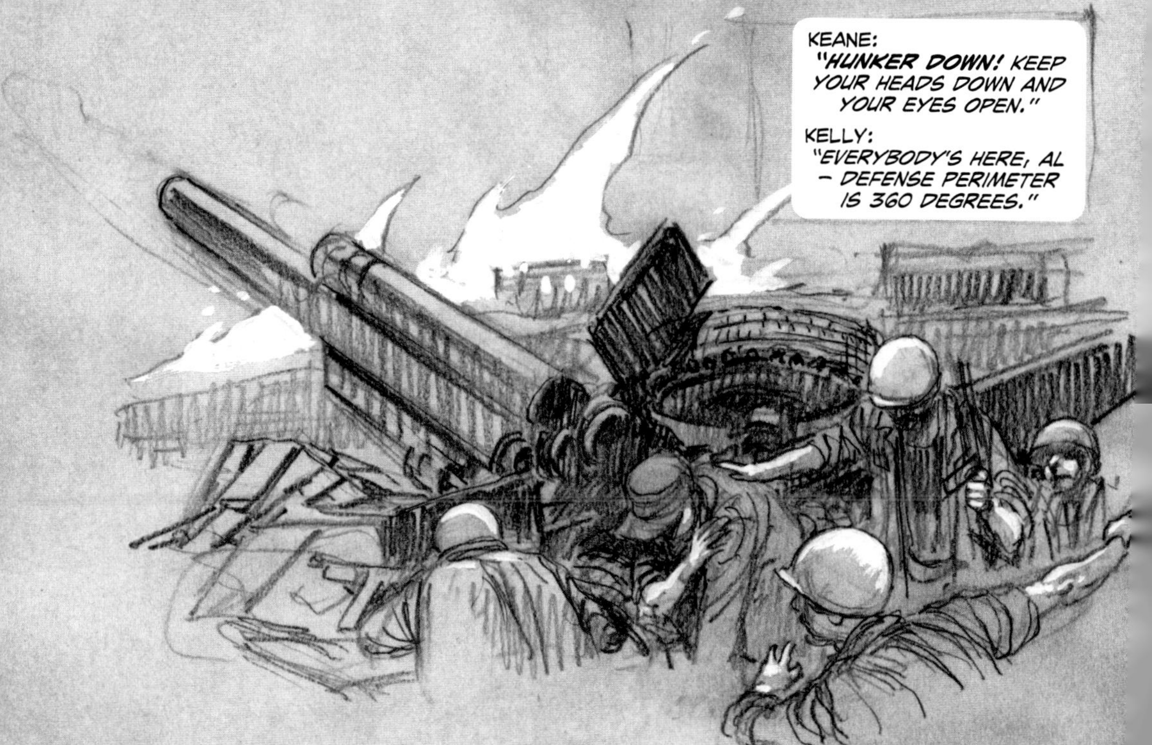
KEANE:
"HUNKER DOWN! KEEP YOUR HEADS DOWN AND YOUR EYES OPEN."
KELLY:
"EVERYBODY'S HERE, AL – DEFENSE PERIMETER IS 360 DEGREES."

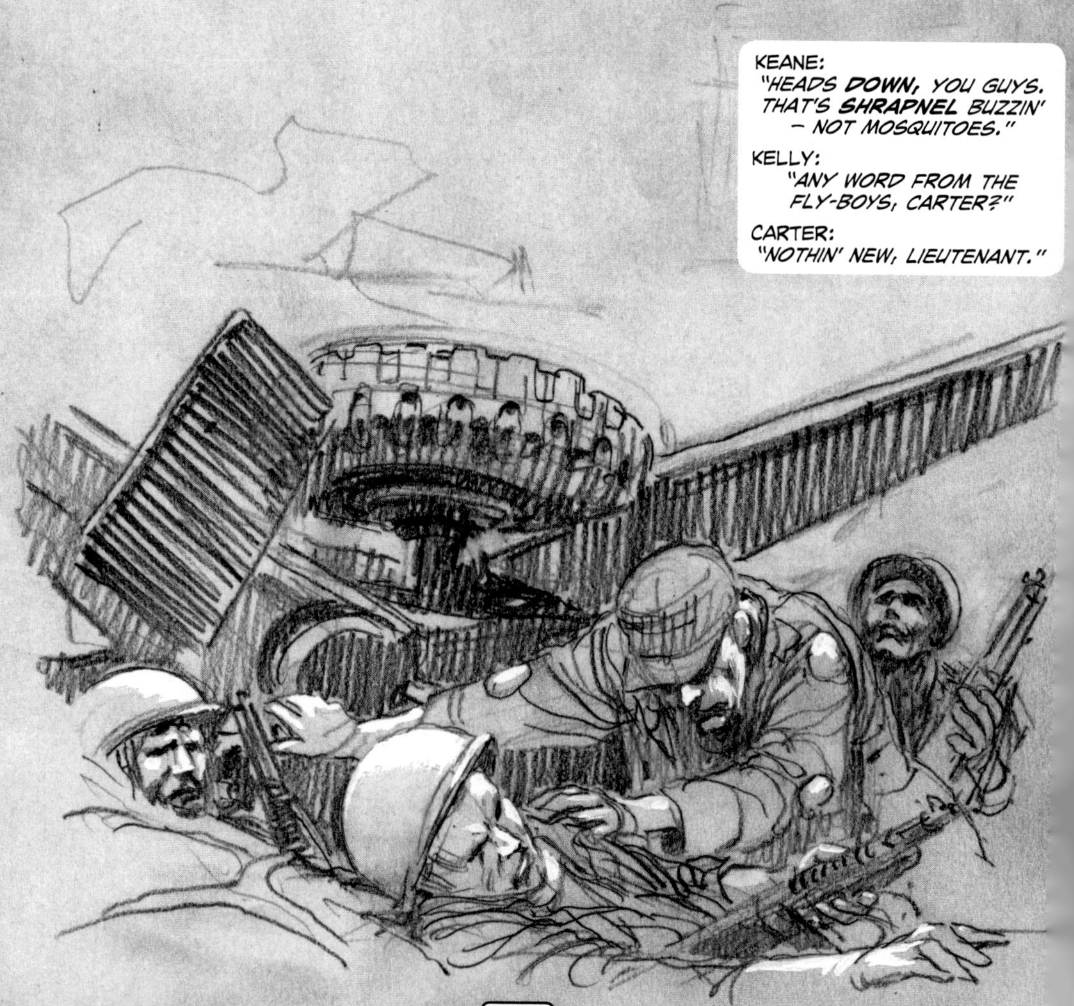
KEANE:
"HEADS DOWN, YOU GUYS. THAT'S SHRAPNEL BUZZIN' – NOT MOSQUITOES."
KELLY:
"ANY WORD FROM THE FLY-BOYS, CARTER?"
CARTER:
"NOTHIN' NEW, LIEUTENANT."

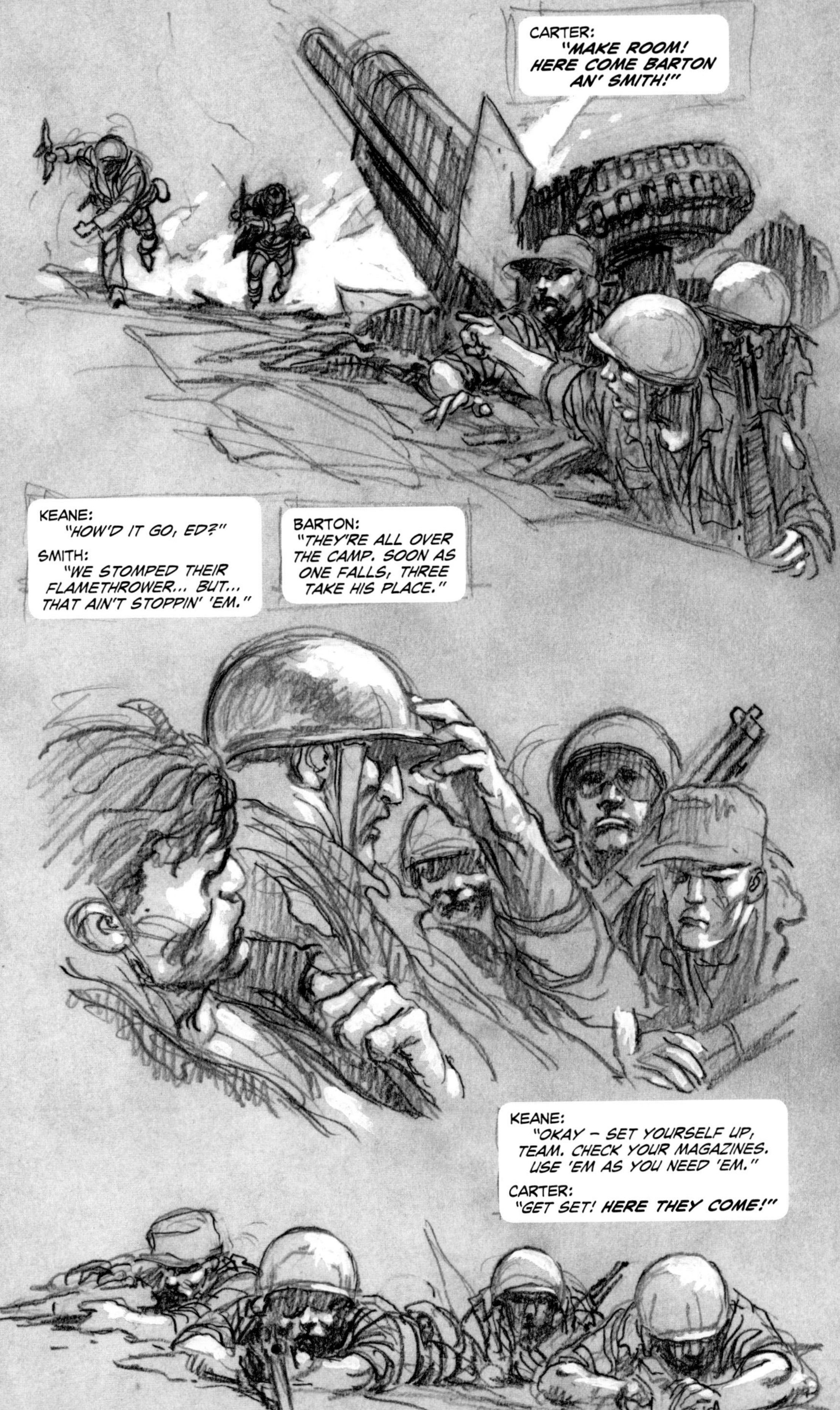
CARTER: "MAKE ROOM! HERE COME BARTON AN' SMITH!"
KEANE: "HOW'D IT GO, ED?"
SMITH: "WE STOMPED THEIR FLAMETHROWER... BUT... THAT AIN'T STOPPIN' 'EM."
BARTON: "THEY'RE ALL OVER THE CAMP. SOON AS ONE FALLS, THREE TAKE HIS PLACE."
KEANE: "OKAY – SET YOURSELF UP, TEAM. CHECK YOUR MAGAZINES. USE 'EM AS YOU NEED 'EM."
CARTER: "GET SET! HERE THEY COME!"

KEEPING COUNT OF EACH SPENT SHELL, THE DEFENDERS PICK OFF TARGETS AMONG THE CHARGING V.C. CONTINGENT.

BUT THE ATTACK DOES NOT SLACKEN — AS FALLEN V.C. ARE QUICKLY REPLACED BY FRESH AND EQUALLY COMMITTED SOLDIERS.

ONLY WHEN A REPETITIVE FLAP-FLAP-FLAP IS HEARD ABOVE THE DIN DOES THE ASSAULT STOP IN MID-CHARGE.

McCABE:
"CHOPPERS!
IT'S OUR
GUYS!"

THE FLAPPING
GROWS LOUDER AND
LOUDER — JOINED
BY THE METALLIC
CLATTER OF O.30 IN.
BROWNING MACHINE
GUN FIRE.

DESPITE THE RETURN OF SMALL ARMS FIRE, THE HELICOPTERS BEAR DOWN ON THE MASS OF ROILING V.C.

KELLY:
"OUR GUNSHIPS'LL BE COMIN' IN ON THE TAILS OF OUR CHOPPERS. GET YOUR STUFF TOGETHER — HELP THE WOUNDED! *PREPARE FOR EXTRACTION!*"

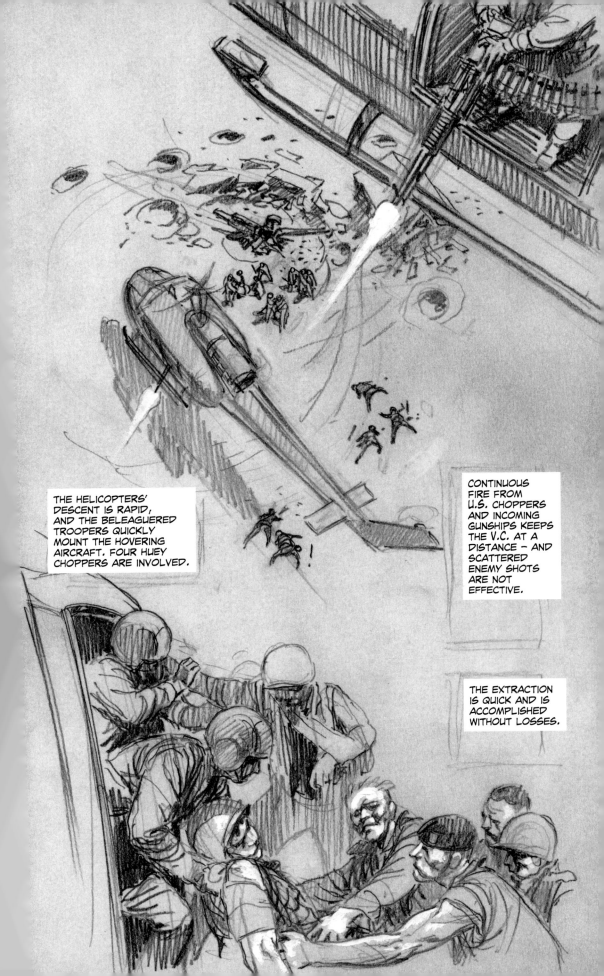

THE HELICOPTERS' DESCENT IS RAPID, AND THE BELEAGUERED TROOPERS QUICKLY MOUNT THE HOVERING AIRCRAFT. FOUR HUEY CHOPPERS ARE INVOLVED.

CONTINUOUS FIRE FROM U.S. CHOPPERS AND INCOMING GUNSHIPS KEEPS THE V.C. AT A DISTANCE — AND SCATTERED ENEMY SHOTS ARE NOT EFFECTIVE.

THE EXTRACTION IS QUICK AND IS ACCOMPLISHED WITHOUT LOSSES.

ALL SURVIVING
PERSONNEL MEMBERS
ARE AIRLIFTED OUT OF
THE BURNING CAMP...

...EXCEPT
FOR SEABEES
STEWART AND
BALASCO.

EARLIER DURING THE BATTLE –
BOTH SUSTAINING DEBILITATING
WOUNDS – ESCAPED DEATH BY
ELUDING THE INVADERS. EACH,
SEPARATELY AND UNKNOWN
TO EACH OTHER, HAD TAKEN
REFUGE IN THE VILLAGE.

STEWART, WITH A
BULLET IN HIS ARM, HAD
HIDDEN IN A SAWDUST
PILE – WHILE BALASCO,
WITH A SHRAPNEL-
DAMAGED FOOT, DUG
HIMSELF INTO A HOLE.

FROM THEIR HIDING
PLACES, THEY WATCHED
THE AIR EVACUATION –
EACH CERTAIN THAT
THEIR COMRADES WOULD
RETURN FOR THEM.

EVENTUALLY THE TWO WOUNDED SEABEES MEET ON THE EDGE OF THE BURNING – AND STILL OCCUPIED – ENCAMPMENT.

STEWART:
"WE TOOK A BEATING, BALASCO, BUT – SO DID THEY."

BALASCO:
"YEAH... BUT THAT DON'T MAKE ME FEEL ANY BETTER."

STEWART:
"HOW'S THE LEG?"

BALASCO:
"HURTS... SO I GUESS IT'S STILL THERE, MAC. LET'S FIND A PLACE FOR COVER AN' WAIT. OUR GUYS'LL BE BACK – FOR US."

STEWART:
"YEAH... AN' WE CAN LOOK ON THE BRIGHT SIDE – WE GOT ONE **GOOD** PAIR OF ARMS AND LEGS BETWEEN US."

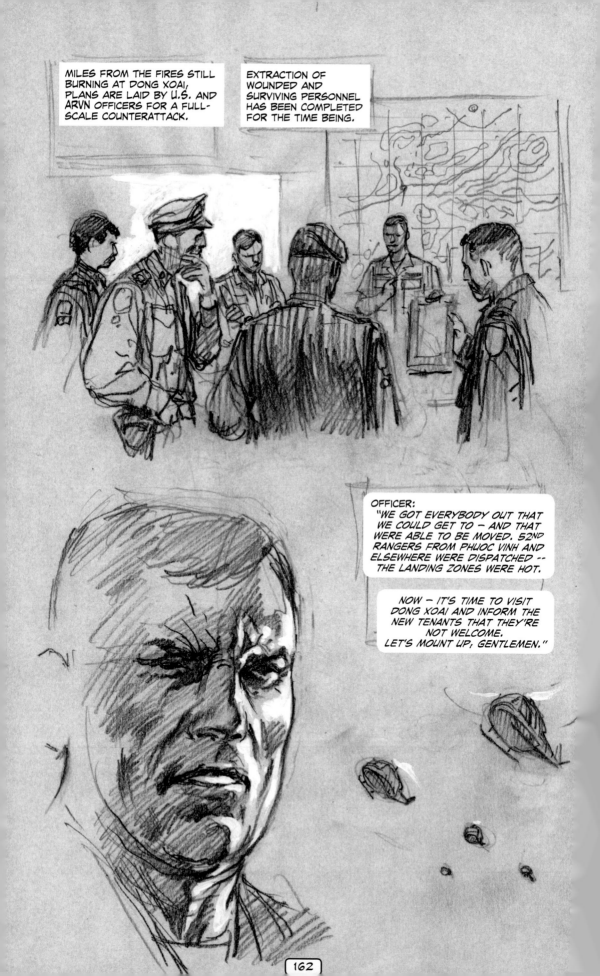

MILES FROM THE FIRES STILL BURNING AT DONG XOAI, PLANS ARE LAID BY U.S. AND ARVN OFFICERS FOR A FULL-SCALE COUNTERATTACK.

EXTRACTION OF WOUNDED AND SURVIVING PERSONNEL HAS BEEN COMPLETED FOR THE TIME BEING.

OFFICER:
"WE GOT EVERYBODY OUT THAT WE COULD GET TO — AND THAT WERE ABLE TO BE MOVED. 52ND RANGERS FROM PHUOC VINH AND ELSEWHERE WERE DISPATCHED -- THE LANDING ZONES WERE HOT.

NOW — IT'S TIME TO VISIT DONG XOAI AND INFORM THE NEW TENANTS THAT THEY'RE NOT WELCOME. LET'S MOUNT UP, GENTLEMEN."

NO TIME IS LOST BEFORE THE SKIES OVER DONG XOAI ARE FILLED WITH HUEY HELICOPTERS IN THE PROCESS OF DISCHARGING U.S. AND ARVN TROOPS TO STRIKE BACK AT THE V.C. OCCUPIERS.

STRONG RESISTANCE IS ENCOUNTERED, BUT NOTHING CAN STOP THESE SOLDIERS FROM RETRIEVING THE DEAD AND MISSING LEFT BEHIND.

11 JUNE 1965

VIETCONG RESISTANCE IS BOTH
SIGNIFICANT AND COSTLY
– BUT – ON JUNE 11, ONLY ONE
DAY AFTER THE ENCAMPMENT
FELL TO THE OVERWHELMING
ENEMY FORCES, DONG
XOAI IS REOCCUPIED BY A
COMBINATION OF VIETNAMESE
SOLDIERS AND A SMALLER
CONTINGENT OF USSF.

THEY WOULD NOT
ACCEPT DEFEAT.

DONG XOAI IS ONCE AGAIN IN CONTROL OF ARVN TROOPS AND USSF ADVISORS. THE WORK OF FULL RECOVERY IS BEGUN.

THEIR WOUNDS BANDAGED AND AWAITING THEIR RIDE OUT, BALASCO AND STEWART WATCH... AS SLOWLY AND WITH GREAT CARE... THE BODIES OF SLAIN COMRADES ARE PLACED ABOARD IDLING HELICOPTERS.

CAMBODIA

NORTH VIETNAM

SOUTH CHINA SEA

BU GIA MAP

NHA TRANG

PHNOM PENH

DONG XOAI

SOUTH VIETNAM

SAIGON

CALLED IN TIMES OF WAR, THESE MEN ARE TRIED AND TESTED IN STEEL AND FIRE. BATTLES ARE WON AND LOST... COUNTRIES ARE BROKEN AND RISE AGAIN... BUT THE BRAVERY OF SOLDIERS IN WAR NEVER FLAGS OR FALTERS.

EACH MAN'S RESPONSIBILITY IS FOR THE MAN WHO STANDS BESIDE HIM. IT'S A STRONGER BOND THAN ANY POLITICAL PHILOSOPHY. IT IS A PLEDGE TO HIS FELLOW SOLDIER... FUSED IN BLOOD.

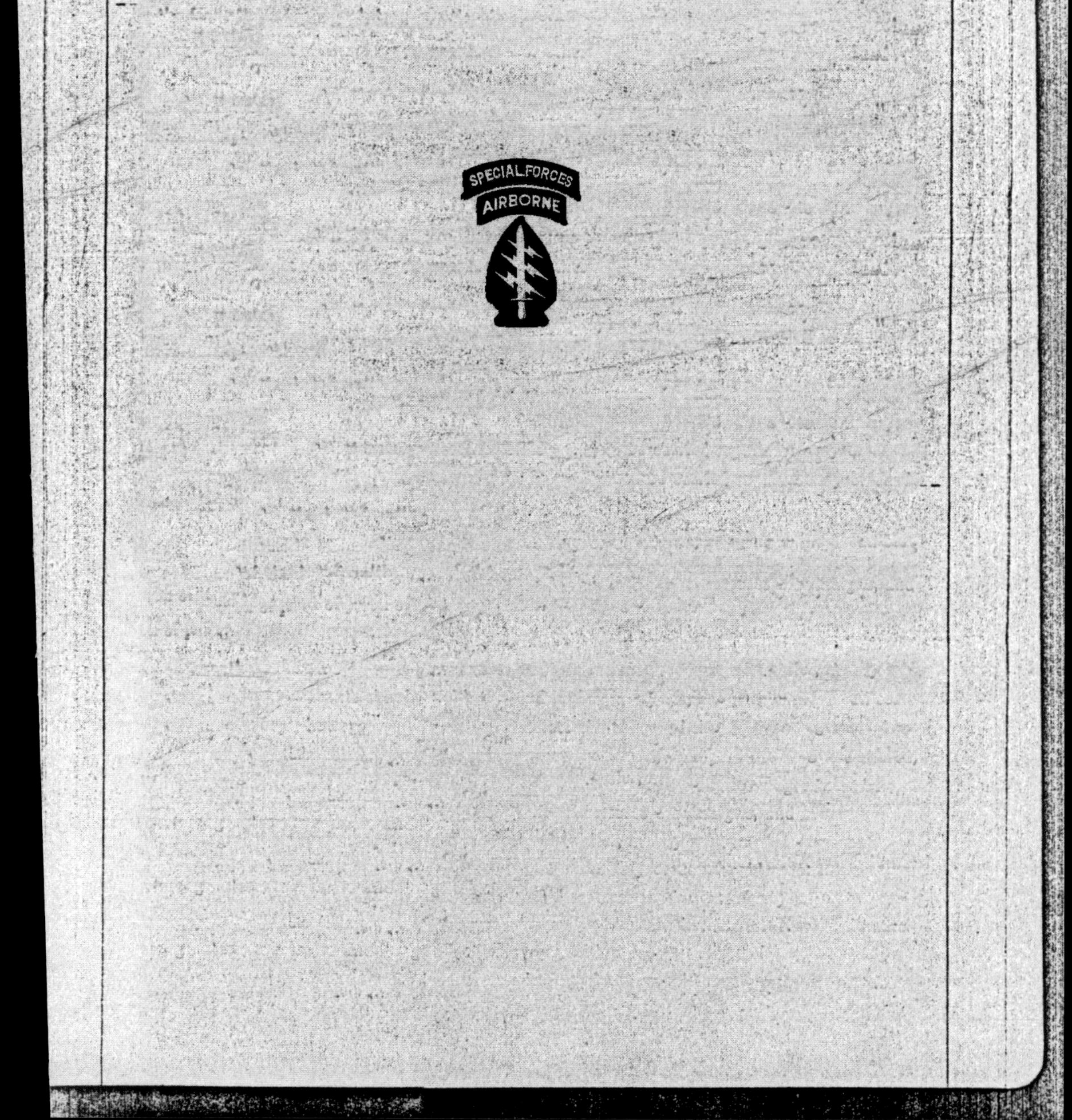
SPECIAL FORCES
AIRBORNE

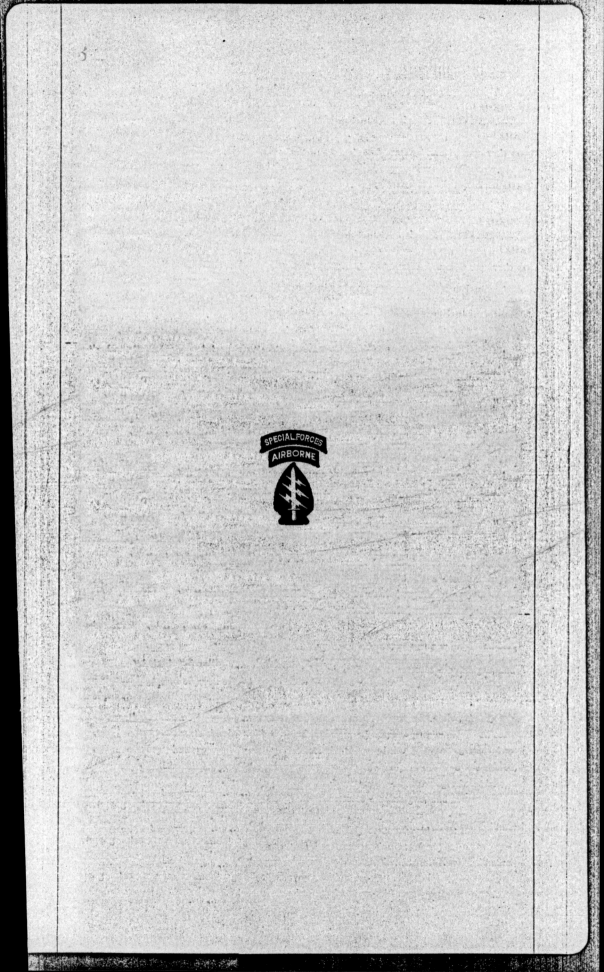

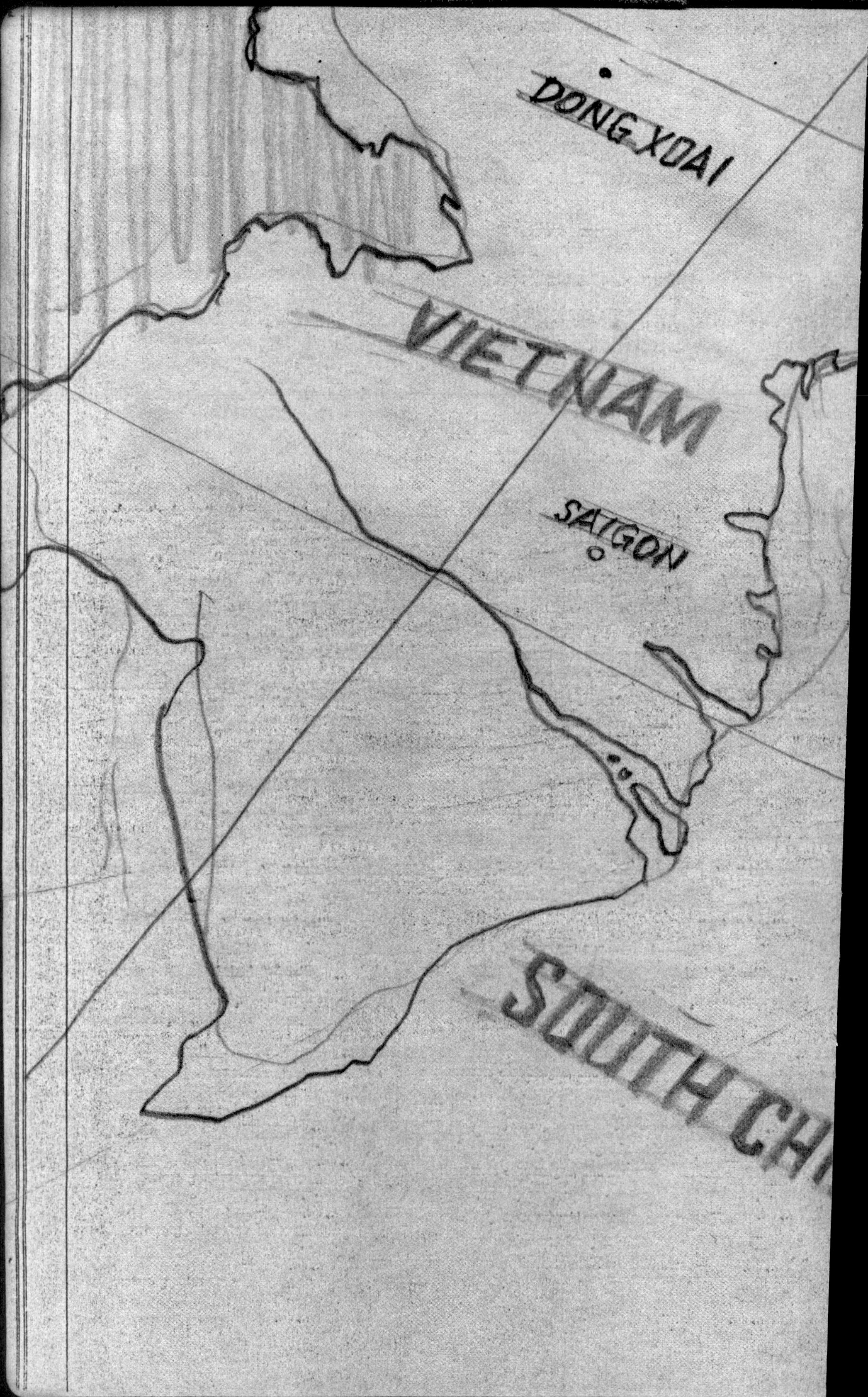
DONG XOAI
VIETNAM
SAIGON
SOUTH CH

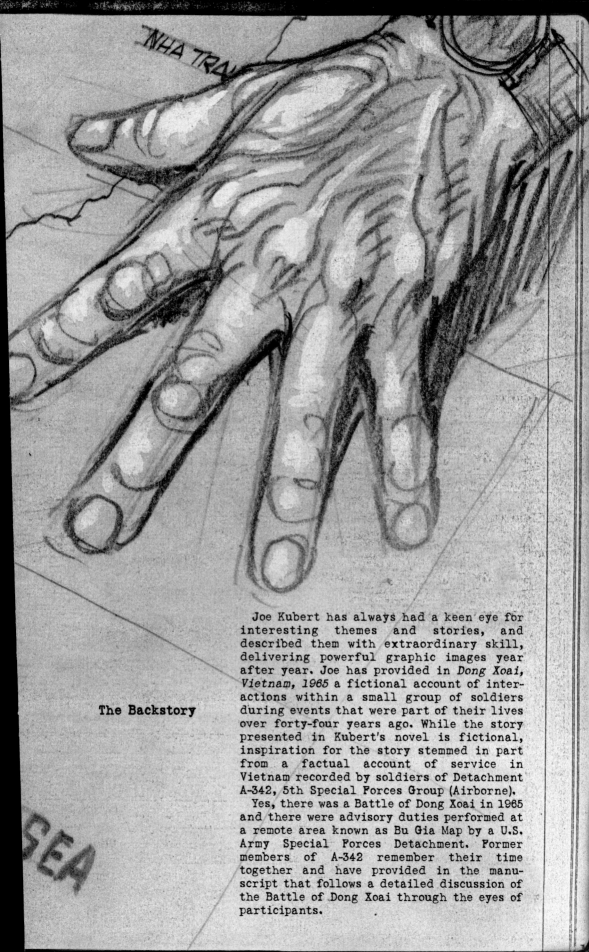

The Backstory

Joe Kubert has always had a keen eye for interesting themes and stories, and described them with extraordinary skill, delivering powerful graphic images year after year. Joe has provided in *Dong Xoai, Vietnam, 1965* a fictional account of interactions within a small group of soldiers during events that were part of their lives over forty-four years ago. While the story presented in Kubert's novel is fictional, inspiration for the story stemmed in part from a factual account of service in Vietnam recorded by soldiers of Detachment A-342, 5th Special Forces Group (Airborne).

Yes, there was a Battle of Dong Xoai in 1965 and there were advisory duties performed at a remote area known as Bu Gia Map by a U.S. Army Special Forces Detachment. Former members of A-342 remember their time together and have provided in the manuscript that follows a detailed discussion of the Battle of Dong Xoai through the eyes of participants.

As the early portion of the Kubert story suggests, there was a small U.S. detachment or team advising a Vietnamese Special Forces element at Bu Gia Map, a remote camp near the Cambodia border north of Saigon. The team's missions, not unlike tasks assigned other such units located throughout the Republic of Vietnam, included training duties, assistance to various Montagnard tribes, and combat operations with members of the CIDG along border infiltration routes. The team at Bu Gia Map was trained in the fields of intelligence, operations, communications, weapons, medical, and combat engineering, and all members were combat infantrymen or medics who accompanied indigenous forces on their missions.

In late May 1965, the team moved to Dong Xoai, a village about fifty miles north of Saigon, to establish a new Civilian Irregular Defense Group (CIDG) camp and serve as advisors to the local district officials, a Vietnamese Special Forces unit, and CIDG contingent. In addition to varied training and civic action tasks, the Team was given the mission of conducting operations against the infamous Viet Cong havens known as War Zones C and D. The Viet Cong attacked the District Headquarters and newly arrived CIDG forces in early June 1965. The Battle of Dong Xoai was horrific by any measure and one the major battles in Vietnam up to that point — indeed, of the entire war. The account of the Battle of Dong Xoai that follows presents a comprehensive account of the ground action in which Detachment A-342 and its small complement of Navy Seabees

fought with Vietnamese forces against a multi-regimental enemy attack.

Although the factual account of the Special Forces team differs somewhat from the foregoing novel, we are pleased that our story of service, mutual respect, and friendship warranted the inspiration that gave rise to *Dong Xoai, Vietnam, 1965*. Together, the fictional and factual segments provide an excellent portrait of a small unit of American soldiers performing military advisory duties in a far-off land and fighting together in one of the major battles of the Vietnam Conflict. The members of Detachment A-342 have presented an overview of events as they happened, and Joe Kubert has deftly animated this slice of history in his own graphic-novel style. We are ever mindful of the enormous contribu-

tions made by other Special Forces units in Vietnam, and the skill, courage, and accomplishments of such teams deployed in harm's way since the end of the conflict in Southeast Asia.

Today surviving team members remain as close as ever, and that fact is an important part of the story. No one member holds all the pieces of the team's history, but discussions over the years have led to a coherent picture of the team and its legacies. The manuscript that follows records an important segment of Special Forces history and the relationships among a few men who mattered then — and matter now.

Special Forces Detachment A-342
5th Special Forces Group

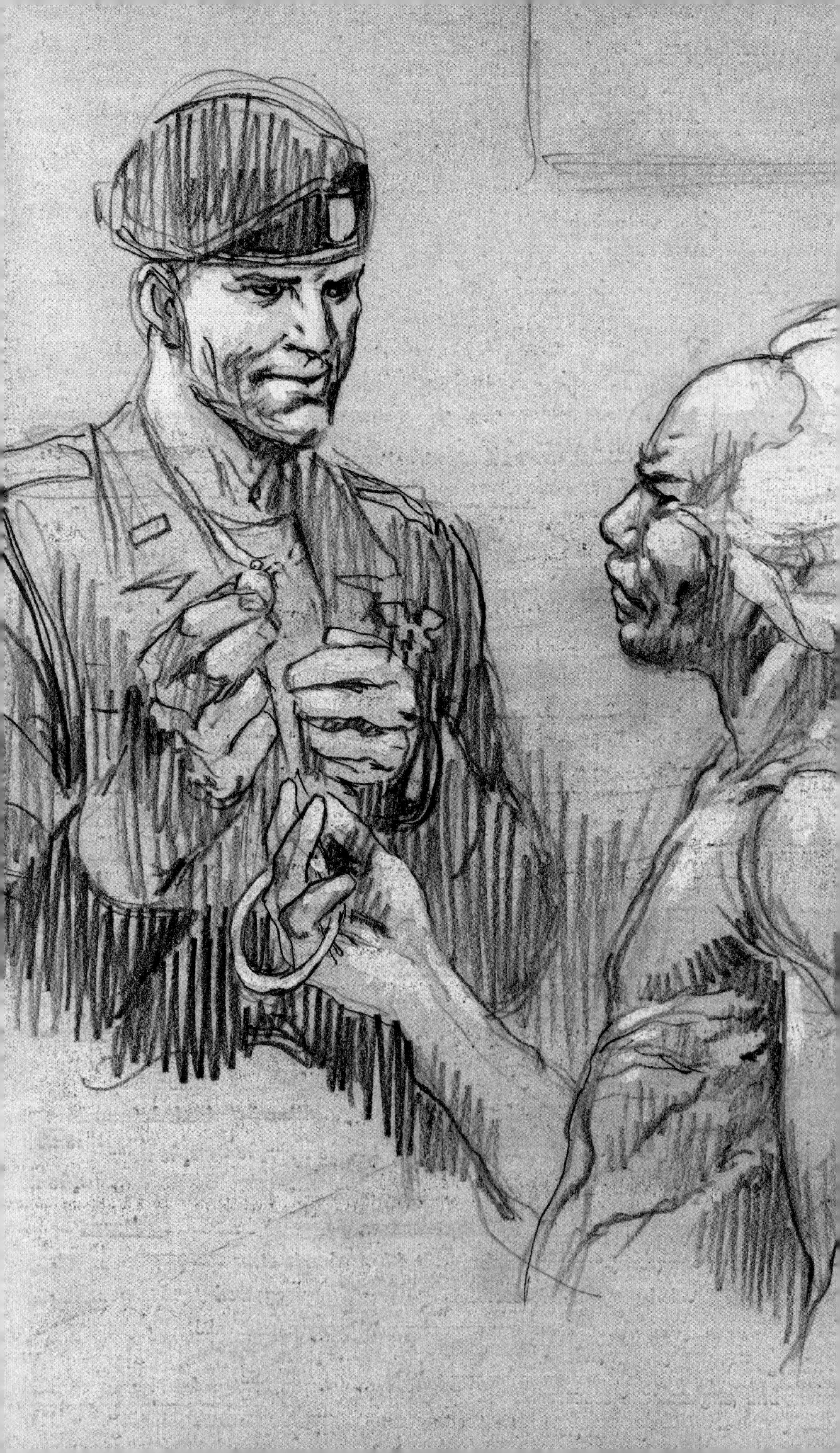

DETACHMENT A-342
5TH SPECIAL FORCES GROUP
(AIRBORNE)
1964-1965
OUR SERVICE TOGETHER

PREPARED BY MEMBERS OF DETACHMENT A-342 2009

INTRODUCTION

Members of Detachment A-342, 5th Special Forces Group (Airborne), did not fight a long war together in 1965, as did the Band of Brothers of the 101st Airborne in the stressful days of World War II. In fact, the team, which was originally designated A-414 at Ft. Bragg, North Carolina, served together only about nine months, five Stateside and four in Vietnam.

The team was a diverse one, pulled together quickly to support the growth of Special Forces in the early stages of US involvement in the Vietnam War. Team members were from all over the country, and ranged in rank from private first class to captain. The youngest member was twenty-one, the oldest thirty-seven. Experience levels varied greatly, as the ages and ranks would suggest. Five members of the deploying team had previous Vietnam combat experience.

After deploying to Vietnam in late February 1965 the team was designated A-313 and operated with Civilian Irregular Defense Forces from a remote camp near the Cambodian border. As ground combat goes, this initial phase was fairly benign, but the experience allowed the team members to bond and hone their operational skills.

In late May 1965, the team was deployed into a crucial location between the infamous War Zones C and D north of Saigon and designated A-342. The team and its supporting Seabee detachment were involved in the horrific fight to defend Dong Xoai village, seat of the district government in that area. The Battle of Dong Xoai, one of the most intense of the Vietnam War, would leave no doubt about the mettle of the US defenders there and the cohesiveness, endurance, and professionalism of the team. Detachment A-342 and its supporting Seabee were awarded two Medals of Honor, three Distinguished Service Crosses, six Silver Star Medals, and a number of Bronze Stars. All the Americans who defended Dong Xoai on the ground received the Purple Heart for wounds. Three members of the team and two Seabees died in the battle.

After the Battle of Dong Xoai, team members were dispersed to a variety of other combat and staff duties to complete their overseas tours. Later most members of the team continued their military careers, reaching the highest noncommissioned officer grades, and in three cases, moving from the enlisted ranks to serve as officers; two left the service to pursue civilian endeavors.

The passage of time and careers were impediments to continuing close relationships. Yet, after over forty years surviving team members are perhaps closer than ever. There appear to be several reasons for the endurance of the team's friendship and respect by members for one another. One reason has been simply that team members have retired, giving them more time to contemplate times past, visit with one another, and correspond. Another self-evident reason is that e-mail has made the exchange of messages easy and fun. Yet another stimulus has been the queries of children of team members who died at Dong Xoai. The sharing of information with children people too young to have known their fathers required thoughtful reflections on team activities in 1965 and interaction among the team members themselves. Finally, in 2000 and 2002 team members met at Special Forces conventions, and over the course of those several days and correspondence that followed, they were able to discuss activities from the fall of 1964 to the summer of 1965 in great detail. No one member held all the pieces of the team's history, but detailed discussions have led to a coherent picture of the team and its legacies. The "quiet team" is now beginning to share its story.

The narrative and photographs that follow simply record a small slice of Special Forces history and relationships among a few men and their families that mattered then -and matter now.

PRE-DEPLOYMENT

Gathering of the Team

Detachment A-414, 5th Special Forces Group (Airborne), later designated A-313 and A-342, was among many A-detachments organized at Ft. Bragg, North Carolina, in 1964 to fill a pressing need in Vietnam. In many cases training was shortened to meet deployment demands, and the levels of experience varied among teams and within them. Within A-414, for example, ages ranged from twenty-one to thirty-seven and ranks from private first class to captain. Five members of the team had previous Special Forces experience in Vietnam and seven did not. From the time of deployment onward the team benefited from strong cohesion and experienced NCO leadership. The photo below pictures A-414 as it was constituted in late fall 1964.

During the late fall of 1964 formal skill training was completed and time was devoted to language and area studies, weapons training, survival activities, and parachute jumps for proficiency.

Detachment A-414, Later Designated A-313 and A-342 Front Row (Left to Right) CPT Bill Stokes, SSG Don Dedman, MSGT Rick Enriquez, SP4 Dan McLaughlin, SGT Chuck Jenkins, 2D LT Charlie Williams Second Row (Left to Right) PFC Mike Hand, SGT Lamar Sale, SFC George Zacher, SSG Harold Crowe, SSG Tony Sova, SSG Jim Taylor (Team Photo)

Jump Time for Enriquez, Jenkins, Sale, and Crowe (Team Photo)

Final Preparations

During the final days before deployment the team completed its immunizations, packing, and individual preparations.

Carol and Rick Enriquez treated the team and its families to a grand Tacada (taco feast) just prior to departure. The event featured a variety of superb Mexican food and provided the perfect opportunity for the families to get to know each other better before the deployment. Thirty-eight years later members of team would gather again at the Enriquez home for great food and friendship.

DEPLOYMENT
Checking In

The physical deployment was uneventful, but long and tiring. The team departed Pope AFB, North Carolina, on an older C-118 aircraft – propeller-driven and not comfortable by any stretch of one's imagination. The scheduled flight by Boeing 707 had been scrubbed, reportedly so the aircraft could be used in evacuating dependents from Vietnam. The trip was about a four-day affair. The team arrived in Saigon on 24 February 1965, and after spending several hours there, flew on to Nha Trang, where it received a three-day orientation at 5th Special Forces Group Headquarters. The in-processing at 5th Group Headquarters was routine, but by the end of the first day the team was ready to get out of the replacement-depot environment and go to work. There was time for a final beer in beautiful Nha Trang before departure and a parachute jump with unforgettable views of what later would be called Cam Ranh Bay. While in Nha Trang the team was quite surprised when the Intelligence NCO was pulled off the team without warning or explanation for another task, leaving the group without a key member the day before deployment into Bu Gia Map. The team was to assume the designation of A-313 upon arrival at its operational camp.

The Final Leg –
Destination Bu Gia Map

The team was flown to Bu Gia Map on 28 February 1965 by Australian C-7 Caribou. There were spectacular views of vast jungle areas as the team flew into the interior of Vietnam. Bu Gia Map was located roughly one hundred miles north of Saigon in the III Corps Tactical Zone. Administratively, Bu Gia Map was in Bu Dop District of Phuoc Long Province.

Immediately upon arrival at Bu Gia Map some team members and their LLDB counterparts took advantage of a dozen or so parachutes on board the Caribou and made a quick jump on the airstrip. On or about 2 March 1965 Detachment A-313 assumed responsibility for Bu Gia Map camp from Detachment A-223, an Okinawa-based team.

Jump Time for Enriquez, Jenkins, Sale, and Crowe (Team Photo)

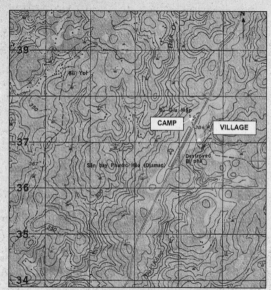

Bu Gia Map Area (Map, Army Map Service, 1:50,000, 1963)

BU GIA MAP
Missions, Area, and Forces

The basic missions of Detachment A-313 at Bu Gia Map were to train Civilian Irregular Defense Group (CIDG) forces, advise a Vietnamese Special Forces unit (Luc Luong Doc Biet or LLDB), and interdict Viet Cong (VC) infiltration routes.

The camp, the most remote in the III Corps Tactical Zone, was well established physically. Areas of interest included the local Bu Gia Map area, the camp itself, the contiguous village, and, of course, the tactical area of operations. The forces available included CIDG companies, US and Vietnamese advisers, and a small local force.

Bu Gia Map camp was on a ridgeline that had been shorn of vegetation and leveled for construction of the compound and airstrip. The village of Bu Gia Map was just below the camp to the east. Except for areas under cultivation by the Montagnards, the camp and village were surrounded by dense jungle.

The camp living conditions were quite good — folding cots, generator-driven electricity, shower (sometimes warm), septic system with flush toilets, butane stove, water treatment capability, and three kerosene refrigerators, at least one of which always seemed to be on the blink. The medics, Taylor and Sale, supervised the kitchen effort and work of the indigenous cooks. Several wives of Strike Force members were paid to take care of laundry and cleaning of the teamhouse and latrine.

The compound held a variety of buildings and fortifications. Structures included billets for the CIDG troops, US Special Forces (USSF) team, and LLDB; tactical operations center; supply building; Strike Force kitchen; and barber shop. The fortifications included bunkers, mortar pits, protective wire, and a perimeter trench, but no interconnecting communication trenches. Most buildings had partial protection with sandbag blast walls. Sova and McLaughlin undertook a review of the protective wire, minefields, trip flares, and booby traps that served as part of the camp defense. Some mines and booby traps were old, fragile, and somewhat primitive, requiring removal by physical probing and replacement with newer ordnance. Improvements were made to the protective wire, and gasoline was mixed with a thickener to create homemade napalm, which was integrated into the defensive system.

Hello, Bu Gia Map (Team Photo)

Aerial View of Bu Gia Map Camp (Team Photo)

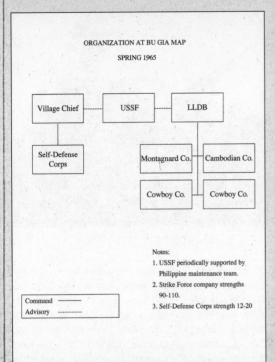

ORGANIZATION AT BU GIA MAP

SPRING 1965

Notes:
1. USSF periodically supported by
   Philippine maintenance team.
2. Strike Force company strengths
   90-110.
3. Self-Defense Corps strength 12-20

Command ————
Advisory ------------

Bu Gia Map Organization

Montagnard Work Detail (Team Photo)

There were four Strike Force companies at Bu Gia Map — one Cambodian, one Montagnard, and two Saigon "Cowboy." The term "Saigon Cowboy" was used to describe young urban troublemakers. Reportedly, these men were rounded up and advised that they could perform service in remote areas as CIDG troops for several years, then be relieved of further military service — or they would be enlisted into the Army of Vietnam (ARVN) with an indefinite wartime obligation. Initially there was also a Nung platoon at Bu Gia Map. The Nungs, Vietnamese of a Chinese extraction and somewhat larger in stature than other CIDG forces, had an excellent reputation as fighters. Regrettably, the Nung platoon was withdrawn from the camp after several days.

The village contained about one thousand Stieng Montagnards and several hundred dependents of CIDG soldiers. The local economy was essentially a barter one, and the slash and burn technique was largely used for agricultural development. The closest store was about forty kilometers to the southwest. About every ten days a small trading truck came to the village after paying VC taxes. The Village Chief had available a very small self-defense force of minimal capability, perhaps twelve to twenty men.

The villagers, who were animists, slept in longhouses. They spent their days in the fields, and nights were often filled with chanting to ward off evil spirits. (*Note: The Stiengs of Bu Gia Map were resettled in mid-1965 to an area near Song Be because of the difficulty in protecting the remote village.*)

Intelligence

There was very little information available on VC activity or the area of operations. Johnson's first task after joining the team as Intelligence NCO was to develop a relationship with his Vietnamese counterpart, Nghi, and establish a network for gathering information. Productive intelligence relationships did not develop automatically, but required establishment of personal rapport and nurturing of trust. Even with all sources considered there was sparse threat data.

Operations

Operations consisted primarily of camp defense and patrolling. The improvement of camp defenses was a continuing task — improvement of bunkers and trench walls, repair and upgrade of defensive wire, placement of trip flares, review of fields of fire, and practice alerts. There were several 60 mm mortar and machine gun positions manned by Strikers, and alerts seemed adequate. The USSF teamhouse, to include the 81 mm mortar pit and communications bunker; LLDB teamhouse and operations center; and main tactical operations center were fairly defensible, but the absence of communication trenches would have made it difficult to reach the perimeter without exposure to fire.

Downtown Bu Gia Map (Team Photo)

Protective Wire, Striker Billet, and Gun Position (Team Photo)

Harold Crowe Ready to Go (Team Photo)

One observation post/listening post (OP/LP) was manned by CIDG personnel on high ground about seven hundred fifty meters west of the camp. The camp had not come under attack previously, so the defenses were largely untested.

During the period 1 March – 25 May 1965, Bu Gia Map elements generated a significant number of patrol days, exclusive of local security missions. Some examples of patrol activity include:

Montagnard Patrol: The Montagnard company was commanded by an intelligent young man referred to as Bu. At the time of the camp turnover Bu was on patrol southeast of camp, without advisors. The patrol had contact and captured a rifle and other items.

Stokes – Taylor: During the period 7-12 March 1965, Taylor and Stokes accompanied the initial patrol that left Bu Gia Map after A-313 became operational. LT Luc, the LLDB commander, led the forty-man CIDG patrol. This patrol was helpful in acquainting USSF personnel with the area of operations. The patrol mission was to perform reconnaissance west of Bu Gia Map and link up with a

Rick Enriquez Checking CIDG Position (Team Photo)

CIDG force from Bu Dop on the Dak Huit River about ten miles from camp. The main objective was to flush out any VC from one side of river boundary into the force on the other side. The beginning leg of the patrol was without incident; the patrol found recent campsites, but no VC. The patrol took up a position on the east side of the river at the proposed link-up point, but was unable to reach the Bu Dop force by radio.

Throughout the next morning the patrol heard heavy woodcutting on the opposite side of the river, and the USSF advisers suggested to the Lieutenant that he send people across the stream to investigate. The Lieutenant argued that the woodcutters were civilian and that there was no need to verify this point. He said that the river was the boundary given him and that he would not cross the boundary and defy his instructions. Years later this general area revealed corduroy trails made and used by the VC. Whether the patrol heard civilian or VC woodcutters was never known. No reason was ever offered for the failure of the Bu Dop force to arrive at the link-up point. Had this force reached the designated point, it would have come right through the woodcutting area.

Later the patrol moved toward Bu Dinh hamlet to evacuate a sick Striker, possibly a malaria case, and take advantage of that helicopter sortie for resupply. At one point in the deep growth the patrol lost communication with base camp but was able to restore it successfully by extending an auxiliary antenna on a very long bamboo pole — a common expedient in heavy vegetation. The patrol remained in the area near Bu Dinh overnight and while there arranged a night medical evacuation for another ill Striker. The following day the patrol proceeded to Bu Gia Map, exploring both sides of the Song Be -Bu Gia Map road.

Dak O Patrol: During the night of 17 March 1965, the team was advised by a MACV team (US Military Assistance Command, Vietnam) that the Dak O hamlet, for which MACV was responsible, had been attacked and burned that evening. The MACV team asked if the Bu Gia Map detachment could check out the report. Dak O was about four miles south of Bu Gia Map on the road to Song Be. The LLDB sent out friendly agents a short time later to assess the damage and determine if the VC had undertaken actions to ambush relief forces. When the agents had not returned by late morning on 18 March, Sova,

"CQ" Williams Checking Area (Team Photo)

armed helicopters, followed by three A-1E Skyraiders. On 13 April the patrol briefly encountered a VC squad. Williams was subsequently awarded the Bronze Star-V and Crowe the Army Commendation Medal-V for their performances on 12 April. The patrol returned after having no further VC contact.

Stokes – Johnson: This patrol, 18-23 April, was basically one of reconnaissance to examine path networks and stream areas southeast of Bu Gia Map. The patrol was lead by the Montagnard company commander, Bu. There were no LLDB on the trip. The patrol was to link up with a Vietnamese Ranger unit near a burned-out Catholic mission. The CIDG patrol had spent the night at the church site, Easter Sunday 1965. There was some so-so fruit around — mostly green bananas and pineapple — and the resourceful troops also found some sweet potatoes.

An ARVN captain led the Ranger unit. Stokes and Johnson recall the link-up, after which the other troops immediately stopped for lunch — and of course that two-hour midday snooze known as "pak time." The jungle setting notwithstanding, a fancy spread was set out for the Vietnamese captain — checkered tablecloth, nice eating utensils, and fare quite different from the troops, possibly duck or chicken.

There was a stream with steep banks not far from the destroyed church. The most expeditious way across was a log that spanned the creek. Stokes, about midway in the gaggle crossing the log, lost his balance and to a roar of Montagnard laughter fell about ten feet into the creek. Johnson later recalled the sure-footed Montagnards nimbly negotiated the log with their keen sense of balance, suggesting that the Strikers had an unfair advantage since they could grip logs with their toes because the Bata boots were so thin. (*Note: Bata boots were made by the renowned Bata footwear people, formerly a Czech company, now headquartered in Canada. Bata boots had thin rubber soles and flimsy canvas tops. This footwear was standard issue to CIDG troops. Bata boots wore out quickly and were vulnerable to punji stakes.*)

The balance of the patrol was spent checking possible VC campsites and establishing ambushes on more promising trails. There was evidence of VC movement, but no contact.

Taylor – McLaughlin: In late April, Taylor and McLaughlin, together with an LLDB NCO and forty CIDG Strikers, spent six days south of Bu Gia Map looking for fresh VC activity and possible infiltration routes. The patrol went west of Dak O, then south, with the final leg being east of Bu Gia Map. There was no contact with the VC.

McLaughlin – Hand: During the major VC attack on Song Be in mid-May 1965, McLaughlin and Hand were sent by aircraft to a communications relay site on Nui Bara, a mountain just outside of Song Be. The purpose of the augmentation was to assist in the coordination of aerial reconnaissance and air strikes against VC in the Song Be area.

Enriquez – Taylor: As the ARVN reacted to the Song Be

Taylor, and Stokes accompanied a platoon-size relief patrol to Dak O. The agents returned after the patrol departed. Armed helicopters provided limited security for the patrol. Dak O was indeed gutted. There were no casualties among the people, but the VC did take rice. The village self-defense element, about twenty armed men in the village, fled and did not engage the vastly outnumbered VC, who reportedly had only about five men.

Enriquez – McLaughlin: In late March, Enriquez and McLaughlin accompanied a CIDG patrol north and west of Bu Gia Map, the most remote part of the team's area of operations. There was no VC contact during the patrol. Footpaths were noted in the area, but traffic on them did not appear fresh. The patrol did encounter punji stakes along the route, and several Strikers were injured by them.

Williams – Crowe: During the period 9-15 April 1965, Williams and Crowe accompanied a patrol on a mission to interdict VC forces to the southwest of Bu Gia Map and east of Song Be. The operation was conducted in conjunction with forces from Song Be, and coordinated carefully with the Province Senior Adviser. Arrangements were made for reconnaissance, artillery, and close air support. On 12 April the patrol made contact with elements of a VC company, and after a brief firefight and assault by CIDG forces the VC withdrew. Williams led the CIDG in the assault and Crowe provided suppressive fires with the support element. The VC left behind several rifles, grenades, and other equipment. Two Strike Force members were wounded and evacuated by a helicopter that brought in supplies. Stokes flew with the Air Force Forward Air Controller (FAC), CPT John Lynch, in his L-19 aircraft to provide reconnaissance and communication support to the patrol. Lynch marked areas of interest with smoke rockets, then brought in close air support by three

Bill Stokes Back from Walk with Dallas Johnson (Team Photo)

attack of mid-May, VC elements began to exfiltrate the area toward War Zones C and D. The readiness posture at Bu Gia Map was increased in light of the VC strength and activity in the Song Be area. The US and VNSF B detachments ordered that a reconnaissance team from Bu Gia Map be inserted just south of Song Be to develop information on VC movement in that area. The order was transmitted by radio to both the LLDB and A-313, and Stokes, who was in Phuoc Vinh working on future plans for the team, returned to Bu Gia Map to ensure that the instructions were received and the team was prepared to deploy immediately.

The LLDB team at Bu Gia Map refused to provide the forces for this important special reconnaissance mission. The LLDB CO, the Lieutenant in charge, was visiting his home at the time and an Aspirant (essentially a warrant officer in training to be commissioned a lieutenant) was in charge of the Bu Gia Map camp. The Aspirant refused the USSF request for patrol forces, and, in doing so, violated orders from his B-detachment that were provided by radio, as well as verbally by Stokes. The USSF went over the head of the Aspirant to the commander of the CIDG company consisting predominantly of Montagnards. The CIDG commander provided the troops. (Comment: The incident at Bu Gia Map was frustrating, but not dangerous. Helicopter support was literally on the way to pick up the reconnaissance team, and the Acting LLDB CO remained adamant in his refusal to cooperate. The USSF personnel were imbued with the need for cultural understanding in dealing with indigenous people and the need for advising the Vietnamese Special Forces, not directing them in a high-handed manner. There was never a lack of cooperation on the part of the Strikers.)

Enriquez and Taylor led the patrol because of their in-country experience and medical capability. The Strike

Force element included about six members — a very small element. The LLDB elected not to participate. The team was directed to conduct reconnaissance in the designated area and look for VC movement associated with the Song Be attack and movement between War Zones C and D. The rules of engagement made clear that the patrol was for reconnaissance purposes and should not fire, except in self-defense. There was no opportunity for preparation and barely time to draw rations and ammunition before the helicopter transportation arrived. There were no detailed plans, briefings, or rehearsals. The team simply flew away on about a one-hour notice, with sketchy guidance at best.

The initial helicopter insertion was aborted just before darkness because of a hot landing zone. The team went to Song Be for the night and was inserted at first light the following day. The team was extracted after three or four days. Only one helicopter showed up for the extraction, so a second sortie was required to pick up Enriquez and Taylor. The patrol report prepared by Enriquez and Taylor suggested that there was recent and fairly substantial VC activity in the area, which included crossings over the Song Be River and the corridor between War Zones C and D. (Comment: This hastily prepared reconnaissance patrol placed the team along a major VC infiltration corridor that would be used a short time later in support of the attack on Dong Xoai to the south.)

Training

The US team at Bu Gia Map was responsible for training the CIDG forces and LLDB. While considerable thought was given to a future CIDG training program for Bu Gia Map camp, the operational tempo, demands on trainers' time for other duties, and infrastructure maintenance requirements of the rainy season limited the time spent on formal training. In early March 1965, A-313 was directed to send two NCOs and twenty Strikers to Dong Ba Thin near Nha Trang for about five weeks of special reconnaissance training. The training was designed to create within the Bu Gia Map force a capability beyond that offered by the average Striker. There was no illusion, however,

Chuck Jenkins, Reconnaissance Trainer and Weapons Specialist (Team Photo)

Jim Taylor -Combat Medic, Combat Infantryman, Chef Extraordinaire (Team Photo)

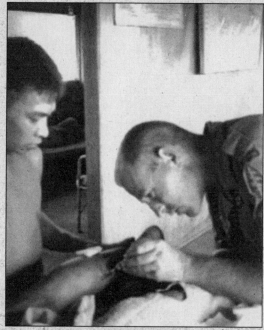
Lamar Sale Providing Medical Treatment (Team Photo)

that this short course would produce highly trained long-range teams that could operate over extended distances for long periods of time. Sale and Jenkins were tasked with the mission. To the degree time permitted some preliminary training was undertaken prior to departure, to include marksmanship, basic formations, and rudimentary map reading.

The group arrived at Dong Ba Thin on 27 March and began its program, which consisted primarily of small units tactics. The course also included a three-day training mission near the Cam Ranh Bay area and a night live-fire exercise. The reconnaissance team arrived back at Bu Gia Map on 30 April, but given the imminent redeployment of A-313 to Dong Xoai there was little opportunity to test these freshly trained CIDG soldiers. A-313, regrettably, was unable to take them to Dong Xoai.

Other than marksmanship training at the camp range, supervised by Dedmon and Jenkins, CIDG training was accomplished primarily by individual mentoring, on-the-job guidance, and suggestions during actual operations. There was continuous informal instruction in a variety of areas, for example, hygiene, supply economy, water purification, weapons maintenance, 60 mm mortar employment, and field fortifications. Patrol operations allowed opportunities for tactical suggestions. Given time, the USSF team would have put in place a more structured training program. The LLDB expressed little interest in sponsoring CIDG training.

The US team took its advisory duties quite seriously and to the degree possible attempted to mentor its counterparts through one-on-one contact and efforts to have the LLDB participate fully in every aspect of camp activity. In the area of operations, for example, the team would suggest the structure of a concept plan, then elicit ideas from the LLDB, constantly refining the plan to include all the necessary detail.

Civic Action

Civic action was also an important part of the mission [at] Bu Gia Map. Medical activity was the most challenging [ci]vic action task undertaken by the US team. In addition [to] care for the US, LLDB, and CIDG forces and dependents, [th]e team was responsible for village health and sanitation, [to] include maintaining a safe water supply. The general health of the local Stiengs was poor — worms, malaria, hepatitis, typhoid, dysentery, skin diseases, and malnutrition. Pneumonia was a common killer. In addition, there was frequent trauma resulting from accidents.

The health care ranged from preventive medicine to first-responder trauma treatment. Basic sanitation, rodent control, anti-malarial actions, and personal hygiene were the basic ingredients of the preventive activities. The US medics, Jim Taylor and Lamar Sale, ran a small dispensary for village care, conducted training for local health workers, and coordinated medical evacuation. Notes from team members indicate that over a thousand civilians were treated in March 1965, most of them in the dispensary. The aerial evacuation procedures were fairly efficient, but the return of patients was typically slow, particularly in the case of Montagnards, who spoke little if any Vietnamese. The Montagnards were quite fearful that children sent to Saigon hospitals might not come back, and their fears were justified. To supplement medical supplies, local crafts were used to barter for items in short supply. A crossbow, basket, or knife might be traded for much-needed antibiotics and other medicines at US dispensaries and hospitals in the Saigon area.

The Montagnards and Strike Force families were in great need of outer garments. They particularly liked colorful western-style clothing and showed little hesitation in mixing American clothing with traditional tribal or Vietnamese items. Some clothes were sent through the US Agency for International Development, but these bundles of garments bore little resemblance to what was needed. The most useful clothing gifts were those thoughtfully arranged by USSF friends and families, churches, and schools. The distribution of clothing was an interesting event. Some villagers, most often women, received their garments, then got back in line for seconds and thirds before all people had been served.

Dan McLaughlin —The Candy Man (Team Photo)

Village Chief, Du Krang (Team Photo)

When team members went into the village the young people, like children everywhere, surrounded the Americans in anticipation of a gift of candy or gum — a scene repeated over and over wherever GIs serve. On one occasion in late April an event was planned at which colorful shirts, balloons, and candy were to be distributed to the children. As a result of poor coordination, for which the Vietnamese Project Supervisor was roundly thrashed, the villagers failed to show up with their children as anticipated. Parents were afraid the children were being gathered to be spirited away or sent to school.

The proposed event could have been a useful one, but as with so many activities, "the devil was in the details."

Vignettes

Witch Hunt: On 1 March 1965, the team's first full day at Bu Gia Map, the Village Chief, Du Krang, came to the camp with his assistant. Over coffee, Du Krang indicated that ten people in the village had died of cholera during the week prior to the team's arrival. He said that they found a man whom they considered to be the witch, possibly because of a deformed arm, and held him responsible for the sickness. To determine whether the man were guilty or innocent, the villagers reportedly poured molten lead into his palm. If the lead were to go through the man's hand he would be considered a witch. Well, the lead didn't eat through the hand apparently, but they killed him and possibly his wife and child, anyway — so the story went. According to the tale, the heads and limbs of the witch and his family were severed and their livers cut out and thrown on the trash site. Later, a second witch was reportedly found and suffered a similar treatment. Although the team was never able to corroborate the events related by Du Krang, the story added some mystery to the Bu Gia Map environment, and served as an excellent pretext for the promotion of village sanitation.

Cocktails with Du Krang, Village Chief: After an unusual visit to the USSF teamhouse, a beer, and some discussion about village needs, Du Krang asked Stokes to visit his longhouse on the following Sunday. There was no particular ceremony going on, just Sunday at home Montagnard-style, with people gathering to play musical instruments and sing after a long week of work. As was customary, the Village Chief seated his company by two rice wine jugs, which were about thirty-six inches high and had three bamboo straws sticking out of them —not straws, really, more like bamboo pipes. Two bamboo pipes were for mutual and simultaneous swigs, and the third provided the necessary air vent to overcome the vacuum in the bottom of the jar. The wine tasted sweet and was not repulsive, as one might expect. The communal drinking was essential for local rapport and simply something that had to be done. One had to suppress thoughts of the many mouths and flies that had been on the pipe, and conditions under which the wine was made. Medic Taylor had prescribed a loading dose of tetracycline and Lomotil as a preventive measure against dysentery — and it worked. Stokes was presented a Montagnard bracelet, one of many the team members received at Bu Gia Map. As a reciprocal gift, Stokes took an Episcopal medallion off his dog-tag chain and gave it to a smiling, grateful Village Chief.

Cambodian Dust-up: From the outset of operations at Bu Gia Map it was clear that the relationship between the LLDB and Cambodian company was strained. On the other hand, the Cambodians got along quite well with the Americans. The Cambodians were mercenaries of the Khmer Serai (Free Khmer) faction, right-wing dissidents opposed to the Sihanouc regime. The USSF were instructed not to intervene in the event the Cambodians, led by their Political Officer, decided to leave the camp and strike out for home. Early one morning before first light, a Cambodian soldier was apprehended by the LLDB trying to sneak back into camp after visiting his wife or girl friend in Bu Gia Map village. The LLDB, armed and menacing, threatened to punish the soldier, backing down only after the Cambodian Political Officer told them that he would order his troops to kill them if the soldier were not released immediately. This offer of Cambodian violence and some early morning advice from the USSF team — put the incident to rest, but not the festering relationship.

Cambodian Sock-hop: On one occasion, the Cambodian invited Stokes and Taylor to a party in their longhouse. There was some reason to be apprehensive about spending a long period of time in the Cambodian billets at night

Mike Hand and Montagnard Supplier (Team Photo)

Dan McLaughlin Back from Patrol (Team Photo)

...t no way to turn down the invitation. The US team ...ped that the occasion might allow a closer relationship ...th the Political Officer and per chance an opportunity to ...in intelligence information of value. The evening was ...stive, with beer and endless singing and dancing. The ...mbodian native dances seemed to be a hybrid of Bali-...yle and the "Twist" — perhaps the "Angkor Wat Two-...ep." With fluid motions of their arms the Cambodians ...ckoned the Americans to participate — and dance the ...mericans did. The evening was productive in terms of ...-Cambodian rapport.

...Crossbow Sales and Much More: The Stiengs of Bu Gia ...ap were essentially subsistence farmers, one step ...moved, it seemed, from being hunter-gatherers. When ...rcraft crews or other visitors came to Bu Gia Map often ...eir first question was about souvenirs, particularly VC ...gs and Montagnard implements, such as crossbows; ...rious baskets; knives; pipes carved with likenesses of ... Gaulle, Special Forces soldiers, and other prominent ...en; and small axes. For metal, the resourceful ...ntagnards often used old vehicle parts, for example, ...af springs. VC flag production was late getting started at ... Gia Map, and perhaps failed to flourish because the ...gs were not dipped in chicken blood, as was the case in ...me other areas. Certainly it would have been difficult to ...stify large quantities of bloody flags during a time when ...stile contact was so sparse. Nevertheless, the local ...onomy was aided by this modest cottage industry — a ...rthy civic action program

...Outgoing Becomes Incoming: The weather during the ...ght in question could not have been worse — driving rain ...d dense fog. Sometime after midnight heavy firing ...gan, and there was much commotion in the camp. ...ither the LLDB nor US team could verify that the camp

was receiving VC fire, yet the thump-thump of mortars and outgoing machine gun fire continued. As nearly as the team was able to determine, the high alert and defensive fire were triggered by a friendly machine gun near the southwest corner of camp, where a Striker claimed to have seen VC crossing the runway. The unusual aspect of the event involved live mortar rounds, which left the tubes and slithered wildly, unexploded, across the ground or into trenches. Why CIDG mortar rounds were not leaving the compound was quickly apparent. The CIDG crews had not placed covers on the mortar tubes or swabbed them, and the heavy rains left water in the tubes, preventing proper ignition. Fortunately, an important lesson was learned without injury and the task became one of explosive ordnance disposal.

Monkey Business: The monkey business began early at Bu Gia Map. Dedmon and McLaughlin had a particular affinity for monkeys. While one could not always pick the enemy out of the crowd, one could be very sure that monkeys were not VC, and that was a good thing. Gertrude was first on the scene, and later local Montagnards brought a smaller monkey to the camp. The baby was named, imaginatively, "Monkey." "Monkey" was a roof-hopper, and expressed disdain for some camp occupants by getting on high perches, then throwing fecal matter at those people out of favor — so typically monkey.

Squad-pot Chow: Strikers typically carried sock rations on patrol, which consisted of rice and other odds and ends stuffed into a cloth sleeve or sock for easy storage. For the evening meal Strikers would boil water in large cooking pots they carried and dump rice, pork, and other items they viewed as edible into the pot, then squat around it with spoons and eat in communal style. Team members on the patrol normally carried rice and US or Japanese long-range patrol rations, which contained bouillon cubes and other items that added taste and nutrients to a squad pot. The USSF often joined in the squad-pot feast, but as Johnson once pointed out, it did not pay to check the Strikers' ingredients too carefully.

Administrative Support — Finally: Despite the remote nature of the camp and operational requirements, administration soon became burdensome. Tying up team members typing reports made little sense, so the team requested an administrative assistant be sent to the field. The team was greatly relieved when the request was approved. Within a few weeks the courier aircraft was on final approach for the camp with its precious administrative cargo. Much to the team's surprise, and early consternation, out stepped a comely young Vietnamese woman in her native dress. The team had clearly expected a male administrative assistant to be sent to the remote Bu Gia Map camp. Two actions were taken immediately. Miss Hwang was fitted quickly with CIDG fatigues and a place was found for her to live in the village. She adapted quickly and was a big help.

Up to Eyeballs in Eyeball: In mid-March 1965, a Montagnard man showed up at the Bu Gia Map dispensary after puncturing an eyeball in the fields. Taylor examined the eye and recognized that the injured man could lose his eye, and that the wound required specialized treatment. Before treating or evacuating the man, steps were taken to insure that the patient and, importantly, the Village Chief, were aware that advanced treatment was needed and the eye could be lost. The incident did not represent a major medical dilemma, but it did suggest that there were not always easy solutions to what seemed to be uncomplicated problems. In this case, otherwise humane treatment, without proper consultation, might have impacted adversely on the team's mission. The action taken by the USSF medics promoted positive relationships, and prevented potential misunderstanding by the villagers.

Deployment to Dong Xoai

In mid-March 1965 there was scuttlebutt at C-detachment level about deployment of the team elsewhere in the III Corps area, possibly Dong Xoai, a district village located south of Song Be between War Zones C and D. A few days later, the C-detachment S-3 indicated that one scenario being considered was to split A-313 between Bu Dop and Bu Gia Map. Under this plan, Stokes and six others would go to Bu Dop and assume district advisory duties, and another captain would come in to head the partial team left at Bu Gia Map.

On or about 21 April 1965, Detachment A-313 was advised officially that it would move to Dong Xoai. Guidance indicted that the team would deploy an Assessment Team to Dong Xoai in early May and turn over the Bu Gia Map camp to a split detachment from Bu Dop in mid-May. Upon redeployment the team was to be designated A-342, and operational control of the team was to shift from Detachment B-31 (Phuoc Vinh) to B-34 (Song Be). In

early May the Assessment Team deployed to Phuoc Vinh and Dong Xoai to perform its tasks. Normal operations continued at Bu Gia Map, to include patrolling, while turnover of the camp began.

DONG XOAI
Overview

Detachment A-342, 5th Special Forces Group (Airborne) was involved in one of the most significant battles of the Vietnam conflict. For fourteen hours, the Detachment, its supporting Seabee team, and small force of Vietnamese and Cambodian defenders, held at bay a multi-regimental Viet Cong attack against Dong Xoai on 9-10 June 1965. Much has been written about the friendly air support, so critical to the survival of the Dong Xoai force, and the heroism of defenders who were awarded Medals of Honor for actions during the battle. There has been less discussion of events leading up to the attack, the full range of activity during the fight, and the heroic actions of other participants in the ground battle.

This section addresses some of the pre-battle activities, describes the roles of team members, highlights strengths and weaknesses associated with the US and Vietnamese forces in the May - June 1965 timeframe, provides observations by participants in Dong Xoai operations, and describes early post-battle activity and establishment of the camp.

New Operational Area --
New Missions

In the spring of 1965, Detachment A-313 was located at Bu Gia Map, in northern Phuoc Long Province. In late April 1965, the Detachment received a warning order for deployment to Dong Xoai village further to the south. The order indicated that the Detachment would:

Be designated A-342 upon redeployment.

Establish an Assessment Team to deploy to Dong Xoai on or about 1 May 1965.

Serve under the operational control of Detachment B-34 (Song Be), effective on or about 1 May 1965, and that control by B-31 (Phuoc Vinh) would cease at that time.

Turn over Bu Gia Map camp to a split A-detachment from Bu Dop camp on or about 15 May 1965.

Upon arrival in the Dong Xoai area, A-342 was to perform three primary missions:

Serve as advisors to Don Luan District.

Serve as advisors to the Vietnamese Special Forces (LLDB). In this role, the Detachment was to expect the deployment to Dong Xoai of an LLDB A detachment and approximately seven hundred fifty Civilian Irregular Defense Group (CIDG) forces.

III Corps
Tactical Zone

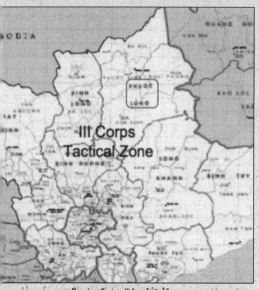

Phuoc Long Province, III Corps Tactical Zone

THUAN LOI
District Headquarters
Old Ranger Camp
DONG XOAI

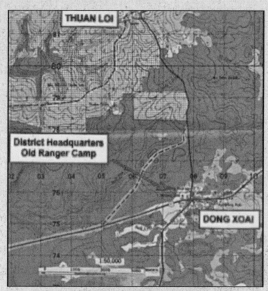

Dong Xoai (Map, Army Map Service, 1:50,000, 1963)

Conduct operations against War Zones C and D within ıe III Corps Tactical Zone.

Dong Xoai Area

Dong Xoai was the location of the District eadquarters for Don Luan District of Phuoc Long rovince. The village sat at the intersection of important oads known as QL 14, LTL 13, and LTL 1A (Song Be – huoc Vinh Road). From a military point Dong Xoai was gnificant because it was located astride critical surface outes between War Zones C and D, major Viet Cong (VC) anctuaries within the III Corps Tactical Zone.

The village of Dong Xoai is located at the center of the ap above left. The major north-south road, LTL 1A, went orth to Song Be and south to Phuoc Vinh. Route QL 14 ent east from Dong Xoai toward the village of Bunard, and TL 13 served as a route westward toward Chon Thanh.

The map above right further defines the location of ong Xoai and its associated geographic features. The istrict Headquarters and an old Ranger camp were locat- d in the upper left quadrant of the highway intersection. huan Loi, site of a major Michelin rubber plantation, lay pproximately seven kilometers to the north. Thuan Loi ould figure prominently in events of the coming month. here was no real airstrip at Dong Xoai, but the shoulders f LTL 13 on the western edge of the village had been raded somewhat and cleared of brush, but even so, there as little tolerance between wing tips of the larger air- raft and high trees that bordered the road. C-7 Caribous nd C-123 cargo aircraft did land there – very carefully. elicopters used a soccer field directly across LTL 13 om the District compound.

Assessment Team

The Assessment Team consisted of SSG Donald edmon, SFC Dallas Johnson, and CPT Bill Stokes. ohnson, Intelligence NCO, was selected for the team ecause analysis of the threat and area of operations was ritical. Dedmon, Heavy Weapons NCO, was chosen ecause of the need to evaluate District defensive positions, establish sites in the abandoned Ranger compound for initial and subsequent CIDG firing positions, and determine how best to coordinate defensive fires.

The Assessment Team went to Phuoc Vinh in early May 1965 for an orientation by Detachment B-31, then deployed to Dong Xoai to conduct an analysis of the area, assess requirements for the team's new role as subsector advisers, and formulate plans for the new camp. With the arrival of the entire USSF component and Seabee support team scheduled for late May, very little time was available, for on-site assessment, camp planning, and logistical preparations. There were no existing assessments available, and the LLDB did not participate. After several days at Dong Xoai the Assessment Team was withdrawn to Phuoc Vinh to complete its plans. The plans were approved by the USSF and Vietnamese B- and C-detachments, subject to several modifications. With plans approved, the Assessment Team was reinserted into Dong Xoai and conducted further assessment of District capabilities, the defensive area, and potential employment of CIDG elements.

Findings of Assessment Team

The notes that follow summarize findings of the Assessment Team as a result of its initial visit to Dong Xoai and subsequent deployment there:

Intelligence: The initial information available on VC capabilities and intentions was quite limited. Other than general information on the VC use of War Zones C and D for logistical support and training activities, and limited local order of battle information, intelligence data available to A-342 was sparse. The District Chief, CPT Con, appeared to have a fairly effective network for collecting local intelligence information. There were periodic reports of VC sightings by observation posts and civilians from the Phu Rieng area to the northeast. Dong Xoai was mortared in early May, with approximately twelve 60 mm mortar rounds landing in the District Headquarters and Ranger areas.

By mid-May, the intelligence picture became clearer. VC mortar fire hit Dong Xoai, possibly for registration, killing

District Chief Con and Bill Stokes (Team Photo)

edge of Dong Xoai and the abandoned Ranger camp contiguous with the northeast perimeter of the District Headquarters compound.

The southern area was flat and open, and provided excellent fields of fire. There was no existing infrastructure there, and coordination with District Headquarters would clearly have been difficult for proper subsector advisory duties and control of defensive fires.

The abandoned Ranger area, which was adjacent to the District Headquarters, lay on terrain that sloped slightly to the southeast, but was dominated by a ridge approximately three hundred meters to the east. Fields of fire from the eastern perimeter were very limited because of residential structures just across the Dong Xoai - Song Be road. Anyone walking along the road could locate firing positions, billets, and storage areas. To the west, undergrowth had been cleared for five hundred meters or so, except for twelve-inch grass; heavily forested terrain existed beyond the clearing. About seventy-five meters of foliage had been cleared to the north of the Ranger camp, the area beyond that consisting of high grass, bushes, and some smaller trees. Approximately five hundred meters to the north and northwest there were dry rice fields. Existing berms and protective wire in the old camp were of marginal potential. Within the Ranger area there were five frame buildings partially sheathed in corrugated steel and a small masonry building in the northwest corner. The area of the Ranger compound was too small to accommodate the incoming force and would require significant expansion. The surface consisted of laterite, which was hard as a rock when dry.

The District Headquarters – Ranger site was the predestined area for the new camp. Other forces were there, all forms of coordination would be easier, and the District Chief was at that location. This site was vulnerable, however, because vegetation would initially restrict fields of fire, it was located in a populated area, and the District compound was open to civilians during the day for normal administrative business.

Existing Forces and Structure: The existing forces at Dong Xoai were located in the District compound. The force and administrative structure consisted of the District Headquarters component, Vietnamese Army (ARVN) howitzer platoon, ARVN armored car platoon, and RF/PF company.

The Headquarters element was housed primarily in a masonry building that dominated the compound. The building contained District administrative offices and a small command element for the existing military presence. Communications included telephone and radio, the latter operating from an underground bunker just outside the Headquarters building to the east. Much of the District activity consisted of basic governmental administration. There was, therefore, a constant stream of civilians in and out of the compound, making it easy pickings for VC intelligence operatives or saboteurs. Preliminary discussions were held with the District Chief regarding security deficiencies.

one Regional and Popular Forces (RF/PF) soldier. About the same time in May, a VC force of regimental size attacked Song Be, approximately fifteen miles north of Dong Xoai. The Song Be camp was not overrun despite the unauthorized withdrawal of an ARVN company on a flank of the US compound. Army and Air Force aircraft dropped flares, brought in supplies, performed medical evacuation, and conducted air strikes. Phu Rieng, northeast of Dong Xoai, was attacked shortly thereafter. Immediately after the Song Be attack a reconnaissance team from Bu Gia Map was inserted just south of Song Be. The patrol, led by Enriquez and Taylor, determined that there had been substantial recent VC movement between War Zones C and D. (Comment: This patrol took place along a major VC infiltration corridor that would be used a short time later in support attacks to the south.)

During the night of 15 May 1965 the Dong Xoai area received a mortar attack (twelve to fifteen rounds). There were several civilian casualties in the village, but none in the District compound. The District 105 mm howitzers responded to the mortars. Also in mid-May, an ARVN battalion pushed its way from Song Be south to deliver artillery ammunition. The battalion was ambushed south of Song Be on the return trip. Three US advisors were reported killed in this action, along with the Vietnamese battalion commander.

The Assessment Team increased its efforts to gain insights into the new area of operations and VC activity. The activity around Dong Xoai, particularly to the north, left little doubt that the area was vulnerable to attack. The question became when would an attack take place?

Camp Sites and Design: The Assessment Team looked carefully at two potential sites for a camp — the southeast

Howitzer Firing Position (Team Photo)

Armored Car Position (Team Photo)

ARVN 105 artillery platoon: There were two 105 mm howitzers in firing positions to the east of the Headquarters building. The crews appeared well trained and reacted quickly to calls for fire. The positions allowed indirect fire in all directions, but direct fire was limited to the north because of a high berm. Ammunition was stored under cover, and concrete bases under the howitzers allowed them to be shifted easily. The unit provided limited harassing and interdictory fires nightly, and responded to such sightings as were made known. The integration of howitzers fires with other weapons of the defense plan had to be adapted to support the existing configuration of the defended areas, as well as the one anticipated upon completion of the CIDG camp. The integrated plan was far from complete as of early June 1965, and ammunition resupply was a major problem.

ARVN armored car platoon: There were six armored cars in the platoon, which was located on the east side of the District compound behind a low berm that fronted on public roads. The vehicles were not deployed in a way that would maximize their use in an attack. The defensive position was weakened further by the location of family living quarters within the area. The poor employment of the armored car platoon was discussed with the District Chief on a number of occasions. Con indicated at the time that he was sympathetic with the US request but was unwilling to give the necessary orders to the ARVN platoon. Detailed USSF discussions with the commanders of the armored car and howitzer platoons were more limited, given the need to avoid usurping the District Chief's authority, but were substantive. The USSF concept included randomly shifting the cars among various areas of the camp. Occupation of alternate and supplementary positions could have confused VC planning, stiffened the defense, and ensured greater security for the platoon itself. Elements of this platoon would also have been useful for periodic road-sweeps. (*Comment: The location of accompanying dependents was always an issue. Dependents often went with CIDG elements where there were civilian communities to absorb them, but normally fewer dependents followed CIDG forces into very remote areas. The location of families within defended compounds was a two-edged sword. Some people argued that the forces would fight harder because they had families with* them to protect. *Others suggested that the presence of dependents created physical obstacles to defense, weakened counterintelligence efforts, and created major distractions.*)

Regional/Popular Forces: The capability of these forces was largely unknown. The RF/PF, ninety or so strong, would muster in the morning, provide perimeter security for the District Headquarters area, and man two observation/listen posts (OPs/LPs), one near the sawmill south of the village and the other just beyond the northeastern outskirts of the village. The RF/PF apparently were rarely used for patrolling and when they did go on limited patrols did not venture far or stay out very long. The District Chief cited the lack of radios as the major reason the RF/PF were not used more aggressively. During the period May – early June 1965, no RF/PF training or patrols were noticed at Dong Xoai. The District Chief brushed aside suggestions for RF/PF patrols to the north and west of Dong Xoai.

National Police Office. This office consisted of a small frame building just outside the District compound to the south, staffed by several policemen.

Fortifications and structures: In addition to the masonry Headquarters building, there were other structures in the District compound, mostly frame, that housed dependents, supplies, and other administrative functions. The Headquarters compound had nice fields of fire to the south, but vision was obstructed to the east and north by frame structures within the compound used for dependents and administrative purposes. There were high defensive berms on the north and west sides of the compound, but a more modest one fronting on the south. There were fighting bunkers on the berms that allowed overlapping fields of fire and observation. Near the point at which the District and CIDG compounds would be joined there was a bunker flanked by an armored car oriented to the northwest. This armored car could have placed effective fire along the west wall of the CIDG area and north wall of the District compound, as well as direct frontal fire on attack positions in the distant wood line. Compound alerts were not routinely held; however, positions were manned several times when VC sightings occurred. Defensive wire was somewhat modest, and little use was made of claymore mines and trip flares. A 60 mm mortar pit was located

West Wall of District Compound (Team Photo)

Some of Dong Xoai Players, Late May 1965 Front Row: CPT Con, Unnamed Interpreter, Interpreter Phee
Back Row: Unnamed Vietnamese, Don Dedmon, Dallas Johnson, Jim Taylor (Team Photo)

outside the Headquarters building to the southwest.

The Assessment Team returned to Dong Xoai in mid-May to refine plans and coordinate the arrival of the remainder of the Detachment, Seabees, LLDB, and CIDG forces. The team continued its efforts to gain insight into the new area of operations, existing capabilities, and VC activity. The VC activity around Dong Xoai was of growing concern.

Full Detachment Deployment

The entire A-342 team closed into Dong Xoai on 25 May 1965 and immediately took steps to refine intelligence information, proceed with camp development, absorb CIDG assigned, establish interim security, and prepare for advisory tasks associated with the new LLDB detachment and District elements.

The Detachment began its District advisory role by matching USSF personnel and functions with appropriate District counterparts, e.g., intelligence with intelligence, medical with medical, supply with supply, operations with operations, and communications with communications. Further, the USSF began to broaden the Assessment Team's outline for camp preparation and operations. The USSF personnel were briefed on their duties prior to arrival and were able to start camp activities immediately, to the degree permitted by available resources.

The Intelligence Situation

Most of the general intelligence information was dated from the middle of June onward and was not available to the Detachment as it was getting organized at Dong Xoai. A number of high-level US sources had been suggesting for some time that the VC were preparing for attacks of larger scale, although little of this information filtered down to A-team level. According to Andrew Goodpaster in mid-June 1965, the VC had been preparing for operations in strengths larger than battalion for some time — training, gathering supplies, and planning. (*Source:* Memorandum For Record, Andrew Goodpaster, "Meeting with General Eisenhower," 16 June 1965)

A mid-June press release from the Office of the Secretary of Defense (OSD) commented that new VC groupings were noted between War Zones C and D and that these areas contained VC headquarters and several combat units. The VC forces, according to the article, appeared to be preparing to launch a surprise attack within the next day or two against Vietnamese villages or district towns. (*Source: News Release, OASD PA, 17 June 1965*) (*Comment: While the dates of the reports above fall after the Battle of Dong Xoai, the information was apparently available for some time, but disseminated poorly.*

The appearance of this threat information seemed to provide justification for B-52 strikes —which should have come earlier from a tactical perspective. The use of B-52s within the Republic of Vietnam involved a political decision of considerable magnitude.)

Later in June CIA commented on a growing VC capability to mount and sustain large-scale military engagements, frequently in reinforced regimental strength. The report also mentioned stepped-up VC activity in May, including the regimental assault on Song Be and an increasing willingness of the VC to risk heavy casualties. (*Source: CIA, 30 June 1965*)

At the local level, the District intelligence network suggested that about one thousand VC were in the Thuan Loi and Phu Rieng areas after the Song Be attack in the late May - early June timeframe. Also, sporadic VC mortar rounds, likely harassing or registration fires, landed in the compounds about this time. This intelligence information was included in Detachment reports to higher headquarters. The District Chief continued to deny US requests that RF/PF patrols work close-in areas to the north and west. The LLDB intelligence net was begun in early June, but no important information was gained solely from its sources. Most intelligence information came from District sources.

Information about the enemy's capabilities and possible intentions became increasingly specific by early June 1965. On 1 June, the VC probed the northeast OP on the outskirts of Dong Xoai. Several days later civilians from the Phu Rieng area to the northeast reported that VC in their village intended to attack Dong Xoai as soon as they had enough food. The villagers also reported truck movement south of Phu Rieng. This information was sent to higher headquarters through Sector and USSF channels. Aircraft en route Song Be from time to time reported vehicle movement in the Phu Rieng area, but there was no feedback from requests for aerial reconnaissance of the area. (*Comment: The informant's information was right on the money.*)

On or about 6 June, a woman, reported to be a VC intelligence agent, was captured by District elements, but escaped before she could be exploited. District personnel indicated that she had been traveling with the VC at Phu Rieng. The VC agent was brought into the District headquarters without a blindfold, most of the defenses within full view. In fact, any citizens coming into the headquarters compound on routine business, e.g., rice permits, had the same access to views of the defenses and could easily have created mischief. After the initial interrogation an aircraft was requested to take the agent to Song Be for further questioning, but before the aircraft arrived, the agent escaped from the National Police Office. The District Chief permitted the woman to be taken out of the District Headquarters area under the guard of only a single RF/PF soldier. During the same twenty-four-hour period three young men, reportedly VC agents, were captured near the airstrip. After interrogation the men were flown to Song Be. The interrogators at District failed to ask meaningful questions or use questions provided to them by the USSF. No feedback was received from Song Be. (*Comment: One can only imagine the impact of the agent's escape. The LLDB and District forces were very weak from the standpoint of counterintelligence operations.*)

No VC indirect fire was received between the time the CIDG arrived and 9 June; however, four or five probes were conducted by the VC near the RF/PF OPs. All areas were probed lightly, except the west and northwest sectors. It is possible that the west and northwest sectors were also probed, but without detection. The areas where no probes were detected became the primary directions of the attack by the VC on 9 June 1965.

Correlated intelligence reports in the late May-early June period suggested two thousand VC were located five-teen kilometers north and west of Dong Xoai. (*Source: 5th SFGA Dong Xoai After Action Report, 7 July 1965*)

Camp Preparations Get Under Way

In preparation for camp development and other missions, A-342 focused on local security, camp construction, and the logistics and administration required to house and feed the troops and their families. The VC complicated fulfillment of requirements by interdicting ground supply routes, resulting in severe shortages of food and other commodities essential for the welfare of the villagers and viable commercial activity. (*Comment: US civilian agencies had an important role to play in cases where nonmilitary populations were in stress because of inadequate food and other important commodities. USSF teams performed important civic action duties around the clock.*)

Operations: The USSF noted the immediate need for increased security. While the conduct of aggressive patrols would need to await the arrival of Strike Forces, there was an imperative requirement for short patrols outside of camp to at least two kilometers. The District Chief continued to refuse requests for such patrols, even with USSF advisors. The USSF made plans to begin active patrols upon arrival of the LLDB and Strike Forces. The USSF maintained active security at night and identified alert positions. (*Comment: Such patrols may have uncovered evidence of VC activity, enhanced the confidence of the RF/PF, and given the USSF an important look at the surrounding terrain.*)

McLaughlin and Interpreter Davis Check Mortar Damage (Team Photo)

Fortifications: There were low berms on the north and west sides of the CIDG area, but no significant berms on the eastern side of the perimeter along the road to Song Be and south side, contiguous with the area occupied by the armored car platoon, its families, and livestock. Claymore mines and trip flares were installed. There was little protective wire available initially. The firing positions left by the Rangers were few in number, shallow, uncovered, and eroded. Major improvements were needed, with priority to machine guns and mortars. The USSF dug an 81 mm mortar pit just outside their billet structure. Jenkins took the lead in preparing the mortar position, which was about chest high on 9 June. (*Comment: Shovels and picks were in very limited supply, and digging positions manually was difficult in the hard-packed laterite soil.*)

Logistics and Administration: Deficiencies in logistics and administration were to become major issues in the overall security at the new camp. The overarching logistical problem was the lack of aircraft to bring people and supplies into Dong Xoai in a timely, well-sequenced manner. Aircraft, the USSF were told, were diverted to assist other US units coming into Vietnam. On the ground, there were issues associated with shelter, food, and equipment.

Shelter: There were five frame shelters with corrugated steel siding in the CIDG compound and one small masonry building. There was no reliable information about the numbers of dependents who would be arriving with the CIDG forces, all of whom would require shelter. The requirement for more and improved shelter was apparent.

Food: There was insufficient food in Dong Xoai village because incoming roads were blocked periodically by the VC. Inadequate rice was made available to the villagers despite urgent pleas from the District Chief to the Province Chief. Parallel USSF requests went through Sector channels with little result. A contractor began to bring some CIDG subsistence in early June. The province United States Operations Mission (USOM) representative made a small quantity of bulgur wheat and cooking oil available to the dependents and civilians. (*Comment: Bulgur wheat, used typically for livestock in the area rather than food for people, was not a big hit for family meals.*)

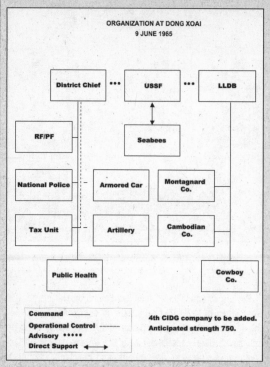

ORGANIZATION AT DONG XOAI
9 JUNE 1965

Command ———
Operational Control - - - -
Advisory •••••
Direct Support ←——→

4th CIDG company to be added.
Anticipated strength 750.

Organization at Dong Xoai

Equipment shortages: Major shortages included engineer and fortification materials, grenades, communications equipment, and medical items. As of 9 June, for example, the dispensary kit had not been delivered, nor had portable radios crucial for patrol operations. (*Comment: The failure to support Dong Xoai with adequate cargo aircraft prevented the delivery of Seabee construction equipment that would have aided immeasurably in security and camp development.*)

Mines and Booby Traps: Vacating Rangers left in place to the west and north of the CIDG compound an unmarked minefield with booby traps. The areas where these obstacles were installed were needed for expansion of the CIDG camp perimeter. The District Chief had no incentive to remove these obstacles because they afforded his compound some measure of security. The initial clearance of these areas was begun by Sova and McLaughlin; the LLDB refused to participate or order Strikers to help. Approximately thirty-five USSF man-hours were spent in clearance activities prior to 9 June. (*Comment: The clearance of these obstacles created somewhat of a dilemma for the USSF. The decision to clear the mines was based upon the need to put Seabee construction equipment to work in these areas immediately upon its arrival. Fortunately, no one was hurt in the removal effort. Unfortunately, the engineer equipment did not arrive prior to the VC attack. The subsequent attack and response facilitated the final clearance effort.*)

Deployment of the LLDB: An LLDB detachment, commanded by CPT Do, arrived about 27 May, the same day as two CIDG companies began arriving, creating some confusion. Do, who had not seen the proposed camp plan nor been briefed by his B-detachment, immediately wanted to change the approved plans.

Continued Operational Activity: Discussions of recon-

naissance, observation, and security operations were held jointly among the USSF, District Chief, and LLDB. The observation post system used only two sites and left uncovered the eastern outskirts of the village and areas northwest of the compounds. The existing observation posts to the northeast and south seemed to be reasonably productive, however. Reconnaissance operations were hampered by the lack of communication equipment and competence. Despite the fact that portable radios were given a top priority in the camp equipment recommendations, as of 9 June none had been received. The USSF borrowed two HT-1A radios and one PRC-10 from Detachment B-31 prior to entry into Dong Xoai; one HT-1A was inoperative on 9 June. The HT-1A was used in the voice command net and the PRC10 for air-ground communications. During the pre-battle phase there were no portable radios on hand for CIDG operations. The District Chief may have had two HT-1s.

Integration of elements: Plans were developed for the integration of District and CIDG forces, but they were very preliminary, given the District Chief's reluctance to get into details and the absence initially of the LLDB team and CIDG forces. The District Chief would not allow CIDG elements to defend from District positions, which complicated reinforcement planning. Practice alerts were conducted nightly in the CIDG camp to ensure that personnel knew positions and that all gaps resulting from absences were filled. The integration of defensive fires was far from complete, and live fire opportunities were limited because of the lack of ammunition.

Seabee Arrival: Most supporting Seabees arrived in early June, and represented a variety of critical construction skills. These Seabees had with them minor engineer equipment. The heavy equipment needed for construction of berms and protective walls could not be brought in because airlift was not available. The Seabees turned their attention to detailed planning, and construction of temporary fortifications and sanitation improvements.

Strike Force Elements: Strike Forces began arriving, unpaid, during the period 26-31 May. As of 1 June 1965, some troops were still awaiting airlift. The Strike Forces arrived by aircraft upon very short notice. The forces arrived in no logical sequence and were accompanied by wives, children, animals, little food, and few comfort items. The Strike Force was to consist of about seven hundred fifty men ultimately, organized into two Vietnamese "Cowboy" companies, one Montagnard company, and one Cambodian company. Company 342, a "Cowboy" company from Phuoc Vinh, was made up of troublemakers, reportedly transferred because of fights with Rangers at their former station. A third CIDG company, Cambodian, arrived on 30 May. The Cambodians demanded to stay initially in a school compound on the eastern edge of town, where they could also accommodate and protect their families. Two CIDG companies were housed in the proposed camp area. The CIDG strength was approximately four hundred men. Many initial man-hours were lost to payday activities at a very crucial time.

Battle of Dong Xoai --
The Setting and Commencement

The weather on the night of 9 June 1965 was miserable -- rain and heavy fog that limited both air and ground observation. The ground was muddy. The weather during the daylight hours of 10 June 1965 was clear.

Friendly forces: The morale of USSF and Seabees was outstanding, a fact that contributed greatly to the tenacity of the defense. The morale of the CIDG soldiers was at best fair, affected adversely by the lack of shelter and food for themselves and their families, unfamiliar surroundings, inadequate supervision by the LLDB, and operational delays. Morale of District forces appeared to be fair generally, and very good among the artillery people. The state of morale among LLDB members was unknown.

US forces were split between the District and CIDG compound at night to reduce their vulnerability in the exposed CIDG area and to provide support in the District compound. Overall, there was better USSF control with USSF personnel in both compounds. USSF forces were to be consolidated in the CIDG area after camp completion. Johnson, McLaughlin, Sale, Williams; Seabees Brakken, Keenan, Mattick, Wilson; and several interpreters were billeted in the District compound. Crowe, Dedmon, Enriquez, Hand, Jenkins, Russell, Stokes, Taylor; Seabees Eyman, Hoover, McCully, Peterlin, Shields; and interpreters were in the CIDG area at night. USSF personnel were providing local security at both sites at the time of the attack. Most USSF were sleeping fully clothed because of earlier probes, and were quickly up and armed.

All the LLDB were located in the CIDG compound. Two Strike Force companies (one Montagnard, one "Cowboy") were also located in the CIDG compound. The third company (Cambodian) was located on the eastern edge of Dong Xoai.

The sketch above right displays the general orientation of the two compounds, reflects the location of friendly elements in relationship to the village, and depicts some of the areas mentioned in subsequent paragraphs, thus helping in the visualization of unfolding events. The CIDG area is in the upper right section of the sketch and the District compound the upper left.

Enemy forces: The VC mission, according to VC sources, was to overrun Dong Xoai and eliminate the US and Vietnamese forces. VC morale was judged to have been high. Although some participating units had been bloodied at Song Be several weeks earlier, they had reorganized, rested and been resupplied. Under the cover of darkness, fog, rain, and thick vegetation, the VC moved within several hundred meters of the camp before launching the assault.

High-angle fire into the District and CIDG compounds was unrestricted. The VC also had good fields of fire on all sides of the camp complex, although earthen defensive walls reduced the effects of direct fire weapons to the west and north. Throughout most of the battle the VC had excellent observation from the high ground east of the compounds

The attack begins: At about 091800 June, the District

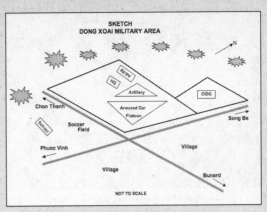

Dong Xoai - A Sketch

Chief received a report that one hundred VC were four kilometers south of the compound. The howitzer platoon fired into the reported area with unknown results. There was no counterfire by the VC.

The assault on the CIDG and District compounds began at approximately 2330-2345 hours, 9 June. The VC attacked in reinforced regimental strength. The primary direction of attack was through the heavily vegetated terrain to the west of the camps. The VC employed supporting weapons around the entire perimeter, and are believed to have used 75 mm pack howitzers, recoilless rifles, rocket-propelled grenades, mortars, machine guns (multi-caliber), flamethrowers, pole charges, hand grenades, and small arms. Ammunition constraints were not apparent. The major weapons were well zeroed on critical elements of the camps, and the attack appeared to have been well planned. (*Comment: The VC unit designations have been variously reported. The PAVN 9th Division was involved according to oral history discussions of MG Vo Van Dan, 9 April 1996. Statements of COL Pham Vinh Phuc, reportedly commander of the VC troops at Dong Xoai, provide interesting detail of the attack plan and execution. COL Pham Vinh Phuc reported that premature firing by one of his units to the south of the District compound required that he move up H-hour, which had been scheduled for 2400 hours.*)

In addition to the main attack against the District and CIDG locations, the VC prepared effective ambushes around likely landing zones for ARVN reinforcements. The VC cut all roads leading into Dong Xoai and occupied the high ground overlooking the CIDG area.

Battle of Dong Xoai --
The CIDG Area

The attack began with heavy concentrations of mortars and recoilless rifle fire focused principally on the masonry building used as a command post and US billets. At the time of the attack, Taylor was on security watch. The immediate tasks were to report the attack to higher headquarters, communicate with elements in the District compound, get friendly forces to their fighting positions, and initiate defensive fires. Taylor and Seabee McCully immediately guided able defenders to firing positions on the berms. Crowe was able to get a brief message off by radio before enemy fire destroyed the USSF billet structure and

Command Post, CIDG Area (Post-attack photo, original source unknown)

Striker Billets in CIDG Area (Source of original photo unknown)

single sideband communications there. The initial firing also severed the phone line to the District compound. Fighting along the berms was violent and continuous.

Stokes, Seabee Hoover, and Do, the LLDB detachment commander, were in the command post at the time of the attack. Stokes and Hoover were both injured when mortar and 57 mm recoilless fire hit the building. Stokes went from the masonry building to the USSF billet area to ensure that the attack had been reported by radio. He found the radio burning from damage to the battery. He then attempted to extract someone wounded from underneath corrugated metal debris, but was hit by mortar fragments in both legs. As Stokes crawled out of the team area, Taylor picked him up and carried him to the west wall. Taylor provided Stokes an M-79 grenade launcher with two rounds, and later Dedmon handed him a machine gun with a short belt of ammunition.

One of the abandoned Ranger structures in the CIDG compound served as the billeting area and temporary operations center for the USSF. The primary US voice communications capability was here. This area was clearly the main target of the initial fires by VC mortars and crew-served weapons positioned on the high ground to the east overlooking the camp. Russell died in this area before he could join Jenkins in the mortar pit in front of the structure. The Striker billets were also subjected to a

heavy pounding during the early minutes of the attack.

After helping to organize the initial defense and treating early casualties, Taylor, despite the heavy VC fire and significant risk of friendly fire, infiltrated the District compound to reestablish contact with other USSF elements and update that group on the situation in the CIDG camp. After he established contact, Taylor returned to the CIDG area where he rejoined the fight, treated the wounded, and helped stiffen the dwindling defense force.

The VC attacked the north and west walls in groups of six to ten men, task-organized into sapper, assault, and other teams — supported by fires from direct and indirect fire weapons. The CIDG machine gun position at the northwest corner was a major focus for the developing VC ground attack. Dedmon, wounded in the head and chest, anchored the northwest corner, moving along the berm encouraging participation by the CIDG and engaging the enemy at close ranges himself with remarkable courage. He was fearless. Hoover, wounded during the initial barrage of mortar and recoilless rifle fire on the masonry building that served as the LLDB CP, fought with others in the vicinity of the northwest corner until his death.

Jenkins manned the 81 mm mortar position alone from the beginning of the attack, braving intense enemy fire from his exposed position and bringing effective counter-fire against the VC. Jenkins was killed at his post in the

USSF Billet Area (Source of original photo unknown)

West Berm of CIDG Area (Source of original photo unknown)

early hours of 10 June after a display of extraordinary bravery.

At approximately 100200 hours, the VC assaulted the northwest corner heavily. This assault was accompanied by a bugle call from east of the compound and an intensified infantry attack. The attacking forces wore distinctive garments for recognition; for example, one group wore armbands and another checkered cloth around their waists. Taylor recalled that yet another breaching team at the northwest corner wore shirts, but exposed one bare shoulder. Most LLDB and CIDG troops then broke into small groups, abandoned the compound, and moved into the village. (*Comment: The VC report found in Selected Battles from the Resistance Wars against the French and the Americans, 1945-1975, Volume II, published by the Ministry of Defense, Hanoi in 1991, has an interesting account of preparations for the attack and command and control issues that arose. While the report overestimated friendly capabilities and casualties, and understated VC losses in a very typical propagandistic way, the discussion of small unit coordination difficulties seems quite plausible.*)

Taylor was the glue that held the CIDG defense together. Without regard for his own safety, Taylor directed people to defensive positions, actively supervised the defense, sought out and tended the wounded, distributed ammunition, reestablished contact with District elements, and employed his personal weapons under close combat conditions.

At about 100230 hours, the VC assaulted the northwest corner with a flamethrower. The operator was shot after his initial burst, but the infantry attack intensified and the perimeter was penetrated. When the VC came over the wall, they cut off McCully and Peterlin from others closer to the west berm. Dedmon received fatal wounds during this major assault. At this point, Peterlin and McCully,

both wounded, went over the north wall and evaded the VC until they were recovered by Vietnamese reinforcements on 11 June. The few remaining CIDG troops went through the eastern side of the perimeter into the village. The commander of the LLDB failed to assist in the control of the defense. His men, however, gave an excellent account of themselves on the west and north berms.

After the unauthorized departure of the "Cowboy" company from its assigned positions, the west berm was defended by just a handful of USSF personnel and Seabees.

After the breach, Taylor and Shields carrying Stokes, and Eyman their weapons, withdrew from the west berm through the armored car and howitzer areas into the District compound, exposing themselves to both VC and friendly fire during the trip. Taylor received a bullet wound to the leg just before they reached the headquarters building. The intensity of the situation, lack of US personnel, and intervening VC forces prevented the evacuation of Dedmon, Hoover, Jenkins, and Russell at this time.

Fighting in the District Compound

The District Headquarters compound was struck by direct and indirect fire — a full array of weapons — at about the same time as the CIDG area. The VC initiated the attack with heavy mortar concentrations, followed by direct fire from crew-served weapons against perimeter bunkers and armored car positions. The direct fire came principally from the wooded area to the northwest of the compound and positions near the schoolhouse to the south, just beyond the soccer field. (*Comment: COL Pham Vinh Phuc, in his report, indicated that his assault battalion for the District Headquarters objective was reinforced by eight 75 mm recoilless rifles, one medium machine gun, and six flamethrowers. The initial mortar concentrations,*

Taylor and Shields Carrying Stokes (Illustration courtesy Joe Kubert, 2007)

Dong Xoai Military Area - After Attack (Source of original photo unknown)

he further indicated, were designed to inflict substantial casualties on the defenders while they were in bed and to provide suppressive fires for assaulting forces.)

Initially the USSF and Seabees in the compound moved to the south and west defensive walls to join RF/PF troops manning positions there. The US forces were armed with individual weapons, two grenade launchers, and a 3.5-inch rocket launcher. All bunkers were receiving fire, and breaching teams were advancing into the protective wire. The US forces focused first on the close-in enemy forces and their supporting teams across the soccer field.

McLaughlin, using the rocket launcher, brought successful counterfire against a VC machine gun in the schoolhouse several hundred meters to the south. (Comment: COL Pham Vinh Phuc wrote that the "enemy infantry threw hand grenades and fired rifle grenades at our breach-points, killing or wounding most of our demolition specialists," and that "a number of our direct-fire artillery positions were struck by enemy shells.")

Johnson, who had gone to the west berm of the District Headquarters compound with others, noticed the lack of defensive firing from the armored cars armed with 37 mm

Johnson Checking Out Destroyed Armored Car After Fight (Source of original photo unknown)

Rear of District Headquarters (Source of original photo unknown)

guns. He tried to get the armored cars to take up alternate positions from which they could engage known targets, but the cars stayed where they were, shooting at targets unknown, until the vehicles were either knocked out or departed the camp. (*Comment: The USSF had asked District Chief and commander of the armored car platoon repeatedly to set up alternate and supplementary positions, and to switch positions regularly, rotating through both compounds. Permission was denied to use the armored car platoon in this manner. One factor in the refusal was the location of the armored car platoon families among the vehicles. Another factor was the apparent disdain in which the ARVN troops held District and CIDG forces. The proper use of the armored cars' weapons could have made an important contribution to the defense.*)

Two VNAF A-1H aircraft were reportedly on station by about 092400 June, but strikes were denied because of cloud cover. A flare aircraft was above the area about 100030 hours. At approximately 100430 June, two USAF A-1Es broke through cloud cover and dropped twenty-four fragmentation bombs. About sixteen thousand rounds of 20 mm cannon fire were also fired into the area to the north of the District compound. (*Source: "Tactical Air Support," Air Force, August 1965*)

Sustained Activity in District Compound

At about 100230 June, the RF/PF machine gun position on the southwest corner of the berm was destroyed, and Williams moved the USSF personnel back to the Headquarters building. CIDG people were noted exfiltrating the compound into the village. Steps were taken to cover approaches into the compound, and defenders relocated within the Headquarters building to cover various hot spots and vulnerable entry points. Johnson made radio contact with Song Be and expressed the team's urgent need for air support. (*Comment: During the early morning, according to COL Pham Vinh Phuc, three assaults were launched against various bunkers. He indicated that infantrymen were required to lie down across*

protective wire so that others could cross the obstacles over their bodies. Once the breach had been established, attack "spearheads" were directed to the Headquarters building, the interior of the west wall, and the RF/PF housing area.)

At about 100350 June, a second aircraft was on station to provide flare support, which was diminished by the overcast weather conditions. C-130 gunships were not available during the night. After approximately 100500 hours supporting tactical air was advised to shoot anything outside the camp perimeter that did not appear civilian. Air support after first light included runs by Army helicopter gunships, twenty-four A-1Hs, thirty-five A-1Es, thirty-seven F-100s, and eleven B-57s. Air strikes included bombing with fragmentation clusters, iron bombs, and napalm; use of rockets; and strafing. The Air Force claims to have destroyed a .50 caliber machine gun in the schoolhouse across LTL 13 from the District Headquarters between 100600 hours and 100800, and dropped ordnance on VC groups in the center of the town. By about 101000 June the fog lifted, followed by substantial air strikes. The work of Air Force forward air controllers was superb; they responded incredibly well to ground requests by PRC-10 radio in very simple terms, e.g., "napalm north wall." To his everlasting credit, Crowe managed to keep the one portable radio functioning. (*Comment: According to a White House Situation Room Report, 10 June 1965, one hundred seventy-three US and VNAF sorties were flown. Bill Fraker, pilot of an Army gunship, Playboy One Six, recalled that shortly after daylight on 10 June he attacked along the west wall of the CIDG compound and north wall of the District compound with forty-eight rockets against what he estimated to be about two hundred VC, disrupting the attack. Fraker further recalled that two USAF B-57 Canberras came through a hole in cloud cover right behind him, the first dropping fragmentation clusters, the second napalm.*)

At about 100900 June, VC in the schoolhouse began firing a .51 caliber machine gun into the District Headquarters building. According to Johnson, the tracers

District HQ - East Side

Commo

East Side of District Headquarters (Source of original photo unknown)

were quite visible and the gunner was shooting about eight feet high — fortunately. Later, Williams and Shields, without regard for their own safety, dashed to the southern berm and destroyed the VC with several rounds from a 3.5-inch rocket launcher. Both Shields and Williams, wounded earlier, were injured again by automatic weapons fire in this action. Williams was able to hobble back to cover. Other defenders moved quickly to extricate Shields from his exposed position and bring him into the Headquarters building. Shields died from his wounds later in the day.

About the same time as the action against the position at the schoolhouse, the airstrip of the Michelin rubber plantation at Thuan Loi was selected by Vietnamese III Corps for the introduction of reinforcements. Reinforcing Vietnamese forces were decimated as they landed on the plantation airstrip, where they, their US advisers, and helicopter crews met heavy preplanned mortar and automatic weapons fire. The VC ambush of the reinforcing troops had been sprung. (*Comment: According to one media source, the Commander of ARVN III Corps declined to call for additional US forces, indicating that he wanted to handle the situation with Vietnamese troops. The Vietnamese commander further indicated that the VC were probably trying to suck in the Americans. The manner in which the VC secured possible reinforcement landing zones and routes suggests that they clearly had their sights on other objectives beyond the District Headquarters itself.*)

Johnson and Taylor defended the west end of the District Headquarters building, a large room outfitted for District administrative transactions, with two exterior doors and multiple windows. From this position Johnson and Taylor fired on and killed a flamethrower team moving in from the west and engaged other infiltrating targets

in close combat throughout the morning and early afternoon. The destruction of the flamethrower team created a fire that engulfed a row of wooden structures between the Headquarters building and the north berm that housed the RF/PF members and their families. The room, completely exposed to the west and south, was subjected to heavy fire from VC machine guns and at one point recoilless rifle fire. Taylor left the area only long enough to treat the wounded with the soon-to-be-exhausted medical supplies.

Most of the remaining US defenders operated out of the eastern end of the Headquarters building. Seabees worked partly out of a room on the north side, but the heaviest activity on that end of the building took place in a general purpose room that opened to the east. McLaughlin, Williams, Hand, and Crowe operated from this area, and US communications were maintained from there. Radio communications, largely managed by Crowe, were absolutely critical in the defense — coordination of air strikes and link to higher headquarters.

As the morning of 10 June wore on, the defenders advised B-34 (Song Be) that they were running quite low on ammunition. By 101200 June, the VC were hitting the Headquarters building with 57 mm recoilless rifle fire. There appeared to be little prospect for early resupply, evacuation, or reinforcement. A little after noon the seriously wounded were moved from the Headquarters building into the underground communications bunker and plans were quickly made to move to take a final defensive stand within the howitzer positions. Shortly thereafter, the remaining defenders, carrying Stokes and Shields, moved through an exposed area to the gun pits approximately fifty meters to the east.

By 101300 June the defenders were running perilously

short of ammunition. Johnson recalled having one magazine left for his rifle and one grenade. At about 101355 hours, a helicopter extraction somewhat unexpectedly took place. The helicopter rescue effort was organized and directed by MAJ Jim Jaggers, Commander of the 197th Armed Helicopter Company. The extraction was complex, not simply a case of dropping in on the defenders and loading them on aircraft. From the perspective of the helicopter units, there were many things to consider quickly — fire support within the compound and outside, routes of approach, touchdown actions, and routes of departure, all complicated further by heavy enemy ground fire. Three helicopters of the 118th Assault Helicopter Company, led by MAJ Harvey Stewart, landed just outside the artillery gun pits in a very exposed location, and took aboard the defenders. A fourth helicopter, a gunship piloted by CPT Bill Fraker, 197th Armed Helicopter Company, also swept in to pull out several remaining friendly troops. Simultaneously with the extractions, helicopter gunships and tactical air provided suppressing fires around the compound. All US personnel were evacuated, except Dedmon, Jenkins, Hoover, and Russell, who were killed in action in the CIDG compound, and McCully and Peterlin, who were able to exfiltrate from the CIDG compound and evade the VC until recovered by friendly forces. Shields died of wounds en route to Phuoc Vinh. All US dead were accounted for on 11 June. (*Comment: Fraker and Stewart were awarded Distinguished Service Crosses for their actions at Dong Xoai. The 145th Combat Aviation Battalion received a unit citation for its participation in the fighting in and around Dong Xoai, and its members were awarded a number of valor awards in addition to the two mentioned above.*)

Dallas Johnson Arrives Phuoc Vinh (Source of original photo unknown)

Post-extraction Activity

After the extraction of friendly forces the fight for the Dong Xoai area continued for several days, followed by camp construction and rehabilitation of the District Headquarters and village.

The most immediate task facing friendly forces as the Dong Xoai defenders were evacuated was to regain control of the area. At approximately 1600 hours, 10 June, the 52d Ranger Battalion, advised by CPT Jim Sterling, was inserted by elements of the 118th Assault Helicopter Company at the soccer field across LTL 13 from the District Headquarters compound. The ARVN 7th Airborne Battalion was helo-lifted to the northern edge of Dong Xoai during the late evening of 10 June 1965. The 52d Ranger Battalion encountered heavy resistance and sustained significant casualties, but recaptured the District Headquarters during the early hours of 11 June. At approximately 110700 June, the 52d Rangers linked up with the Cambodian CIDG company on the eastern outskirts of Dong Xoai. Seabees McCully and Peterlin were recovered alive by Vietnamese forces about 110900 June 1965 after having evaded the VC for about thirty hours. McCully had hidden in the sawmill and woods on the southern edge of Dong Xoai. Peterlin had initially taken shelter in a vulnerable village structure, then later dug himself into an existing depression to obtain cover. (*Comment: Horst Faas, a reporter for the Associated Press at the time, accompanied the Ranger battalion and took extraordinary photographs that later appeared in Life and other publications.*)

Estimates of VC casualties differ widely among sources. First reports from US and Vietnamese sources indicated that about seven hundred VC died (three hundred in and around town, four hundred outside). Other reports reflected a body count of two hundred fifty VC at Dong Xoai, with estimates suggesting that over eight hundred VC had been killed altogether. Yet another report indicated that there were one hundred twenty VC bodies within the compounds and several hundred within small arms range. Early Special Forces reports place VC losses as over one thousand.

Within the District and CIDG areas, three US Special Forces soldiers were killed and the other eight wounded. Among the Seabees, two men were killed and the remaining seven wounded. Additionally, there were deaths among US Air Force and Army helicopter crews, and US ground advisors. Reports indicate that three Vietnamese LLDB members were killed and four wounded. CIDG losses, according to 5th Special Forces Group Headquarters, were forty killed, eighteen wounded, and one hundred twenty-four missing. Many of the missing CIDG soldiers returned to USSF control after relief operations were completed. ARVN forces participating in the reinforcement sustained significant losses, particularly in the Thuan Loi area just north of Dong Xoai.

New and Improved District Headquarters and CIDG Camp (Source of original photo unknown)

Early Hanoi reports announced that five hundred CIDG soldiers and two thousand US troops had been killed at Dong Xoai, and a thousand ARVN soldiers captured. Other North Vietnamese Army reports announced the elimination of two thousand fifty-four enemy troops. The inflation of opposing-force casualties in public was a common VC/NVA practice designed as a propaganda tool directed against South Vietnamese forces and civilians, and the wider international audience. Such manipulated information was also fed to VC/NVA forces, VC sympathizers, and the people of North Vietnam. In response to the Hanoi propaganda regarding Dong Xoai, the Commander of the 5th Special Forces Group immediately promulgated guidance for psychological operations to neutralize its impact. (*Comment: Casualty assessment is always difficult, but especially so when it involves not only organized military forces, but also irregular troops, civilians, and enemy casualties that are removed quickly from battle areas. Reporting is also sensitive to timelines, area boundaries, accessibility, and political requirements. With respect to the political impacts of Dong Xoai casualty reporting, it is interesting to note a Memorandum for President Johnson from Douglas Cater, a high level aide on 11 June 1965:*

"This morning's newspapers casualty reports from Dongxoai are typical of a number of recent accounts from Vietnam. The initial reports of American and Vietnamese dead are subsequently scaled down – but the earlier exaggerated reports always make the headlines. The average reader gets a cumulative picture of casualties that are a great deal higher than reality. A week or so ago the early reports indicated 1,000 Vietnamese casualties, and it subsequently turned out to be only about half that.

You may wish to raise *** with General Taylor whether there isn't a better method of reporting casualties. Certainly, it would seem logical to withhold estimates until sources are reasonably sure of their accuracy.")

The USSF and Seabee wounded were treated initially in Saigon. Eyman, McCully, Peterlin, and Stokes were evacuated to the United States for further medical treatment. Once released from the hospital in Saigon, Crowe, Hand, Johnson, McLaughlin, Taylor, and Williams continued to serve in operational Special Forces detachments. Five Seabees were reassigned upon release from the hospital in Vietnam.

On 13 June, USSF CPT Pete Skamser and several NCOs were sent into the area to stabilize the camp and bring help to the many souls in need. During the next few days clearing operations were continued; a small defense force was created with approximately one hundred Strike Force members located within the Dong Xoai area; Vietnamese dead were evacuated; modest defensive positions were established; weapons were distributed to Strikers; and supplies of food, water, and medicine were distributed to surviving Strikers, their families, and local civilian population.

Detachment A-342 was reconstituted in late June and the stabilization team was redeployed. Enriquez, Sale, and Sova were part of the new group, whose mission was to build the new camp, conduct combat operations, and perform civic action tasks. Additional CIDG troops and a US combat engineer platoon were brought a week thereafter. Throughout the summer of 1965 USSF, Army engineer, and Vietnamese elements rebuilt the defenses at Dong Xoai, conducted civic action programs to restore village vitality, and undertook security operations. Fields of fire were greatly extended; berms, fortifications, and critical operational facilities were constructed; and extensive obstacle systems were installed. Civic action activities included medical care, distribution of food and clothing, and restoration of business infrastructure.

Awards and Decorations

Recognition for participants in the Battle of Dong Xoai developed over time and in a piecemeal fashion. High-level valor awards wind slowly through the military bureaucracies as statements are taken, facts checked, and recom-

President Johnson Presents Medal of Honor to "CQ" Williams
(White House Photography)

Medals of Honor: USSF
(Williams), Seabees (Shields)

Distinguished Service Crosses:
USSF (Hand, Johnson, Taylor)

Silver Stars:
USSF (Crowe, Dedmon, McLaughlin, Stokes),
Seabees (McCully, Peterlin)

Bronze Stars:
USSF two, Seabees seven

Purple Hearts:
USSF eleven, Seabees nine

Unit Awards:
Seabees, Navy Unit Citation

mendations evaluated in light of other heroic acts. The year following the Battle of Dong Xoai (1966), Williams and Shields were awarded Medals of Honor, and Hand, Johnson, and Taylor the nation's second highest award for valor, the Distinguished Service Cross. No attempt is made here to identify dates associated with awards, but rather to summarize those of the Special Forces and Seabee participants.

Williams' Medal of Honor ceremony was a memorable event for the former Members of Detachment A-342. On 24 June 1966, President Johnson presented the Medal of Honor to "CQ" Williams. Williams was cited for extraordinary heroism and leadership at Dong Xoai on 9-10 June 1965. The citation noted that Williams, despite multiple wounds, organized, inspired, and led the defenders in the District compound; coordinated critical air support; displayed great personal courage in the destruction of a VC machine gun position; and skillfully supervised the evacuation of surviving team members. The citation read, in part, "1st Lt. Williams distinguished himself by conspicuous gallantry and intrepidity at the risk of his life above

Team at Medal of Honor Ceremony Left to Right: Enriquez, Sale, Hand, Stokes, Crowe, Taylor, Sova, McLaughlin, Johnson (White House Photography)

Stokes, McLaughlin, Enriquez, Dunnem, Taylor (Team Photo)

and beyond the call of duty while defending the Special Forces Camp against a violent attack by hostile forces." Williams' family and team members were present for the ceremony.

Team Transition

Following the award ceremonies of 1966 team members went to new assignments as their Vietnam tours were completed. Two team members left the military service and others remained. Three team members were commissioned later and served with distinction in Vietnam as company commanders of combat units. Six members of the detachment served additional tours in Vietnam before the war ended.

LATER YEARS Whither the Gang

Any discussion of Later Years should begin with a summary of activities after 1966 by detachment members who served together at Bu Gia Map and Dong Xoai, Vietnam.

Harold Crowe was commissioned after returning to the United States, served as an infantry captain, and completed a second tour in Vietnam as a company commander with the 173d Brigade (Abn.). After retiring from the Army, Crowe served as Range Safety Office at Ft. Bliss, TX, after which he opened a computer service in El Paso.

Donald Dedmon was killed in action on 10 June 1965.

Rick Enriquez served three tours in Vietnam. He retired from military service in 1974 after serving with distinction as Command Sergeant Major (E-9) of the 1/4 Cavalry, 1st Infantry Division. Rick earned a master's degree and held a teaching position with the Fayetteville, NC, public schools for twenty-one years before retiring again in 1996.

Mike Hand entered into private business upon completion of his military service.

Chuck Jenkins was killed in action on 10 June 1965.

His son, Dave, served with distinction in Special Forces and other airborne assignments, retiring as an Army Command Sergeant Major (E-9) in 2007.

Dallas Johnson served with distinction on two subsequent combat tours in Vietnam. He retired as a Sergeant Major (E-9) in 1971 at Ft. Devens, MA. Dallas died in 2008.

Dan McLaughlin left the Army upon completion of his enlistment and became a successful small business entrepreneur.

Bobby Russell was killed in action on 10 June 1965 during the initial attack of the CIDG area.

Lamar Sale was commissioned in 1967 and served a second tour in Vietnam as an infantry company commander in the 82d Airborne Division. After attending the Air Command and Staff College and earning a master's degree, he taught at the Air Force Academy, and served in a variety of important staff positions in the Pentagon and with NATO. After a distinguished military career, Lamar retired as a Lieutenant Colonel in 1989. He later established a highly successful Junior ROTC program for students in Harrisonburg, VA.

Tony Sova was promoted to MSGT and served with distinction in Special Forces units until retirement from military service.

Bill Stokes served a second Vietnam tour in 1971-72 as CO, 2d Squadron, 11th Armored Cavalry Regiment. Bill retired as a colonel in 1986.

Jim Taylor served as Senior Medic with Detachment A-302, Mike Force, after leaving Dong Xoai. He was subsequently commissioned and served as an infantry company commander and staff officer with the 173d Brigade (Abn.) during his third Vietnam tour. He later was an exchange officer with the British Parachute Regiment, serving in both command and staff positions. After retirement as a major in 1977, Jim served as a civilian official with the Department of Navy for eighteen years.

Charlie Williams served in various staff positions at Ft.

Back for Enriquez Tacos Seated Left to Right: Lamar Sale, Rick Enriquez, Dallas Johnson Standing Left to Right: Jim Taylor, Dan McLaughlin, Tony Sova (Team Photo)

Bragg until his retirement as a major. He died in 1982 and was buried in Arlington National Cemetery.

Old Buddy (Kim Tot) was the District Chief's houseboy at Dong Xoai. He became good friends with members of A-342, and during the Battle of Dong Xoai loaded ammunition magazines for the USSF team and gave what comfort he could to the wounded. Kim Tot later worked for the USSF at Trang Sup, where several team members were then assigned. Stokes attempted unsuccessfully to locate Old Buddy in Tay Ninh in 1971.

Ms. Hwang, Administrative Assistant to A-342, was killed in the District compound during the Battle of Dong Xoai.

Dong Xoai Painting

In the late 1990s, a commercial artist painted an excellent scene commemorating the Song Tay Raid. Subsequently, another painting reflected the attack on Lang Vei by tanks. A-342 team members were asked if the Battle of Dong Xoai might be the subject of a third painting. There was agreement within the team that such a painting should portray a general description of the battle and that some depiction should be made of Seabee participation. After considerable study of the proposed painting the project stalled. A-342 members were advised that sales of the previous two paintings had been somewhat

Senior Moment Rick Enriquez and Dallas Johnson (Team Photo)

disappointing and that further painting projects would not be cost effective. In addition, the Vietnam War was becoming more and more distant and there were more recent Special Forces actions that needed to be recorded.

Special Forces Conventions and Reunions

The Internet greatly increased interaction among team members in the late 1990s. The first push toward greater communication seemed to come from the very natural inquiries from children, now adults, who had lost their fathers at Dong Xoai. The many questions required team members to dig into old files and memories for answers, and to intensify their own discussions of the details of service at Dong Xoai and Bu Gia Map.

At the suggestion of Enriquez and Taylor, several team members agreed to meet at the 2000 Special Forces Association Convention held in Boston. The trip provided a wonderful opportunity for old friends to gather with wives and talk over old times and life since Vietnam — and perhaps tell a tall tale or two. The reunion also gave the team the opportunity to meet Al and Judie Dunnem. Al, who served on a previous Vietnam tour with Enriquez and Taylor, became a strong supporter of the team, and one might say an adopted member.

The successful get-together in Boston encouraged team members to gather once again using a reunion as the vehicle, this time at the 2002 Special Forces Association Convention held in Fayetteville, NC. Enriquez, Johnson, McLaughlin, Sale, Sova, Stokes, and Taylor mustered for the occasion. Dave Jenkins, Chuck Jenkins' son, stood in for his father and became an adopted teammate. Al Dunnem also joined in team events. Some members had not seen each other since 1965. There was no agenda at the Ft. Bragg reunion, just an opportunity to enjoy friends.

Since 2002 the team members have adopted a mini-reunion format that allows them to gather socially as they pass through each other's hometowns — or areas of operation (AOs) in lingo of the past. The first such get-together took place in Fayetteville in August 2005 as several members gathered at the Enriquezes' — an opportunity to catch up on life events, reminisce a bit, and break bread. An overnight visit to Fayetteville by the McLaughlins in May 2006 allowed another such mini-reunion.

Memorial for Teammates

On 14 October 2005, members of Detachment A-342 gathered in the garden of the Airborne & Special Operations Museum, Fayetteville, NC, to honor teammates who died so bravely at Dong Xoai in 1965. The team members were joined by families and friends to dedicate a Memorial Paver in memory of Don Dedmon, Chuck Jenkins, and Bobby Russell. Several team members spoke of the heroism and sacrifice of their friends, and a message from the Deputy Commander, 5th Special Forces Group, was shared with the attendees. CSM Dave Jenkins, son of Chuck Jenkins, spoke of the team and his father, and together with Rick Enriquez, removed the bunting

Ladies at Boston Reunion Becky McLaughlin, Shari Taylor, Carol Enriquez, Judie Dunnem (Team Photo)

from the memorial.

Dong Xoai Segment, Oliver North "War Stories" Series, Fox News

On 12 March 2006, the "War Stories" series addressed the history of the Seabees and their activities in past conflicts. Part of the Vietnam segment was devoted to Seabee participation in the Battle of Dong Xoai, with emphasis on the evasion and recovery of Frank Peterlin and Johnny McCully, and the heroism of Marvin Shields, who was awarded the Medal of Honor — first such award for a Seabee. Oliver North interviewed Peterlin and the show's producer interviewed McCully and Stokes.

Later Years and Years Ahead

As the end of 2009 approaches, the surviving members of A-342 remember their fallen comrades, appreciate the soldierly fellowship they have enjoyed over the past forty-four years, and look forward to continued friendship.

Rick Enriquez and Dave Jenkins Remove Bunting from Memorial (Team Photo)

SPECIAL FORCES

AIRBORNE

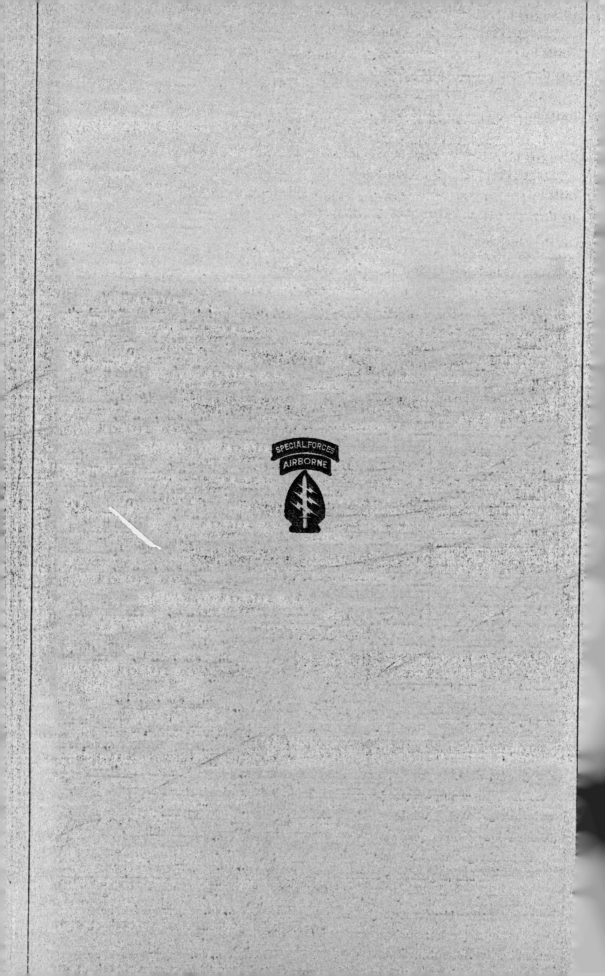

Selected References Detachment A-342,
5th Special Forces Group (Airborne)

Articles

10 June 1965, "U.S. Dealt Worst Blow Yet in Viet Conflict," Daily Advance, Lynchburg, VA, pp. 1-2: Indicated that all twenty-one Americans wounded, missing, or dead, and that casualty reports varied.

10 June 1965, "Vietnamese Forces in Struggle to Retake Town from the Reds: Mortars Open Attack," Jack Langguth, *New York Times*: Provided media map and early description of situation.

11 June 1965, "Battle for Dong Xoai Ends: Casualties Heavy," *Daily Advance*, Lynchburg, VA, p. 1: Described immediate aftermath of battle.

11 June 1965, "Big Viet Cong Attack Curbed," *Lynchburg News*, Lynchburg, VA, p.1: Discussed casualties and reinforcements.

11 June 1965, "Bold Viet Gamble Turns Enemy Stab; U.S. Losses High," *Washington Post*, pp. A1, 20: Provided further description of battle and aerial photo of District compound.

11 June 1965, "Some 150 Civilian Bodies Among Slain at Dong Xoai," Horst Faas, *Daily Advance*, Lynchburg, VA, p.1: Described casualty situation, mentioned Peterlin's recovery, and provided photo of woman with dead child.

11 June 1965, "Special Forces Soldier Tells of VC Attack," *Daily News Briefs*, Command Information Branch, MACV: Noted interview with McLaughlin.

11 June 1965, "Steady Fire Thwarted Dongxoai Rescue 'Copters," *Washington Post*, pp. A20-22: Described difficulty getting helicopters in and provided aerial photo of camp.

11 June 1965, "Vietnam Rangers Recapture Town in Heavy Battle," Jack Langguth, *New York Times*, pp. 1-3: Described casualties and ranger action.

12 June 1965, "Army Lists GI Casualties in S. Viet Battle," *Chicago Tribune*, p. 5: Mentioned casualties.

12 June 1965, "It Was Really Hell, Yank Hurt at Dong Xoai Says," *Chicago Tribune*, p. 5: Quoted Williams and Crowe.

13 June 1965, "Guerrilla Units Hit Again at Battered Vietnam Area," *New York Times*: Discussed follow-on actions at Dong Xoai.

13 June 1965, "Viet Reds Resume Attack on Dong Xoai," *Washington Post*: Included recovery of McCully.

14 June 1965, "Dong Xoai: Grim Graveyard," *Lynchburg News*, Lynchburg, VA, pp. 1-2: Described aftermath of battle and provided photo of Thuan Loi with caption, "Dong Xoai Battle Aftermath ... Even the Trees Were Dead."

14 June 1965, "Little Life Left: Dong Xoai: Grim Graveyard," Peter Arnett and Horst Faas, AP, *Lynchburg News*: Described destruction at Thuan Loi and suggested essentially VC division was involved around Dong Xoai area.

14 June 1965, "U.S. Paratroopers Move to Protect Airfield, "*Daily Advance*, Lynchburg, VA, p. 1: Described move of 173d Airborne Brigade to Phuoc Vinh, and presented photo of boy reported to be sole survivor at Thuan Loi.

15 June 1965, "100 Planes Hit Viet Reds Again,"*Baltimore Sun*, p.1: Provided follow-up account and discussion of air action, and identified Peterlin as wounded and Hoover dead.

15 June 1965, "U. S. Bombers Raze N. Viet Barracks; 'War Regime' Set Up," *Philadelphia Inquirer*, pp. 1-3: Identified casualties and provided media map.

15 June 1965, "U.S. Jets Destroy Barracks in North; Battle's Tolls at 600," *Baltimore Sun*, pp. 1-2: Provided information on Thuan Loi and recovery of Hoover and Peterlin.

15 June 1965, "Viet Base Bolstered," *Washington Post*, pp. 1-2: Described reinforcement of Dong Xoai and provided Faas photo of RF/PF soldier who lost family.

17 June 1965, *News Release*, OASD (PA), p. 1: Mentioned B-52 action; described VC tactics, including concentrating forces in uninhabited areas, concealment under jungle canopy, and sneak attacks against district towns; and outlined tactics used at Dong Xoai.

June 1965, "Flinton Soldier Killed in Rugged Viet Nam Battle," date and source unknown, Patton, PA, p. 1: Reported Jenkins' death.

June 1965, "Hero 'Jittery' in Viet Traffic," Howard Brodie, source unknown: Provided interview of Williams with AP sketch.

18 June 1965, "Heavy Toll at Dong Xoai," *Peking Review*, pp.26-27: Indicated pronged attack on Dong Xoai; forces took town, camp, and airstrip in " lightning raid, annihilating the puppet troops"; booty included two howitzers; "skillful tacticians and masters of the ambush ... knocked out relief battalion;" knocked out 1,500 enemy troops and 50 Americans, and brought down 16 aircraft.

18 June 1965, "North Cambria Soldier Killed in Vietnam," *Altoona Mirror*: Provided photo of Jenkins and story.

June 1965, "Red Victim Doing His Duty," source and date unknown: Provided obituary of Bobby Russell.

18 June 1965, "South Viet Nam," *Time*, pp. 28-30: Provided general description of battle.

21 June 1965, "South Vietnam: Anxious Days," *Newsweek*, pp. 49-51: Contained Crowe quote and photo of little wounded girl in compound.

29 June 1965, "Intelligence Memorandum: Developments in South Vietnam during the Past Year," CIA, Office of Current Intelligence: Provided broad description of events and mentioned Dong Xoai.

2 July 1965, " New Fury in Viet Nam," *Life*, pp. 31-40A: Consisted largely of photos by Horst Faas, including recovery of McCully, 52d Ranger Battalion in action, and scenes of destruction.

2 July 1965, "Research Institute Recommendations," Research Institute of America, p. 1: Called action "some of ... bloodiest fighting in ... entire guerrilla war" and described drastic change in VC tactics that reduced wooing of peasants and employed more terror).

4 July 1965, "Vietnam – The Escalating War," *New York Times*, Section 4, p. 1: Discussed widening war and US operations in War Zone D.

21 July 1965, "GI's Widow Given Medals," source unknown, Altoona, PA: Described presentation of Jenkins' Bronze Star and Purple Heart to wife.

August 1965, "Tactical Air Support – Balancing the Scales in Vietnam," Kenneth Sams, *Air Force*: Provided good discussion of tactical air support at Dong Xoai.

1965, "Army Copter Pilot Wins DSC for Evacuation at Dong Xoai," *Army Times*, date unknown: Announced Harvey Stewart's DSC and mentioned other awards.

December 1965, "Silver Star for SF Soldier," USARV-IO: Announced McLaughlin's award of Silver Star.

17 December 1965, "City Native Gets Silver Star," *Lynchburg News*, Lynchburg, VA: Provided Walter Reed press release on Stokes' award.

21 December 1965, "Lest We Forget," *Lynchburg News*, Lynchburg, VA, p.6: Editorial mentioned Stokes and LT. Shannon, who was killed elsewhere in Vietnam, and urged people of Lynchburg to give thanks for sacrifices being made for them.

"Carter County Soldier Awarded Medal for Heroism in Vietnam," source and date unknown: Announced Crowe's ARCOM-V.

19 January 1966, "Where the Action Was," *Army Times*: Provided map depicting biggest engagements of 1965, including Dong Xoai.

22 February 1966, "Hit Twice, Helped Wounded: Hero in Viet Battle Wins DSC," *Pacific Stars & Stripes*: Announced Hand's award and described actions.

23 February 1966, "Hero in Viet Battle Wins DSC," *Pacific Stars & Stripes*: Described presentation of Hand's DSC — evacuated seriously wounded; fought from mortar pit, found unattended, which he used effectively against insurgents until gun jammed, body sprayed with shrapnel.

6 April 1966, "DSC Awarded Msgt at Bragg," *Army Times*, p. 39: Stated that Dallas Johnson, "although wounded, continued to move from position to position, exposing himself to enemy fire as he rallied the South Vietnamese force."

25 April 1966, "Local Tots Receive Dad's War Medals," Altoona, PA, evening paper: Described presentation of Jenkins' Vietnamese awards (Cross of Gallantry with Palm and Military Merit Medal) and displayed Bronze Star and Purple Heart.

June 1966, "Victim of Viet Nam War Learning to Smile Again," AP: Provided picture and follow-up story about little girl featured in Faas' story of Dong Xoai. Girl most likely was daughter of RF/PF soldier, who lived in District Compound. She was often seen before attack.

24 June 1966, "Fourth Veteran of Vietnam Awarded Medal of Honor," *New York Times*, Described Williams' Medal of Honor ceremony and provided photo. President said act was "a patriot's gift to his country."

24 June 1966, "Johnson Gives Viet Hero Medal of Honor," *Philadelphia Inquirer*, Described Williams' Medal of Honor ceremony.

24 June 1966, "Medal of Honor Awarded Lieutenant Wounded Five Times in Viet Battle," *Washington Post*: Described presentation ceremony.

24 June 1966, "Viet Cause Called Just," *Baltimore Sun*, p. 1: Described Williams' Medal of Honor presentation.

29 June 1966, "Special Forces Hero Awarded Highest Honor," *Commander's Digest*, p. 4: Announced Williams' Medal of Honor — rallied men and led them personally without regard for five wounds.

13 September 1966, " Medal for Seabee," *Kansas City Star*: Provided short summary of rocket launcher action involving Shields and Williams and announced Medal of Honor for Shields.

28 September 1966, "Heroic Seabee Earns Nation's Highest Medal," *Navy Times*, pp. 1, 10: Commented on Crowe's communication efforts and noted that Shields was wounded, fighting as infantryman, and volunteered to help stop VC before mortally wounded.

20 November 1966, "This Thanksgiving, I'll Remember the Brave Men of Dong Xoai," *Family Weekly*, pp. 20-22. Provided Williams' interview with Jack Ryan.

December 1966 "Camp Dong Xoai," *The Green Beret*, p. 8: Described actions by Hand and Williams and mentioned post-battle operations at camp.

22 February 1967, "Citation for Co A, 101st Avn Bn," *Army Times*, p. 5: Announced Distinguished Unit Citation for action near Dong Xoai, June 1965.

February 1967, "Brave Men of Dong Xoai," *All Hands*: Described battle, highlighted role of Seabees, and included sketch of compounds.

March 1967, "The Navy's Fabulous Seabees," *Our Navy*, pp. 2-43: Provided description of Seabee participation in Dong Xoai battle.

15 May 1967, "Distinguished Service Cross Recipient Graduates from OCS," *The Coatesville Record*, p. 8: Reported Taylor's award of DSC and provided photo of Taylor shaking hands with President earlier.

31 May1967, "Four More Soldiers Awarded DSC," *Army Times*, p. 39: Included Taylor.

18 August 1967, "Green Beret Sergeant Commissioned 1st Lt," *Veritas*: Announced Crowe's commissioning and provided photo.

October 1967, "Battling Seabees," *Saga*, pp. 16-21: Discussed Seabees generally, Seabee story of Dong Xoai and Shields' MOH.

6 November 1967, "Attacked by Reds, GIs Get Orders to 'Kill or Be Killed': Night of Blood – Night of Valor," Part 1, Tom Millstead, *Philadelphia Inquirer*, p. 1: Contained Kubert illustration.

December 1967, "Lt. Williams Takes Over Command: Night of Blood – Night of Valor," Part 2, Tom Millstead, *Houston Chronicle*, Section 2, p. 7: Contained Kubert Illustration.

December 1967, "At 0400 Hours, a Time for Decision, Night of Blood – Night of Valor," Part 3, Tom Millstead, *Houston Chronicle*, Section 5, p. 9: Contained Kubert illustration.

13 December 1967, "Kentucky Windage Blasts a Gun Nest: Night of Blood – Night of Valor, " Part 4, Tom Millstead, *Houston Chronicle*, Section 5, p. 3: Provided stylized version of period 0600-1000 hours, 10 June 1965 and contained Kubert illustration.

14 December 1967, "Ready for the Last Stand at Dong Xoai: Night of Blood – Night of Valor," Part 5, Tom Millstead, *Houston Chronicle*, Section 4, p. 9: Provided stylized discussion of period 1000-1400 hours, 10 June 1965 and contained Kubert illustration.

15 December 1967, "The Man Who Fought Like a Tiger: Night of Blood – Night of Valor," Part 6, Tom Millstead, *Houston Chronicle*, Section 5, p.5: Provided post-battle account with photo of Williams and Crowe.

17 May 1971, "Taking Honors," *Armed Forces Journal*: Announced launch of USS Marvin Shields (DE1066) named for Medal of Honor winner at Dong Xoai.

January 1972, "The Seabees at Dong Xoai ... a New Kind of Fighting Man," William Middleton, *U.S. Naval Institute Proceedings*, pp. 30-32: Described Seabee participation.

October 1990, "Seabees at Dong Xoai," John Wukovits, *Vietnam*, pp. 18-24: Summarized events and reported that Michelin plantation manager took aerial photos and gave to VC.

20 March 2003: "Beutel, Ex-anchor and Host for ABC," *Raleigh News & Observer*: Provided obituary for Bill Beutel, who interviewed Crowe at 3d Field Hospital after Battle of Dong Xoai.

Books

Green Berets at War: U.S. Special Forces in Southeast Asia, 1956-1975, Shelby L. Stanton, Novato, CA, Presidio Press, 1985, pp. 106-108: Provided superficial treatment of battle and criticized defense.

"The Attack by the 2nd Infantry Regiment against the Dong Xoai District Capital during the Night of 9-10 June 1965," COL Pham Vinh Phuc, Selected Battles from the Resistance Wars against the French and the Americans, 1945-1975, Volume, II, Ministry of Defense, Military History Institute of Vietnam, 1991: Some overstatement, but provided good description of attack details.

Correspondence, Military and Other Government

5 April 1965, Letter, HQ, MACV Detachment, Phuoc Long Sector, Song Be, Vietnam: Thanked A-313 for report on burned-out Dak O Hamlet.

10 June 1965, Memo for the President, "Situation in Dong Xoai, South Vietnam:" Indicated situation remained "fluid" and mentioned relief force briefly.

11 June 1965, Brief, "Situation in Southeast Asia," White House Situation Room: Provided casualty update, mentioned reinforcement, and described activity.

11 June 1965, Memorandum to The President, Douglas Cater: Took issue with Maxwell Taylor's casualty reports.

11 June 1965 (estimated), statement, LTC Miguel de la Pena: Described visit to Dong Xoai shortly after evacuation, stating: "It was evident to me that a fierce battle had taken place in this compound....I returned to the aircraft extremely impressed with the stand made by our forces at Dong Xoai."

12 June 1965 (estimated), statement, CPT James Sterling, Advisor to 52d Ranger Battalion: Statement, made shortly after ARVN recaptured area said: "Evident that defending personnel had conducted remarkable defense."

14 June 1965, Letters of Appreciation, Stokes to Crowe, Enriquez, Hand, Johnson, McLaughlin, Sale, Sova, Taylor, and Williams: Covered pre-deployment, Bu Gia Map, and Dong Xoai.

14 June 1965, Statement, Stokes: Responded to Seabee request for information to support Navy award recommendations.

14 June 1965, Statements of Seabees Larry Eyman, James Keenan, Frank Peterlin, and James Wilson: Provided participant's view.

Undated Statement, SFC Dallas Johnson: Provided comments of actions by McLaughlin at Dong Xoai.

Undated Statement, SFC Dallas Johnson: Provides details of actions by Taylor at Dong Xoai.

Undated Statement, SFC Jim Taylor: Provides comments of actions by Hand at Dong Xoai.

16 June 1965, Memorandum for Record, "Meeting with General Eisenhower," Andrew Goodpaster: Described VC preparations.

20 June 1965, Intelligence Memorandum, "Developments in South Vietnam During the Past Year," CIA: Indicated situation deteriorating, larger-scale VC capabilities, VC capabilities for multiple actions, growth of main force units, major attack Dong Xoai by reinforced regiment or elements of two regiments.

1 July 1965, Letter, "The True Facts of Dong Xoai," HQ, 5th Special Forces Group: Promulgated fact sheet to counter VC/NVA propaganda.

7 July 1965, Memorandum for COL Spears, "Dong Xoai After Action Report," CPT Bill Holt, HQ, 5th Special Forces Group: Provided very brief report.

4 January 1966, Letter, Stokes to William Wollenberg: Provided general comments regarding Dong Xoai and Special Forces.

10 July 1966, Message, CDR JTF-FA Honolulu to SecDef, Oral History Program, MG Vo Van Dan: Provided interesting notes of VC battalion commander who fought at Song Be and Dong Xoai.

14 September 1966, Recommendation for Award (Distinguished Service Cross) for Taylor: Upgraded previous Silver Star.

Undated Citation, Secretary of the Navy: Commended Seabee Team 1104, and authorized wear of Navy Unit Commendation Ribbon.

Undated, Extract, 145 CAB (V) History, "Battle of Dong Xoai Information for 118 AVN and A-342 SFG Det:" Provided brief synopsis, with emphasis on aviation participation.

Letters, Non-military

18 August 1966, Letter, Stokes to David Brinkley: Corrected commentary that CO at Dong Xoai was killed, and mentions entire team. No response from Brinkley.

15 May 1994, Note, Steve Sherman to Stokes and others: Provided correspondence related to Geisell proclamations of his association with A-342 and Battle of Dong Xoai.

19 July 1994, Letter, Stokes to B.G. Burkett: Provided initial data for use in Geisell refutation. Later phone call resulted in ABC "20-20" segment regarding Geisell's misrepresentation of awards and other facts. Taylor represented A-342.

24 February 2006, Note, Stokes to Ayse Weiting, Producer Fox News / War Stories: Commented on report by COL Pham Vinh Phuoc, 1991.

Note: In addition to the correspondence above there are numerous personal letters and e-mail messages among team members and between team members and their families that provide first-hand accounts of team activities during the period 1964-65. These letters provided the best primary sources of information available on the Battle of Dong Xoai.

Other Documentation

4 January 1966, "Personal Observations, Dong Xoai," Stokes: Personal notes addressed pre-entry, camp planning, occupation by CIDG of camp area, and attack and post-attack activities.

2006 Video reflecting Williams' Medal of Honor Ceremony, Beutel's interview of Crowe and related war footage, "20-20" repudiation of Geisell by Taylor, and elements of Fox News' "War Stories" regarding Seabee participation in Battle of Dong Xoai.

JOE KUBERT

Born in 1926, Joe Kubert began his comics career at the age of eleven as an apprentice in Harry "A" Chesler's comic book production house. He has worked in the industry ever since, and in his more than sixty years in the field he has produced countless memorable stories for countless characters, including DC's Hawkman, Tarzan, Enemy Ace, Batman and the Flash. Kubert also edited, wrote and illustrated the DC title SGT. ROCK, which, beginning under its original title OUR ARMY AT WAR, he contributed to for thirty years.

In 1952, Kubert was a principal in the creation of the first 3-D comic book (*Three Dimension Comics* Vol. 1, No. 1), and his pioneering development of 3-D comics continued with the early appearances of what would become his best-known creation -- a heroic caveman named Tor and his adventures "One Million Years Ago."

Kubert was also one of the first creators to embrace the long-form version of comics that became known as graphic novels, with his first two works in this medium being a graphic novel of *Tor* and the war adventure *Abraham Stone*. In 1996 he produced *Fax from Sarajevo*, a gripping graphic narrative that earned him accolades in the mainstream and trade press alike. He followed that success with two more historical graphic novels: *Yossel: April 19, 1943* (2003) and *Jew Gangster: A Father's Admonition* (2005).

Kubert has also been a pioneer in the realm of comics education. In 1976 he founded the first and only accredited school devoted solely to the art of cartoon graphics: The Joe Kubert School of Cartoon and Graphic Art in Dover, New Jersey, which has since produced many of today's leading cartoonists. Pursuing this educational path further, in 1998 he established a series of correspondence courses under the banner of Joe Kubert's World of Cartooning, and in 1999 Watson-Guptill published his book *Superheroes: Joe Kubert's Wonderful World of Comics*, a guide to the art of creating powerful comic book characters.

Kubert lives in New Jersey. Two of his five children, Adam and Andy, have also achieved great popularity as comic book artists.

MORE TITLES IN THE JOE KUBERT LIBRARY

SGT. ROCK: THE PROPHECY

TOR: A PREHISTORIC ODYSSEY

TOR ARCHIVES VOL 1-3

VIKING PRINCE

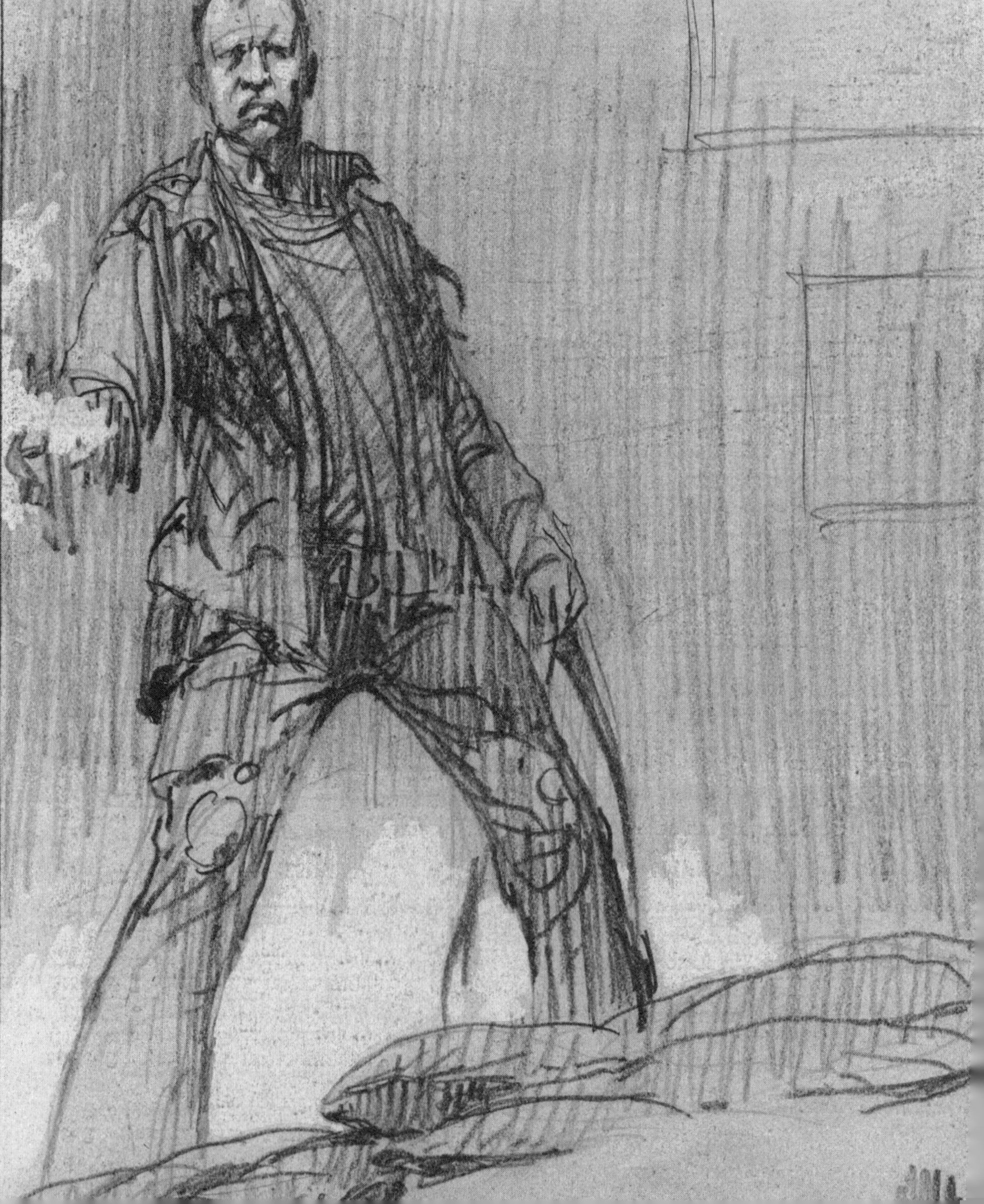

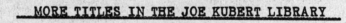